JESUIT MISSIONARIES TO NORTH AMERICA

FRANÇOIS ROUSTANG, S.J.

JESUIT MISSIONARIES TO NORTH AMERICA

*Spiritual Writings
and Biographical Sketches*

Translated by
Sister M. Renelle, S.S.N.D.

IGNATIUS PRESS   SAN FRANCISCO

Original French edition:
Jésuites de la Nouvelle-France
Desclée de Brouwer, 1961
Published with ecclesiastical approval

Originally published by Herder & Herder in 1964
The title of the English edition was
*An Autobiography of Martyrdom:
Spiritual Writings of the Jesuits in New France*
Used by permission.

Interior art and map:
Map of Seneca Villages, circa 1931
John S. Allen and St. John Fisher College Library
Map illustrator: Helen M. Erickson

Seneca villages' historian and archeologist: Alexander M. Stewart,
a Baptist minister who worked with Catholic clergy
and a Jewish businessman to uncover the history of the French
period in upstate New York and to place monuments (some
illustrated on the map) at historic locations.
John S. Allen is the Grandson of Reverend Stewart.

Cover art: © Bettmann/CORBIS
Illustration of Jean de Brébeuf Speaking to an Indian Council

Cover design by Riz Boncan Marsella

© 2006 Ignatius Press, San Francisco
All rights reserved
ISBN 978-1-58617-083-7
ISBN 1-58617-083-X
Library of Congress Control Number 2005933373
Printed in the United States of America ∞

Contents

Foreword	9
Preface	17
Abbreviations	19
General Introduction	21

PAUL LE JEUNE

Introduction	59
A Brief Account of the Voyage to New France	66
Hardships We Must Be Ready to Endure When Wintering with the Savages	71
Diary of the Trip	85
Various Thoughts and Feelings of the Fathers in New France	97

ENEMOND MASSÉ

Introduction	111
Letter to Reverend Father General, December 8, 1608	114
Letter to Reverend Father General, June 10, 1611	117
Spiritual Notes	119

SAINT JEAN DE BRÉBEUF

Introduction	123
Important Advice for Those Whom It Shall Please God to Call to New France, Especially to the Country of the Hurons	139
Instructions for the Fathers of Our Society Who Will Be Sent to the Hurons	153

Letter to Reverend Father Le Jeune, October 28, 1637	157
Graces, Visions, Illustrations, and Comments Excerpted from the Writings of Father Jean de Brébeuf	160
The Holy Deaths of Father Jean de Brébeuf and Father Gabriel Lalemant	176

PIERRE CHASTELAIN

Introduction	187
Letter to Reverend Father Le Jeune, August 8, 1636	193
The Love of Christ	195

SAINT ISAAC JOGUES

Introduction	205
Letters to His Mother, 1636–1637	222
In the Land of the Hurons: A Dream, 1638	231
Prisoner of the Iroquois: A Dream, 1642	234
Prisoner of the Iroquois: Several Visions, 1642–1643	240
Prisoner of the Iroquois: Letter to the Governor of New France, June 30, 1643	244
Prisoner of the Iroquois: Letter to His Provincial in France, August 5, 1643	247
Account of His Escape: Letter to Father Jérôme Lalemant, August 30, 1643	294
After His Return to France: Letter to a Priest, January 5, 1644	305
After His Return to France: Letter to Father Charles Lalemant, January 6, 1644	307
Mission to the Iroquois: Letter to Father Jérôme Lalemant, May 2, 1646	308
Martyrdom of René Goupil by the Iroquois	311
New Holland	321

Final Departure: Letter to Father Castillon, September 12, 1646	327
Final Departure: Letter to a Fellow Jesuit, September 1646	330

SAINT CHARLES GARNIER

Introduction	335
Letter to His Brother, June 25, 1632	348
Letter to His Brother, March 31, 1636	352
Letter to His Brother, July 20, 1636	355
Letter to Reverend Father Le Jeune, August 8, 1636	358
Letter to His Brother, April 30, 1637	360
Letter to His Father, 1638	364
Letter to His Brother, June 23, 1641	371
Letter to His Brother, May 22, 1642	374
Letter to His Brother, May 14, 1646	378
Letter to His Brother, August 12, 1649	381
Letter to Reverend Father Ragueneau, December 4, 1649	384

SAINT NOËL CHABANEL

Introduction	387
Brief Sketch of the Life of Father Noël Chabanel	388

PIERRE CHAUMONOT

Introduction	395
Letter to Saint John Eudes, October 14, 1660	400
Letter to Saint John Eudes, September 27, 1661	402
Letter of Father Chaumonot to His Confessor	404
Bibliography of Works Cited	419
Index	423

Foreword

Anyone who wants to do so can learn that there are eight Jesuit martyrs called, depending on what side of the border one is on, the Canadian or the North American Martyrs and that they met their deaths by the Iroquois between 1642 and 1649. All now canonized saints, they are René Goupil (September 29, 1642), Isaac Jogues and Jean de la Lande (October 18–19, 1646), Antoine Daniel (July 4, 1648), Jean de Brébeuf and Gabriel Lalemant (March 16–17, 1649), Noël Chabanel and Charles Garnier (December 8–9, 1649).

In the pages that follow Father François Roustang has given us excerpts from the writings of four of these men and to these he has added four more selections written by their companion missionaries, who were spared the grace of red martyrdom. In doing so he has broadened the seven-year time frame into which the martyrs are generally placed, and he has expanded the field of what is certainly one of the most heroic chapters in religious history. Many of these writings originally appeared in *The Jesuit Relations* and all serve to give the experiences of each man the animation and life of a modern novel. Roustang has also done us a great favor in giving, by way of introduction, a snapshot of his eight subjects, allowing us to study each man's background, his sanctity, idiosyncrasies, defects and talents and the circumstances of his narrative. The result is that we can learn much, not only about eight Jesuits of heroic virtue and about the times in which they lived, but also about human nature itself, how grace builds on that nature and, from our vantage point almost four hundred years later, how the hand of Providence can reconstruct the seemingly inscrutable messiness of life into a beautifully designed masterpiece. The writings themselves, like the authors who wrote them, are worthy of reflection for each is marked by a distinctive mannerism, but it is Roustang's presentation that helps us to ask ourselves if the world has ever seen anything like those Jesuits who were sent as missionaries to New France between 1610 and 1660.

Of course, this was the golden age of spirituality in old France, where the eight men were born and molded. It was the age that began with Pierre de Bérulle in the first decade of the 1600s and ended with St. Louis Grignion de Montfort one hundred years later. In between there were such giants as Jean-Jacques Olier, Louis Bourdalou, Jean de Bernières, Marie de l'Incarnation, Charles de Condren and Jacques-Bénigne Bossuet and saints like Vincent de Paul, Louise de Marillac, John Eudes, Julien Manoir, Francis Regis, Jeanne de Chantal, Francis de Sales, Claude de la Colombière and Margaret Mary Alacoque. Very much part of that school was the Jesuit Father Louis Lallemant, who personally formed some of the eight men in this study and who exerted a powerful influence on all of the Jesuit missionaries of New France. Modern readers used to affirming the goodness of human nature will understandably feel uncomfortable with the insistence on such themes as discarding the world, the sinful condition of man as opposed to the grandeur of God and the need for a radical love for the cross, the symbol of absolute self-annihilation, which are found in the writing of representatives of such spirituality in general and in the letters and reflections of these missionaries in particular. Without defending or excusing such themes, they explain the mindset and the motives of action of all the Jesuits highlighted in this book, and it must be admitted that these are also themes, however limited, not foreign to the teaching of Jesus in the New Testament. No one can claim that these eight Jesuits were unaware of the New or the Old Testament. All of them peppered their correspondence with copious citations from Scripture, and since frequently they did not have Bibles at hand when they composed their letters, it must be concluded that such citations were deeply fixed in their memories. One gets the impression that these missionaries were in the habit of penetrating the Word of God, not merely spouting Biblical verses for the edification of their readers.

The golden age of French spirituality coincided with the golden age of French literature, architecture and political hegemony. It was the age of Corneille, Molière and Racine, of Versailles, Charles Le Brun and Madame de Sévigné, of Richelieu and the Sun King. Jacques Amyot, the great Renaissance humanist of whom Montaigne said, "He taught France how to write", died the year Jean Brébeuf was born. Meanwhile, throughout the cities of France the Jesuits were successfully applying the norms of the *Ratio studiorum* in their numerous *collèges*, with the result that a number of young men imbued with humanistic learning as well as the spirituality of the age were taking their places in society. Paul Le Jeune's accounts of the mission of New France, into which he sometimes slips sly humor, and St. Isaac Jogues' descriptive letters remain compelling evidence of the literary and cultural presence of that humanism among those Jesuits missioned to New France. Both men fascinated their readers by recounting in unparalleled Classical style anecdotes that told what life was like living among the "savages of New France"—and the reader should remember that the term *savage* in French does not carry with it the pejorative connotation associated with the same word in English.

Not all of the missionaries were stylists, a fact that Roustang makes clear. Enemond Massé's nervous notes owe their charm in part to chopped, hurried phrases that but enhance their spiritual depth, and there is no example given of any writing of René Goupil, whose gentle and perceptive personality is described by Jogues. The physically strong, handsome giant Jean de Brébeuf is a chronicler who writes in laconic straightforward, no-nonsense sentences, whereas the onetime picaresque Pierre Chaumonot can be chatty. His reflections on the Mass, however, should be compulsory reading for today's priests and seminarians. Both the style and content of Charles Garnier's letters inspire one to doubt that if there is free seating at the celestial banquet the place next his will not be quickly filled. But then one would be immediately shaken from such musings by reading of his fearless courage. Courage was the virtue that shines forth in the lives of each of these men, but it took on an almost holy arrogance in the demeanor of Garnier. Cicero teaches that fortitude is the chief quality among men, and Aristotle observed that cowards are necessarily pessimists because they fear everything. By contrast a courageous man is confident, optimistic. Optimism is not a Christian virtue; hope is. And if there is any virtue that is made evident from the words and actions of these men it is hope, a hope built on what God has done in the past through the life, death and resurrection of Christ, and what he promises for the future, the sharing of that same life for all eternity. Such hope, riveted on a fathomless faith, enabled these men to live in the present with that purity of heart which is having no other desire than being opened to God and his grace that Lallemant taught his disciples was the shortest way to perfection. But generally it took long nights and a weary route through dry deserts to learn how to disentangle the designs of God from those that were not from God; to arrive at that stage of total self-annihilation that enabled these missionaries to live intimately united with God at every moment. How else does one explain the serenity with which Brébeuf underwent such barbaric tortures before his death or how Jogues and Goupil suffered their captors to pull out their nails and bite and saw off their fingers? But most of all, how else does one explain that, after continuous, day-by-day frustrations and sufferings, Pierre Chaumonot could vow never to leave his Indians, who all but despised him?

The Huron mission began with an irresistible momentum of success; quickly floundered and ended in dismal failure. Brébeuf, who after six years of work baptized only one single adult, blamed it on the Indians' immorality, on a lack of their creative energies and on the epidemics that reduced the population more than fifty percent within a few years' time. By 1650 the Iroquois were in complete control of what had been the Huronia. And so was all of this hope impracticable? Ironically the opposite is true, although the missionaries did not live to see it. The popularization of letters from the missionaries of New France was a decisive event in the subsequent history of the Catholic Church. The enthusiasm they generated in Jesuit *collèges* in France, particularly at Rennes, where many of these missionaries had matriculated or taught, resulted in a veritable mission mania. This of course, is another story. For our purposes, suffice it to say that the reports of the Jesuit missionaries in New France eventually inspired former students from the *collèges* to establish the *Missions Étrangères* seminary in Paris from which generations of priests brought the faith to many parts of Asia. Then there is the subsequent history of the Iroquois, the protagonists in the drama of the Jesuit martyrs.

Over the course of the next two hundred years many of the different tribes of this nation submitted to baptism. The most famous of their number, Kateri Tekakwitha (1656–1680), has been since beatified by the Catholic Church. In the early decades of the nineteenth century, a shortage of food forced some two-dozen members of the Iroquois nation to migrate west, where they finally settled beyond the Rockies and were adopted by the Flatheads. These Christian Iroquois taught their pagan hosts the prayers they had learned and prepared them to receive the faith of Jean de Brébeuf and his companions. Between 1831 and 1839 the Flatheads sent four delegations to St. Louis to beg that Blackrobes come and teach them what their predecessors had tried to teach the Hurons and their own Iroquois ancestors. Finally in 1840, the Jesuit superior at St. Louis appointed Peter De Smet to reconnoiter the territory and give a report on the prospects of establishing a mission. His report was positive, and following year, he, two priests, one of whom was Nicolas Point, and three lay brothers were participants in the historic first wagon train to the Oregon Territory where they established the famous Jesuit Rocky Mountain Mission. As a teenager in France, Point read some of the same letters contained in the pages of this book, and he determined at that moment to follow in the footsteps of the heroic men who wrote them. He had no idea that Jesuits still existed, and when he found out they did, he joined the Society and was eventually sent to the United States where he attempted to carry on the titanic labors begun by Jogues, Le Jeune and Brébeuf among the Flatheads, Cœur d'Alènes and Blackfeet.

Almost seventy years after Nicolas Point had pondered the letters that changed his life, a newly ordained French Jesuit read the same letters and underwent a similar experience.

The result was that Louis Ruellan shocked his superiors when he asked to be sent to North America to work among the native peoples. Father Ruellan gave promise of becoming an outstanding Jesuit academician, a professor or a writer of scholarly articles, and so it was after some time and with great reluctance that in 1884 he was at last assigned to the Rocky Mountain Mission, where he hoped in some way to replicate the lives those he had read about in the *Jesuit Relations*. But when he arrived in Spokane he was told to forget the Indians and direct his talents to building a *collège* for the whites, the future Gonzaga University. Here he learned the hard lesson that imitating Jogues and his companions did not mean performing great and splendid exploits. Rather it meant imitating their fidelity to grace in all matters, and this called for the same kind of quiet self-annihilation that characterized their lives and enabled them to hope in God's providence. Such a state was the by-product of detachment from all self-interest—and that included working with the Indians; of seeing God's presence in all people and events and of his ascertaining God's will in whatever task was given to him under obedience.

Ruellan learned this lesson painfully but in record time. He lived less than a year after coming to America, but the news of the untimely death of this exceptional young man had a miraculous effect. His death so greatly shocked religious Superiors in a number of European countries that they sent scores of missionaries into the American West and Alaska—once again changing the course of the Church's history and once again demonstrating the miraculous and continuous power of the seventeenth-century Jesuit martyrs and missionaries to North America. Hopefully some modern-day *collègien*, some Point or Ruellan reading this book, will feel the power and attraction of the lives, reflections and exploits of these Jesuit Missionaries to North America and will respond to the challenge they continue to offer.

                              Cornelius Michael Buckley, S.J.
                              Thomas Aquinas College
                              Santa Paula, California
                              October 19, 2005

Preface

The spiritual writings of early Jesuit missioners in Canada, chiefly those who worked among the Hurons, form the content of this work. The selection of texts and the introductory essays preceding the groups of writings of the individual men, as well as the general introduction, are those of Father François Roustang, S.J. They are translated from his book *Jésuites de la Nouvelle-France* (Bruges, 1961), published by Desclée de Brouwer. The selections that were written originally in Latin, however, are here translated directly from that language without recourse to Father Roustang's French rendition. Passages that are included in *The Jesuit Relations and Allied Documents*, edited by Reuben Gold Thwaites (Cleveland, 1896–1901), have also been completely retranslated into English and in several places show a marked deviation from that publication, chiefly because of comparisons with documents that seem to be more authentic. These documents for the most part have been procured in microfilm form from the Archives of Canada (Quebec), the Archives of the Collège Sainte-Marie (Montreal), the Archives of the Society of Jesus in Rome, and the Bibliothèque nationale in Paris. Abundant information and documentation was also supplied by the collection of *Jesuitica* housed in the Saint Louis Room and in the Knights of Columbus collection of microfilms at the Pius XII Library of Saint Louis University, Saint Louis, Missouri. To all of these our most sincere thanks are tendered.

We wish also to thank the Bruce Publishing Company, Milwaukee, Wisconsin, for their generous permission to quote from the Kleist-Lilly translation of the New Testament and the Kleist-Lynam translation of the Psalms, wherever these citations occur. All other scriptural quotations are taken from the Confraternity edition of the Holy Bible.[1]

The list of individuals to whom special recognition and gratitude for assistance are due is almost endless. To all of them, chiefly to my religious superiors and companions, to Father Roustang, S.J., and other Jesuit friends, I offer my heartfelt thanks and ask the holy martyrs, saints of the Church, whose spiritual treasures are here revealed, to obtain for them from God an abundance of blessings.

Sister M. Renelle, S.S.N.D.

Christmas, 1962

---

[1] The present edition (2006) retains the Scripture translations chosen by the author. However, for the convenience of the third millennium reader, Scriptural names are given in the form more currently in use. Psalm references have, in addition to the older numbering, in parentheses the numbering now commonly in use (including in the New Vulgate edition). The reader should also note that Sister M. Renelle has slight adaptations for the American reader.

Abbreviations

ARSJ	Archivum Romanum Societatis Jesu, General Archives of the Society of Jesus, Rome
Écrits	Marie de l'Incarnation. Écrits spirituels et historiques. Solesmes 1929–
MHSJ	Monumenta Historica Societatis Jesu. Madrid and Rome 1894–
MHSJ Ep. Xav.	MHSJ Epistolae S. Francisci Xaverii
MS de 1652	*Manuscrit de (Manuscript of) 1652*
Rochemonteix	C. de Rochemonteix. Les *Jésuites et la Nouvelle-France au XVIIe siècle*. Paris: Letouzey, 1895.
Thw.	R. G. Thwaites, ed. *The Jesuit Relations and Allied Documents*. Cleveland 1896–1901.

General Introduction

The history of the early French Jesuit missionaries—about thirty in number—who arrived in eastern Canada between the years 1632 and 1637, together with excerpts from the spiritual writings of many, are contained in the following pages.[1] For a period of twenty long years, alone and unaided, they bore the responsibility of the apostolate in this region, including parts of the north-eastern United States. Their hardships included not only the harshness of the climate, scarcity of food, and inadequate lodging, but also the constant menace of those whom they had come to evangelize. Nevertheless, working and praying unceasingly, they endured these hardships for the love of Christ, and the song that welled up in their hearts pealed forth free and unrestrained until their deaths, resounding with tones and overtones of joy and thanksgiving, even of exultation, that they were allowed to suffer something for Christ.

They were not the first, impelled by missionary zeal, to come to this savage land. In 1611 Fathers Pierre Biard and Enemond Massé had left their native France for Acadia but were obliged to return three years later.[2] In 1625 Father Massé came back, this time accompanied by Fathers Charles Lalemant and Jean de Brébeuf, their party including also

---
[1] We are greatly indebted throughout this whole work to Father Campeau, of the *Institut historique de la Compagnie de Jésus*, who has most generously encouraged and guided us to its completion.
[2] Cf. *Lettres du Bas-Canada*, March 1961, "Mission d'Acadie, 1611–1961".

several Coadjutor Brothers. The second attempt to bring the Gospel to the Indians aborted because of the fall of Quebec into the hands of the English in 1629. These are merely two episodes in the long and deplorable rivalry between France and England to establish foundations in the New World. A genuine understanding of the missionary history cannot be grasped without surveying the backdrop of economic, political, and social factors against which their apostolic activities unfolded.

First on the scene were the fishermen who scanned the famed shores of Newfoundland and the surrounding coasts for cod and whales. These men settled on the islands of Saint-Pierre-et-Miquelon and at Saint-Jean-de-Terre-Neuve. About 1540, realizing that they could ship a much larger quantity of fish if they took the time to dry it, they established settlements for processing it on the shore of the North American continent. In the second half of the century, they included fur trading with the natives as a means of increasing their profit. Giovanni da Verrazano in 1524 and Jacques Cartier (1491–1557), with the encouragement and support of François I, took possession of these coastal islands in the name of France, but no political policy was defined. Until the end of the sixteenth century there existed "no solid organization of merchant companies, no attempt of any importance at colonization".[3]

The true founder of New France was to be Samuel Champlain (1567–1635). His long-cherished dream for his

---

[3] C. de Rochemonteix, *Les Jésuites et la Nouvelle-France au XVIIe siècle* (Paris: Letouzey, 1895), 1:6. The three volumes that comprise this work still today furnish the best and most complete discussion of the early days of Catholicism in Canada. This introduction draws quite copiously from this source. Hereafter, references to this work will be made thus: Rochemonteix 1:6.

country, fostered during his voyages to the West Indies and to New Spain, was to found permanent French settlements on this continent. Hence, when he returned in 1601 from one of these voyages, he broached the matter to Henri IV, who wisely acquiesced to his plans and named him geographer. After a few exploratory voyages, a group of settlers with the Sire de Monts as leader and Champlain as guide endeavored to found a colony in North America. The king empowered the Sire de Monts to distribute the land, to grant offices, and to make war and peace; and, most important economically, the colony obtained the monopoly of the fur trade for ten years. But the merchants and fishermen—Basques, Normans, and Bretons—felt themselves injured, and with complaint after complaint, each one more bitter than the last, they finally prevailed upon the court and succeeded in obtaining the revocation of the "royal prohibitions". Thus deprived of all means of sustenance, the small colony that had been established in Acadia was obliged to abandon the place in 1607.

Unfortunately, this was not the last time that the lucrative permits of the fur trade compromised the development of New France. For example, at the end of the year 1610, a group of colonists, financed by a society of merchants, was preparing to depart for Acadia, but the Protestants refused passage to the Jesuits Biard and Massé, despite the formal order of the queen regent, Marie de Médicis. Only through the efforts of Madame de Guercheville, an ardent promoter of the missions in Canada, was their embarkation made possible the following year. To accomplish this, she personally made a subscription at the court and purchased the interests of the Calvinist traders belonging to this society. The quarrels, however, continued under various guises and pretexts, until at length the harassed French were weakened and the English were able to destroy the colony in 1613.

During these years, however, Champlain had energetically continued and multiplied his explorations. He had penetrated farther and farther up the Saint Lawrence, even to Ontario and to the present state of New York. In 1612 he had been appointed lieutenant to Charles de Bourbon, at that time governor of New France, and he had organized a group whose members gave him their full support. Scarcely one month after the death of Charles de Bourbon, Charles' nephew Henri (father of *le grand Condé*) took the title of Viceroy of New France. Champlain was still his lieutenant, but his former powers were now curtailed. It was at this time that the merchants once more refused to subordinate their profits to the good of the distant motherland. Instead of establishing forts, clearing and cultivating the soil, and helping the Recollets who had come with Champlain in 1615, the French who were settled on the banks of the Saint Lawrence devoted all their energies to trading and gave the missionaries no help at all in doing the work for which they had left France. The complete dependence of the latter on the colonists precluded all success in the work of the apostolate.

The government of the colony had passed from the hands of Henri de Bourbon to those of the Duke de Montmorency, then to the Duke de Ventadour; the society of merchants had been transformed several times, but the intentions of the traders had not changed. When Fathers Charles Lalemant, Enemond Massé, and Jean de Brébeuf reached Quebec in 1625, accompanied by the Coadjutor Brothers François Charton and Gilbert Burel, no one wished to receive them and it was only because of the great charity of the Recollets, who gave them half their house, that they overcame their strong desire to re-embark.

Realizing immediately that the mission had no future if the Fathers were not independent of the colonists as well as of the food supplies that arrived each year from France, the Jesuits embraced the idea so dear to Champlain and began to cultivate the land. Father Charles Lalemant wrote:

> The months of July and August passed, partly in writing letters, partly in acquainting ourselves with this new country and in looking for a place suitable for establishing our residence, in order to convince the Reverend Recollet Fathers that we are eager to relieve them as soon as possible of the inconveniences which we have imposed upon them. After due consideration of all the suggested places and much conversation with the French, especially with the Recollet Fathers, on the first day of September, with all possible solemnity, we planted the holy cross at the place we had chosen. The Reverend Recollet Fathers and the most prominent of the French colonists were present. After dinner all began to work. We five had continued to clear and dredge out the land as much as the weather permitted.[4]

The other preoccupation of the missioners was the study of the language. Contrary to all expectation, the interpreters who had refused their help to the Recollets favorably received the request now made to them by the Jesuits. To attain greater fluency in the language, Father Jean de Brébeuf left in 1626 to spend the winter with the Indians.

The following year, Fathers Noyrot and De Nouë, together with Brother Gaufestre, arrived with twenty men engaged in their service. Let us allow Champlain himself to describe their coming:

---

[4] R. G. Thwaites, ed., *The Jesuit Relations and Allied Documents* (Cleveland, 1896–1901), 4:208. Hereafter, references to this monumental work will be made thus: Thw. 4:208.

Father Noyrot brought twenty workmen whom Reverend Father Allemand (Charles Lalemant) employed in clearing the land and building houses. They lost no time, being vigilant and laborious men who all walk in the same intention without discord. This harmony and diligence brought it about that in a short time they were able to provide food for themselves and to be independent of the supplies from France. Would to God that for twenty-three or twenty-four years the trading societies had been so united and activated with the same desire as these good priests; there would now be several habitations and households, even countries, that would have been founded except for the fears and apprehensions that had been shown.[5]

A decisive point was now to be settled. If the Calvinists remained masters of the society of merchants, called "De Montmorency", there was no hope of founding a permanent mission. For this reason Father Charles Lalemant decided to send Father Noyrot back to Paris immediately, so that he could describe the situation to the viceroy, the Duke de Ventadour, and have the colony established on a new basis. Indefatigably Noyrot wrote report after report and visited men of the greatest influence to call to their attention the enormous possibilities that lay beyond the Atlantic and to solicit their cooperation. As the doors closed one after the other and he was put off time and again because no one wished to compromise himself, he determined to stake all on a final chance by going to the very top—to Richelieu himself, who had been in the ministry office for two years. For reasons of domestic politics the minister wished to weaken the Calvinist party. He listened willingly to Noyrot's exposé and immediately took effective action. He

---

[5] Rochemonteix 1:157, n. 1, cites the text of the *Oeuvres de Champlain*.

suppressed the company of the Duke de Montmorency, which had not fulfilled its obligations to colonize the lands or to evangelize the Indians. On April 29, 1627, he established the Company of One Hundred Associates, or the Company of New France. In addition, Richelieu personally took over the direction of the colony in place of the Duke de Ventadour, who had resigned in his favor.

This date marked the definition of a precise and solid political statute for New France. With the minister himself as the new viceroy and with Champlain as governor on the spot, the missioners would be better protected against the cupidity and the shortsighted commerce of the merchants. In addition, a policy of colonization was defined, which Colbert was later very happy to follow. The monopoly of the fur trade was granted to the new society as an attraction for Catholics to go to Canada. The bait was successful; during the following fifteen years, four thousand colonists emigrated and were granted cleared lands for their homes.

These generous grants, however, did not go far in removing the Jesuits' difficulties. Not only did the French Calvinists continue to impede their efforts, but during the siege of La Rochelle (1628), England decided to sustain the Huguenots and to carry the war to New France. Helped by the renegade French Calvinists, who revealed the ways of approach and the weakened condition of Quebec, the English forced the city to surrender on July 19, 1629. All the French were obliged to evacuate the city and to return to France.

The overthrow by the English was an act of marked piracy, since Admiral Kertk, chief of the English expedition, knew very well that the peace between France and England had been signed at Suse three months before his aggression. Restitution was, then, merely justice. The court of Louis XIII, however, did not lack timorous spirits who preferred to see their country hold itself apart from these difficult and burdensome enterprises. The obstinacy of Champlain had been ineffectual without the support of Richelieu. Detained in the Alps by the war of succession of Mantoue, the minister did not think it desirable to threaten England immediately. But after having strengthened the French influence in Italy by the peace of Cherasco, he armed ten ships and ordered them sent to Quebec. The London cabinet hurried to sign the peace of Saint-Germain-en-Laye (1632), which restored to France all the posts occupied by the English in Acadia and in Canada.

Champlain then resumed his post as governor. The Calvinists were evicted, and Richelieu, who, to secure the unity of the apostolate, wished only one religious institute in the new colony, offered the mission to the Capuchins, whom he held in special esteem. They did not accept the offer since it seemed to them that it ought to be made first of all to one of the two Orders expelled in 1629. The cardinal preferred the Jesuits.

Thus, in 1632 the Jesuits again began to clear the land, to build, and to study the Indian languages. Rather quickly, Father Le Jeune, superior of the mission, decided upon a precise manner of conducting their apostolate. His first effort was to resume an earlier attempt of the Recollets. He established a mission compound at Silléry, very near Quebec, with a view to a gradual stabilization of the Indians whose nomadic way of life impeded their being evangelized. He gave the reasons for this project in a letter to his provincial:

> If I can draw some conclusion from the things I see, it seems that we must not hope for many conversions among the savages so long as they are migratory. We instruct them today and tomorrow hunger takes our hearers away from

us, constraining them to go to seek their livelihood in the rivers and in the woods. Last year, with my tongue repeatedly stammering over the Indian syllables, I taught the catechism to a number of children. The boats left, my birds flew away, some in one direction and some in another.

This year, since I am speaking a little better, I expected to see them again, but having built cabins for themselves beyond the great Saint Lawrence River, they have frustrated my expectations. If we wished to follow them, it would take as many religious as there are cabins, and even then we would never come to an end of it, for they are so busy seeking their livelihood that they haven't the leisure to save their souls, so to speak. Moreover, I do not believe at all that, of one hundred religious, there would be ten of them able to bear up under the hardships they would have to endure in following them. I wanted to remain with them last fall; I was there only a week when a violent fever seized me and made me seek again our little house in order to regain my health. When I recovered I tried again to follow them during the winter; I was very sick most of the time.

These reasons, and many others that I could present were it not that I fear being overlong, make me believe that we will work for a long time and advance very little if we do not stabilize these wandering barbarians. We wish them to cultivate the lands themselves, without being helped, but I doubt very much that we can accomplish this soon, because they are completely ignorant of the ways of farming. Besides, where would they store their harvest? Their cabins are made only of bark, and the first freeze would spoil all the turnips and pumpkins they would have garnered. To sow peas or Indian wheat in their miserable settlements would be impossible. Who would feed them while they were beginning to clear the land? They live only from day to day and have no provisions stored away. Finally, after half killing themselves with work, they would be able to extract from the earth

> only a portion of their living until their fields should become fruitful and they would know how to draw profit from them.
>
> Even so, with the help of a few robust workers, we have succeeded in settling a few families who had previously spoken to me about it. Little by little they are accustoming themselves to drawing something from the earth unaided (Thw. 6:146–48).

Indeed, the stabilization of the Indians was always to remain very limited, and it was only by a combination of methods that their evangelization was accomplished.

There is a record of the establishment of thirty Algonquin families at Silléry in 1641. Another compound was founded at Three Rivers, and these two sites became the hub of a vast missionary movement. The Indians passed through in great numbers, remaining there for some time to be instructed, and then rejoining their tribes, where frequently they aroused the desire to receive the missionaries. The latter, after a stay of six months or a year with a tribe, returned to their original house. In this manner they won over the Algonquins, the Attikamegues, and the Abenaquis, and the Gospel was spread among the Indians along the Saint Lawrence River.

Similarly, Le Jeune sought to reach the Hurons, who dwelled in permanent settlements—although they lived by fishing, hunting, and a little agriculture. Their influence extended over all the neighboring tribes: the Petuns, the Neutrals, the Eries, the Andastes, the Ottawas, and the Nipissings. "The Huron mission", wrote Father Bressani, "comprised all these immense regions. Our project was always to seek out new tribes, and we hoped that a colony among the Hurons would provide the means" (Thw. 38:238). The total population of these regions did not surpass ten thousand persons; the people were united by similarities of customs, but even more by a common hatred of the Iroquois, whose confederation was established in the southwest, beyond Lake Ontario. The mission was eventually to perish because of this hatred. The Iroquois, supported by the Dutch and the English, crushed the Hurons, to whom the French had allied themselves long before the arrival of the Jesuits.

The apostolic plan of Le Jeune was, then, very simple: to stabilize as much as possible the itinerant tribes; to radiate from Quebec and Three Rivers to the interior of the land, on both banks of the Saint Lawrence; and to utilize the privileged position of the Hurons to contact all the neighboring regions. He also opened a college-seminary, which, despite several attempts, failed completely; for the young Indians, even with a very liberal regime, could not stand to be closed up for a long time within four walls. On the other hand, a boarding school for young girls, entrusted to the Ursulines, was a more durable success.

Undoubtedly, the conditions of life imposed on the Jesuits were among the harshest that missioners have ever known. They themselves will tell us about it (see the text of Le Jeune, pp. 71ff.), but we can hardly imagine how men who had been abruptly transplanted from one climate to another could survive, in particular, a winter more rigorous than that of Siberia, a winter lasting nearly six months. How could they bear interminable voyages of hundreds of miles by waterways and portages from one river to another; or, clumsy in their unfamiliar snowshoes, make long trips over ice and snow and in whirlwinds? How did they escape death from exhaustion, having nothing to protect them but the sky or miserable huts; nothing to nourish them but a little Indian corn and fish? Finally, how could they endure patiently the intolerable discomfort of dwelling closely with the natives?

Physical strength alone, certainly, could not be sufficient for them.

The most formidable trial for these men, however, was the failure of their mission. The apostolic fruits seem to have been numerous among the wandering tribes near the Saint Lawrence, since in 1653 Father Bressani could write: "There, where on our arrival we found not a single soul who knew the true God, today, in spite of persecutions, poverty, hunger, war, pestilence, we do not meet a single family in which there are no Christians, although some of the members may not yet be baptized. This is the work of at least twenty years" (Thw. 39:44). The situation, however, was not the same in the region of the Great Lakes, the field of labor for most of those whose writings are included in this collection. In the beginning, under the direction of Jean de Brébeuf, a pilot team had stayed among the Hurons before dispersing among the surrounding nations. In 1638 the enterprising and austere Jérôme Lalemant, superior of that mission, changed the methods of the apostolate. He had a census taken of the country, and a map was drawn. Then, instead of multiple residences, he set up a single one, to which he attached some mission posts. His idea was to regroup the Huron country around a village in which the residence was to be established, in order to make of it a sort of fort, like those of Paraguay. This center was to be fixed, surrounded by lands that were to belong to no individual and that could be cultivated for the needs of all.

These ingenious adjustments did not prevent the Huron mission from remaining almost completely sterile. In 1637, three years after his arrival, Brébeuf wrote that the sacrament of baptism had been given to a man fifty years old, the first healthy adult upon whom it had been conferred. In 1641 the Christian colony numbered sixty Hurons and later was to reach the maximum of several hundred. It is difficult to determine the reasons for such meager success. Pestilence had broken out some time after the coming of the missionaries, and they had been accused of causing it by their presence.[6] It seems also that the moral license of the Hurons, proverbial among the Indians, scarcely favored their submission to Christian laws.[7] In 1646, however, after the martyrdom of Jogues, there was a strong movement of conversion, which was accentuated in the following years.

Providence, nevertheless, was not to permit enough time for these fruits to ripen, for the mission soon disappeared, crushed by the Iroquois. The latter had rapidly realized the weakness of the French; from year to year the Iroquois became bolder and bolder, attacking unexpectedly those who ventured out on the rivers and even harassing the forts constructed on the Saint Lawrence, then disappearing again into the forests. Several hundred well-armed soldiers would have sufficed to bring them under control, but Richelieu was dead, and his successor, Mazarin, had other interests. The good will of the new governor was not able to replace the genius of Champlain, whom the colony had lost in 1635.

Thus, the effort to establish peace with the Iroquois was fruitless except in local and spasmodic truces. With surprising strategic ability, these Indians, armed by the Dutch, in

---

[6] The missionaries certainly were innocent of any crime in this regard, but we must recognize the fact that contacts with the Europeans were deadly to the Indians. The Indians lacked resistance especially against the contagious diseases from across the Atlantic that frequently decimated whole tribes. Cf. F. Larivière, *La vie ardente de saint Charles Garnier* (Montreal: Éditions Bellarmin, 1957), pp. 103–5.

[7] Let us note, among others, the judgment of Brébeuf: "I am afraid that they become stubborn when we speak to them of putting on Jesus Christ, of wearing his livery, of distinguishing themselves as Christians from what they were before, by a virtue of which they scarcely know the name" (Thw. 10:314).

1648 and 1649 destroyed successively all the Huron villages. Fathers Antoine Daniel, Jean de Brébeuf, Gabriel Lalemant, Charles Garnier, and Noël Chabanel were massacred, along with a great number of Hurons. Those Hurons who escaped abandoned their country either to spread into the neighboring nations or to put themselves under the protection of the French at Quebec. They were reassembled at the Ile d'Orléans, where Father Chaumonot, who had accompanied them, made model Christians of them.

Can we use the term "failure" to characterize this missionary venture among the Indians? First of all, we must recall once more that the result was very different among the tribes living near the Saint Lawrence. Secondly, is it wise to decide whether or not the evangelization of these peoples was well conducted, since the Jesuits worked there for only about fifteen years? How effective is so short a time in the introduction of customs entirely opposed to the age-old traditions of these people? For the missionary work to be fruitful, peace was indispensable; the absence of which would render equally sterile the pains the missioners would endure among the Iroquois in later decades. Doubtless a sad situation existed here, but we must remember that the descendants of the Huron and Iroquois Christians that were spared from the wars still live today on the "reservations" set up for them in the seventeenth century near Quebec and Montreal.

Did the Jesuits in Canada lack the spirit of adaptation that had accomplished such marvels in China under Ricci and in India under Nobili? Is it reasonable to compare historical situations so far in the past? When Valignano directed the work of Ricci and Ruggieri from Macao, he found himself in the presence of a civilization a thousand years old and a people perhaps even more refined and more cultured than the Europeans. In any case, they were certainly as informed and as confident in regard to their own beliefs. There, as in the Indies, with the help of those who practiced the local rites, patient work enabled the missioners to discern the native character and culture. The Hurons, the Algonquins, and the Iroquois were, in the ethnic sense of the word, primitives; or, as the missionaries said—without any derogatory connotation since the words were used at that time by those who admired these Indians—they were both savages and barbarians. Under these conditions, it was a great deal more difficult to interpret the meaning of their language and religious practices. Even if they had had our libraries at their disposal, it is not certain that these Jesuits would have been able to unravel very easily the complexity of the traditions they met.[8] The religion of these peoples—farmers, hunters, fishermen all at the same time—was a confluence of many complex currents that had had time to be degraded to such an extent that magic had penetrated without a struggle into the totality of the constitutive elements of their culture.

What is particularly admirable is that, in spite of these enormous obstacles, the Jesuits had arrived at this profound discernment—a work that many historians reproach them for not having achieved. To convince ourselves of this, it suffices to read several pages of Jean de Brébeuf, who declared that he was not very bright (cf. Thw. 34:178), but whose perception was keener and more accurate than that of any of his contemporaries.

---

[8] If we listen to the priests who in our own time work among the better preserved nations of Africa, we can form some estimation of the difficulty of the problems confronting the Jesuits of Canada. Even with the help of modern specialists in the history of religions, missionaries very often find it almost impossible to judge the significance of some of the practices they encounter.

They have recourse to Heaven in almost all their necessities. They have greater respect for the immense heavenly bodies than for all other creatures, and they reverence in a very special manner some divine celestial force. This is, after man, the most exact image of the divinity that we have; there is nothing else that represents it to us so clearly. We notice it in the cult of these Indians, in the all-powerfulness of this force in the prodigious effects caused here below; its immensity is perceived in the vast expanse of woods and fields; its wisdom in the order of their movements; its goodness in the benign influences that this divine force pours out continually on all creatures; and its beauty is seen in the sun and in the sheen of the stars.

I say this to show how easy it would be, with time and the divine assistance, to conduct these peoples to the knowledge of their Creator, since they already honor in a very special manner a creature who is so perfect an image of him. And still, I would tell you that it is God they honor, though blindly, for they imagine there is in the heavens an Oki, that is, a daemon or a power, who rules the seasons of the year, who holds the reins of the winds and of the waves of the sea, who can favor the course of their navigations and assist them in their necessities; they even fear his anger and call him to witness their inviolable faith when they make some agreement or treaty of peace with the enemy. These are the terms that they use: "Heaven understands what we are doing today"; and they believe that if after this declaration they fail to keep their word or if they break an alliance, the heavens will infallibly chastise them. More than that, they consider it very bad behavior to make fun of Heaven.[9]

---

[9] Thw. 10:158–60. Father Latourelle, in his work *Brébeuf* (coll. "Classiques canadiens", Montreal and Paris: Éditions Fides, 1958), cites a certain number of texts that reveal the missioner as a competent ethnologist. See also, by the same author, *Étude sur les écrits de saint Jean de Brébeuf* (Montreal: Éditions de l'Immaculée-Conception, 1952), 1:134f. However, Brébeuf is not the only

It would be interesting to know whether or not these statements would be contradicted by the pen of some modern and rigorous ethnologist. Contrary to the opinion of Champlain and of the Recollet Father Sagard, Brébeuf knew how to find the traces of belief in a Being on whom all depends, and he had perceived the force of the symbols used by the Indians. Furthermore, he also understood their manner of taking vengeance, their gestures of supplication and sacrifices addressed to Heaven. He wished that the Christians would be as faithful to divine inspirations as the savages were to their superstitions.[10] He admired their tranquillity in the face of death and their solicitude for proper burial.

If these missionary priests had been content merely to superimpose Christianity upon the life of these Indians, if they had sought just to pique the curiosity of their French readers, would they have put so much care into describing not once, but ten or twenty times, the habits, customs, and beliefs that make their *Relations* a mine of information for the historian of religion? On the contrary, their incessant effort to understand and to experience the background and mentality of those with whom they lived is beyond question.

---

one to entertain such opinions. In the *Relation* of 1648, edited by Ragueneau, there are remarks of the same type (cf. Thw. 33:224–25). It remains true, nonetheless, that the understanding of the Indian mentality by the Jesuits of New France was limited. We will see examples of this defect in our selections from Le Jeune.

[10] Father de Rochemonteix, who several times ridiculed the belief in dreams entertained by the savages, nevertheless did not hesitate to point out the importance of a dream in the missionary vocation of Le Jeune (1:143). Without yielding to the blind credulity of the Indians, the Jesuits had received graces outside the state of wakefulness. That is why Father Le Jeune, who was always very exact in his statements, affirmed to his superiors when relating his winter sojourn among the Indians: "I was consoled, even in my sleep" (Thw. 6:38). We shall see that several times Jogues, too, had similar experiences.

Submitting themselves to the slowness of the ways necessary to evangelize the Indians, they were often accused of not wishing to educate—that is, make French—the Indians, in order to preserve their dominion over them. This was a supplementary proof that in totally different conditions the Jesuits desired to make themselves "all things to all men"—here as in China, the Indies, Paraguay—by sharing the life of the people, learning their languages, espousing even their manner of thinking and speaking. Brébeuf and Chaumonot could harangue for hours on end, exactly like the Huron chiefs; and Jogues, after his sojourn as prisoner, knew all the fine points of the Iroquois language.

If we insist on the spirit in which these religious worked, if we show that it is identical to that which prevailed in other places and times in the labors of other Jesuits, it is because these men all utilized the rules and practices of the apostolate characteristic of the Order in which they had been trained. Recollets and Capuchins had done and were doing the same thing: establishing bonds between the Indians and the traditions that came to them from Saint Francis. It was only after 1640 that in France the missionary idea was to pass beyond the frontiers of a few religious institutes and extend more and more widely to the diocesan clergy and to numerous lay Christians.[11] Canada benefited more than any other country from this vast movement, since Canada was set up as an apostolic vicariate (1658) and thus received secular priests. Later the Sulpicians came, then the Recollets returned. An entirely new epoch opened up for the missions, one very different from that which we are going to describe here.

---

[11] Cf. G. de Vaumas, *L'éveil missionnaire de la France au XVIIe siècle* (Paris: Bloud et Gay, 1959).

By publishing each year the *Relations*, that is, accounts of their works, the Jesuits had contributed a notable share in the development of this new trend. Since we are quoting a certain number of their texts in the pages that follow, it is useful to show how they composed and presented their narratives to a wide public.[12]

From the very beginning of the Society of Jesus, Saint Ignatius had set forth the principle of writing letters to describe the apostolic fruits reaped by the missionaries— letters that could be shown to persons who were not familiar with the work of the Order. Dissatisfied that Peter Favre had not followed his directives in his correspondence, the Founder wrote to him:

> I am repeating what I said in the past so that all of us may be in agreement on all these points. For the love and reverence of God, our Lord, I demand, then, that in our correspondence we write so as to ensure the greatest service to his divine goodness and the greatest utility to our neighbor. In the principal letter, you will write what each of you does—sermons, confessions, spiritual exercises, and other works—according to what God our Lord has directed in regard to each of you; this shall be for the greatest edification of your hearers or readers. If the apostolic field is sterile and there is nothing to be said, you will write a few sentences concerning your health, interesting discussions you may have had with one or another, or some similar subject, without including anything unsuitable. You will reserve more private matters for letters attached to these: dates on which you received letters, the spiritual joys and the sentiments they evoked, any illness, business,

---

[12] Cf. L. Pouliot, *Etude sur les Relations des Jésuites de la Nouvelle-France, 1632–1672* (Paris: Desclée de Brouwer, 1940).

or other news. You can amplify it if you wish by words of exhortation.

On this subject, to assure myself that I am not misunderstood, I shall tell you what I do and hope to continue to do in the Lord in my correspondence with members of the Society. The principal letter I write once. I recount therein the edifying things that are in my heart, then I examine and correct it, taking cognizance of the fact that all will see it. Then I write it a second time, for what is written must be much more carefully thought out than what is said. Writing lasts; it can always be used for reference and is not so easily altered or explained as the spoken word. Even after all this, I do not imagine that it is perfect, and fear that errors may still be present. I leave the less important matters and those less likely to edify for the letters to be included with this principal one. These supplements I write rather quickly, from the abundance of the heart, without necessarily putting things in order. This freedom is not permissible in the principal letter, which must be written with a special effort to edify those to whom it may be shown advantageously.[13]

These lines define specifically the limits to which the accounts of the Jesuits of New France later adhere. They are not documents written to include all that happens, for anything that could possibly wound or scandalize is systematically eliminated from them, and they retain only what can "edify"— the word recurs often under the pen of Saint Ignatius.

Doubtless these letters of the first Jesuits were addressed to a restricted circle of friends or of persons who were especially interested in a particular question. But soon they were circulated more widely, and even printed. We know, for example, that a letter of Saint Francis Xavier, the first apostle

---

[13] Saint Ignatius, *Lettres* (Paris: Desclée de Brouwer, 1959), pp. 85–86.

in a distant mission to send such documents, appeared in Paris in 1545. During the following decades, the collection of his letters was entitled *Lettres annuelles*, and later, *Lettres édifiantes et curieuses*. These letters were distributed widely and were a powerful influence in arousing numerous missionary vocations, not only in France but throughout Europe.

The literary production of the preceding centuries had furnished many descriptions of voyages, beginning with those of Marco Polo. The idea of writing memoirs or annals is as old as our Western culture. Before Saint Ignatius, however, neither the Franciscans nor the other missionary congregations had conceived the idea of making known their apostolic labors in any systematic way and of utilizing these reports to stimulate generosity toward the mission projects.

The Jesuits of New France were eager to continue a tradition already old in their Order. We must note, however, that the first *Relations* had a more limited purpose and were designed only to inform the superiors in France of the missioners' activities, according to the rules contained in the *Constitutions* of the Society (cf. *Const.*, pt. VIII, chap. 1, no. 9 [673]). The letters of Father Biard, one of the two Jesuits who participated in the ephemeral mission of Acadia, were written to the Father Provincial in France, but judging from their tone, Biard must have thought their publication in the *Lettres annuelles* was at least possible.

The *Relation* of 1626 was at first only a missive of Father Charles Lalemant to his brother Jérôme. Its appearance in the *Mercure de France* of that same year certainly must have surprised its author. In the strict sense of the word, then, Father Le Jeune is the first author of the *Relations*. Although the account he composed in 1632 was addressed to the provincial in Paris, the latter granted to Cramoisy the privilege of publishing it. Even if the text was not explicitly destined for publication, it is possible that Le Jeune foresaw this result since he already knew the fate of Father Charles Lalemant's letter. He must have remained editor of the *Relations* until 1642, that is, until several years after he had been relieved of the superiorship of the mission. It is indisputably to him, to his literary talent, and to the vigor of his mind that the widespread popularity of the journal of the missions of New France is due. Later, a certain monotony pervaded these documents, resulting in interminable volumes no longer animated by the inspiration of a great soul and of a vast project.

In 1673 the *Relations* ceased to appear, for a dissension arising over the Chinese rites had caused Rome to require a special permission from the Congregation of Propaganda before publication of any writings concerning the missions. In France, however, the "Gallican liberties" did not recognize any jurisdiction of Roman Congregations. Neither Louis XIV nor the University of Paris could tolerate the Jesuits' asking this authorization. Since these latter did not wish to disobey the pope on the one hand or to dissatisfy the king on the other, there remained no alternative but silence.

The purpose of this present collection is certainly not an attempt to complete the former collections nor an attempt to furnish the reader a sampling of sketches from the *Relations*.[14] Rather, our aim is to eliminate, insofar as it is possible,

---

[14] This task was undertaken by G. Rigault and G. Goyau in their work entitled *Martyrs de la Nouvelle-France* (Paris: Spes, 1925). The small volume of Father Rouquette, *Textes des Martyrs de la Nouvelle-France* (Paris: Éd. du Seuil, 1947), has also widely disseminated the history of these missions. These two books are now out of print, so we thought it worthwhile to resume the task on a larger scale. On the one hand, we include extracts that do not appear in Thwaites; on the other hand, we cite not only those men who were martyred but also quote texts of other Jesuit missionaries.

the official and anonymous character of these narrations, which are addressed to seventeenth-century French readers, and to retain only those passages in which the missionaries expressed directly their most personal lives,[15] either in notes written for their confessor, in letters addressed to their superiors under the eyes of God, or in their personal spiritual diaries. Although the writings of only a few of these men are included, an effort was made to select those that reveal the spirit that animated them, those that shine forth from the invisible hearth on which was forged the strength of their apostolate—one of the most austere, the most onerous, the most excruciating, and yet one of the most momentous apostolic labors in the history of the Catholic missions.

When an inventory of the documents written during more than a century and a half was taken, it became clear that much light was concentrated around the first group, those whose works introduced this volume; yet more especially was that light focused on the group in charge of the Huron mission.[16] The accounts began in 1632 with the second arrival of the Jesuits at Quebec. Already by 1652, as if putting an end to an epoch, Father Ragueneau gathered

---

[15] That is, we are not publishing here all the works of these Jesuits, merely their spiritual writings. Jogues, however, is an exception; we cite all his extant writings.

[16] Except for Le Jeune and Massé, all those whose works we include belonged to that mission. Charles Garnier was correct when he wrote to his brother that if Canada was a "holy and consecrated temple", the Huron country was the "holy of holies" in it (letter of July 20, 1636). A collective success of such magnitude could be accomplished only by the most careful selectivity on the part of the superiors. On the advice of Fathers Le Jeune and Brébeuf, the superiors sent only men of exceptional virtue, capable of enduring every hardship. Cf. for example Thw. 6:66.

together, in a manuscript burning with blood and love, a few of the literary spoils of his martyr-brothers.[17]

More astonishing still was the fact that the pens of these religious of such varied temperaments, not only those whom God found worthy of martyrdom through the violence of the Iroquois, but others as well, reveal the same facility of expression, the same capacity to expose their interior experiences in a language sometimes archaic yet always clear, the same fundamental calm that makes them tower above the dissensions of their times and the infinite pains of their journeyings and labors, the same bursts of joy, the same unceasing zeal to use the last ounce of their strength to establish the Kingdom of God. To the heroism exacted by a painful departure was added a spiritual flowering and a literary success that can be appreciated but not explained.

Another force that cannot escape notice is the multiple bonds that unite the Canadian missionaries to Father Louis Lallemant, whose strong, unique personality dominated his entire generation. During these years, he "had for his disciples", his biographer notes, "the most spiritual and the most interior men that the Society ever had".[18] He exercised a strong influence on those men who left so profound a mark on the history of the mission. For example, Father

---

[17] We are alluding here to the *Manuscrit de 1652*, preserved in the archives of the Collège Sainte-Marie at Montreal. Because the reproduction of this text in the *Rapport de l'archiviste de la Province de Québec* of 1924–25 was very defective, Father Arthur Melançon made a very faithful multicopy in 1936. The present archivist of the Collège Sainte-Marie, Father Paul Desjardins, very kindly sent us a copy as well as other very precious documents and information without which we would have been quite handicapped. In our translation we always cite the pagination of the actual manuscript, not that of the copy.

[18] *La vie et la doctrine spirituelle du Père Louis Lallemant* (Paris: Desclée de Brouwer, 1959), p. 61.

Le Jeune, whose role was most decisive in Canada, made his third year of probation under his direction; Ragueneau, who became superior of the Huron mission in 1645 and whose own deep spirituality understood immediately the outstanding value of the spiritual writings of his companions, was subject to him as prefect of studies in 1633 and as rector in 1634–1635.[19] Antoine Daniel and Isaac Jogues, two future martyrs, received their novitiate training from him.[20] The latter, before leaving for New France, spent another several years under him at Rouen. There is reason to believe that Father Lallemant had been Brébeuf's spiritual director when in 1619–1620, as a young teacher, Brébeuf instructed the sixth form and when the following year he suffered the great trial of his illness (cf. Latourelle, *Études*, 2:193–95). Also, during the time (1628–1631) that Father Louis Lallemant was directing the third year of probation at Rouen and when his spiritual authority was greater than ever, Brébeuf, who had recently returned from Canada, was also there, preparing himself, with the burning fervor revealed in his journal, to pronounce his final vows.

Besides these direct influences, there were others that complemented and amplified them. Brébeuf was at the college at Eu from 1631 to 1633; during this same period Father Rigoleuc, the closest disciple of Louis Lallemant, was professor of rhetoric there. Garnier also was there as teacher of grammar, making contact with these two great figures before returning to do his theology at Paris with Chastelain, and

---

[19] Ibid., pp. 55–56. Although Ragueneau was a very holy man and an excellent superior, he took too active a part in political and temporal affairs. He was a member of the council of the governor of New France, to whom he often dictated what decisions should be made.

[20] Cf. A. Pottier, *Le Père Louis Lallemant et les grands spirituels de son temps* (Paris: Téqui, 1927–1929), 3:79.

later with Jogues. Brébeuf and Ragueneau had always been great friends. Chastelain and Garnier also must have been influenced by Father Lallemant, although indirectly, since they made their novitiate with Vincent Huby and Julien Maunoir, direct disciples of Lallemant who later became the apostles of Brittany.

Remarks of this kind can be multiplied indefinitely; those given here are sufficient to show that in this rather restricted circle where changes of personnel were frequent, these strong personalities were not content merely to live side by side, but they fortified each other as they forged their path to God. Thus, it is not surprising that this group of missionaries takes on an inexpressible and marvelous unity despite the variety of their graces and of their characters.

Moreover, their exemplary success contributed in a still wider and more favorable movement. This first half of the seventeenth century, which is noted for its unique extension of missionary activities, was also a golden age for French mysticism. Henri Bremond, in his *Histoire littéraire du sentiment religieux en France*, depicts very clearly the strength of the spiritual current that, despite the troubled times, raised a multitude of souls to the heights of spirituality. Even excluding the Jesuits, whose most outstanding representatives were Le Gaudier and Saint-Jure, in addition to the aforementioned Louis Lallemant and many others, this is still the period made famous by such names as Bérulle, Condren, Saint John Eudes, Madame Acarie, and Mère Marie de l'Incarnation—the latter playing an important part in the religious history of New France. Although they may not have been directly influenced by these great souls, several of whom flourished at a somewhat later period, the Jesuit missionaries profited by the richness of this movement and breathed in the atmosphere of this spiritual wealth.

Father Chaumonot corresponded with Saint John Eudes, and the history of Canada clearly establishes the existence of other numerous contacts between the mystics in France and the laborers in the mission. For example, in 1638 Madame de la Peltrie paid a visit to Condren, at that time superior general of the Oratory, and to Saint Vincent de Paul, to ask their advice and aid in the work she wished to undertake across the Atlantic (cf. Rochemonteix 1:301).

From a literary standpoint, even the least letters of these Jesuits manifest a high quality of expression, an unusual clarity of sentence structure, and a vigorous elegance of language. It is evident that these writings share in the apogee of the development of the French language achieved during that epoch. We must be careful, however, not to attribute the perfection of their style wholly to the times; their personal and individual gifts and literary talents are outstanding. To be convinced of this, all we need do is peruse the accounts of Champlain's trips or the narratives of Sagard. In them, too, is found the same prose of the seventeenth century, but it is padded with redundancies. Many a phrase lacks grace and precision; many a rhetorical figure that would enhance the narrative is simply not employed. We must note also the tremendous differences even from Jesuit to Jesuit. When Father Le Jeune turned over his pen to Father Vimont, a special charm disappeared. We shall notice in the texts we have cited in our collection that between Jogues and Garnier, for example, two martyrs of the same age, there is a huge chasm. The least phrase of the Orléanais vibrates with interior music, while the Parisian, very definitely a competent master of the language, barely escapes bombast and triteness of expression.

How little their pages would influence us had they used the mission confided to them merely as a showcase for their talents! They wrote because they were ordered to do so; Le Jeune complained several times that he was not relieved of the burden of writing the *Relations* when he laid aside that of the superiorship. He clearly had no literary ambitions. If these men wrote well, it was because their souls were at peace; if their ink was clear, it was because their hearts were completely given to the tasks to which they had placed their hands. Even today, what attracts us to them, what fascinates us, is this incredible strength, this heroism, which was as natural to them as breathing. Despoiled of everything, crushed, humiliated, they nevertheless preserved not only an Olympian calm, but also a goodness, a charity toward their persecutors, which was never insincere. They minimized the sufferings they endured; they strove to keep secret the terrible pains that were heaped upon them. If they spoke, it was because they were happy despite their difficulties and because they wanted to arouse in many others the desire to embrace the same sufferings and thus come to know the same happiness. The key word that sums up their entire apostolate is joy—the superabundant joy that transcends the tribulations of the apostle. There is nothing else, no other bond that unifies the pages that follow.

Their mysticism is that of the cross, in which alone resides the supreme consolation of those who carry it in the sight of God. In reading the spiritual journals of these heroic souls, we perceive the fruits of this mysterious unity of spirit, inexplicable to anyone who has not experienced even a modicum of it through his faith. It is incomprehensible to the exterior man, whose spirit is broken a little more each day, but it is perceived and enjoyed fully by him whose strength is vivified from above. "Hunger thought she would kill us," wrote Le Jeune, "but God is so present in these difficulties that the time of famine seemed a time of abundance"

(Thw. 6:38). Chastelain confided to his superior: "As for the state of my soul, in the greatest exterior and even interior abandonments, God has always given me the grace to make me realize that he is doing me a favor for which I shall never be properly grateful until I reach heaven" (Thw. 12:126). Jogues, exhausted by hunger, cold, and nakedness and having become the refuse and infamy of men, heard a voice that persuaded him of the pusillanimity of his heart and invited him to throw himself on the goodness of God; then he added: "The Lord enlarged the soul of his servant so that I regained joy in that village at whose entrance I had thought I would die" (*MS de 1652*, p. 107). A most searching and exhaustive examination of the writings of these men reveals no other motif in the awesome and marvelous symphony of their lives.

Among other traits common to these Jesuits and easily perceived in reviewing their writings, we should call attention to their special devotion to the Holy Eucharist. In those pagan lands where they so often met an obstinate refusal of surrender to Christ, a refusal much more painful to them than the strangeness of the Indian customs, it is easily understood how important the presence of the Blessed Sacrament was to them and how great a refuge was their chapel—even though it was nothing but a miserable cabin—providing for them the sweetness and solace of Heaven itself. Father Buteux, very sensitive to the atmosphere prevailing in the mission, wrote that he would have liked to learn from Father Jogues his manner of making his thanksgiving. "He seemed, as it were, a soul glued to the Blessed Sacrament. Before this hidden God he made all his spiritual exercises—prayers, examens, Office—no matter how intense the rigor of the cold or the importunity of the insects" (*MS de 1652*, p. 72). The visions of Father Jean de Brébeuf, which took place in the presence of the Eucharist, were numerous; those experienced elsewhere usually recalled to him the chapels of one of his former residences. Pierre Chastelain habitually refreshed both his physical and his spiritual strength when he was tired, before the "Venerable Sacrament". His companions frequently found him there, taking a little nap. As for Pierre Chaumonot, his letters to his confessor reveal that his whole spiritual life was centered on the Mass.

As a source for portraying the spirit that dwelled in these priests, most historians cite texts written by Marie de l'Incarnation. Because she was without doubt the greatest expression of French mysticism,[21] because she was witness to the lofty accomplishments of the Church of Canada, because she knew from having experienced them the extraordinary ways of union with God, because even though she was a mystic she was also a missionary, and one of the most active at that, she has been accepted as the exact interpreter of the interior life of these religious whom she knew personally or with whom she was acquainted through letters.[22] Certainly her numerous points of contact with the spirituality of the Society of Jesus cannot be ignored. While still at Tours she had been directed by a Jesuit, Father de la Haye, who had encouraged her submission to the Holy Spirit; and when she came to Canada the Jesuits were her confessors. Long before she knew the Fathers, her spiritual per-

---

[21] It is regrettable that the edition of the *Écrits spirituels et historiques* of Marie de l'Incarnation undertaken by Dom Jamet is not yet complete. Four volumes (1929–1939) have already appeared, and we hope that the Abbey of Solesmes will not keep us waiting long for the last one. [We could find no evidence that a fifth volume has been published.—Ed.]

[22] When she arrived at Quebec on August 1, 1639, she had already had correspondence with Fathers Le Jeune, Garnier, Chastelain, and Adam (cf. *Écrits* 3:106, n.).

sonality had already been formed; the decisive graces of her mystical orientation had already been received. That these Fathers, some of whom she surpassed by her extraordinary graces, were able to direct her to advance with confidence on her own spiritual way, is incontestably a credit to their own spiritual formation.

The text that has become a classic, the basis of historical misunderstanding, is the one in which Marie de l'Incarnation, before explaining what "the spirit of the Holy Word Incarnate" is, states that it had been "given to our holy martyrs, the Reverend Fathers de Brébeuf, Daniel, Jogues, and Lalemant" (*Écrits* 4:255). Her readers do not always sufficiently realize that it is her own experiences she is alluding to, describing to her son "the most precious gift" that has been granted to her. The proof of this is found in the account of her life, written in 1654 (*Écrits*, 2, passim). There she recounts the same experiences with no reference at all to the Jesuits.

Her letter to Dom Claude Martin, in which she bears witness to the heroic lives and deaths of the missionaries, expounds her own deductions that, judging from external signs, these men were invested with the same spirit that had been granted to her, a similar zeal and charity in the face of sufferings and innumerable crosses. "They showed by their generous courage how completely their hearts were filled with that same spirit and that same love for the cross of their good Master", her letter states. It is, then, by a rationalization and not from having received their confidences that she explained the profound motivations for the activities of these martyrs. Besides, as Dom Jamet notes (cf. *Écrits* 4:255 n. 86), she hoped that by describing her own experiences she would clarify the interior life not only of these Jesuits but also that of "other souls that are around her". It is inconceivable that these men revealed to this nun their secret life, the life that only their superiors and their confessors should know. As further evidence of this improbability, she never even met Father Charles Garnier (cf. *Écrits* 3:100 n.), to whom she so glowingly attributes this spirit (cf. *Écrits* 4:291), and it is absolutely unthinkable that this young Jesuit would have been more explicit in his letters to Marie de l'Incarnation than he was in writing to his Carmelite brother or to his superiors. Likewise, when she spoke of Saint Jean de Brébeuf, she referred very simply to what was said about him after his death; she had learned nothing more than the others and was merely sending her son the text of the *Relation* that was later to spread throughout all of France (cf. *Écrits* 4:269–70).

The situation is quite clear: Marie de l'Incarnation, inspired by the martyrdom of these saints, described her own spiritual life, deriving therefrom a parallelism to theirs. This does not necessarily mean that in a very general sense her conclusions were not exact. By and large, the Venerable Mother certainly was right. It was necessary for these men, if they were to bear such quantities and such extremes of pain, to be possessed of a consuming zeal and an outstanding attachment to the Cross of Christ, their only love. Furthermore, since she was here speaking of the end of the mystical life, where union with God is identified with the yearning for his Kingdom, it would be unavoidable that she meet other souls who had arrived at the same point, just as she would meet there, too, all the other Catholic mystics.[23] What we should like to focus attention on here is that there were important differences between the form

---

[23] We are reminded, for example, of Saint Teresa of Avila, who characterizes her seventh mansion by the habitual vision of the Holy Trinity and by apostolic zeal.

of the spiritual life of the Jesuits and that of Marie de l'Incarnation, especially when we consider the manner in which they made their way to Heaven. A lengthy discussion of this difficult problem is impossible here, but perhaps a few remarks can clarify it at least to some extent.

First of all, the double attention—to God in her interior life and to the things of the world on the exterior—is fundamental and constant in the spirituality of this Ursuline of Quebec. Even before her entrance into the religious life, Marie de l'Incarnation was attracted so forcefully by the love of God that she was, as it were, sometimes transported outside herself, although actually in the presence of others (cf. *Écrits* 1:215–16). Most often, however, she was able simultaneously to immerse her spirit in the divine Majesty and to busy herself with the tasks imposed upon her (cf. *Écrits* 1:162). It was characteristic of her mystical life always to live a sort of twofold role. From among hundreds of others, let us cite this text of 1654 in which she described an earlier experience: "It is impossible for me to make known the cries and groans of my soul for the Word Incarnate, so heavy was the cross that I bore *in my interior*—but on the other hand, I had a free and discerning spirit *in my exterior disposition*" (*Écrits* 2:397). This dichotomy was to last until the end of her life. The advice of her confessor, recorded in her journal, gives evidence of this: "As I gave an account of myself to Reverend Father Lalemant, he said that I ought never to refuse any employment in temporal matters provided they did not distract me from the incomparable union with which it pleased the divine Majesty to honor me" (*Écrits* 2:429).

Father Jérôme Lalemant understood perfectly the unique vocation of this Ursuline. It was essential for her spiritual union that she never let the bustle of her active life interfere with her intimacy with God, a treasure that she had to safeguard at all cost, lest she lose the most essential element of her contemplative life. But it is precisely in this respect that his spiritual direction of her soul differs so widely from that given to his colleagues in the Society. Even as their superior, he could never advise them as he did Marie de l'Incarnation before her entrance into the religious life: "Yield yourself completely to intimacy with God, so long as it does not interfere with your work." Although this formula seems more suitable to their active life, it would not have respected their individual vocations, because these missionaries—and they proved it many times over—had to meet God in the apostolate itself. Far from distracting them from union with the divine Majesty, their works furnished them with the principal and most effective means whereby they honored him.

For this reason their spiritual psychology has almost nothing in common with that of the Venerable Mother. She, indeed, may have enjoyed a constant union with God in the depths of her soul, while her spirit, as we have just seen, remained free to undertake exterior occupations, but among the Jesuits a different spirit prevailed: their whole person—soul, spirit, body—participated in the gift of self to God. Even more, they devoted their whole body, their total energies, to God in their daily labors. For them there is no trace of a union with the Lord that could hold itself in a place apart or that could be experienced as an interior isolation undisturbed by apostolic activity. The dreams and visions of Jogues are filled with the events of the mission or those of his captivity; the mystical ascent of Jean de Brébeuf and certain of his struggles with Satan can be explained only by closely following the various vicissitudes of his apostolate and of his missionary trips.

Our discussion of this misunderstanding has already become too long. We hope we have succeeded in suggesting that the problem is not as simple as many would like to believe and that the seeming relationship between the mysticism of Marie de l'Incarnation and that of the Jesuits, attractive as it may seem at first sight, cannot stand under close scrutiny. It is better to consider separately the spiritual experiences of the Jesuits and to attempt to elucidate them as far as this is possible with the slight means at our disposal.

We cannot emphasize too strongly that our missionaries simply bore the exigencies of their apostolic vocation to their ultimate extreme. The graces with which God so magnificently overwhelmed them are inscribed day after day in the tasks from which they never shirked. To us they are specialists in the interior life; to themselves they were merely servants—devoured by zeal for God, it is true, but still useless sinners. In this sense they are close to us and can serve us as models.

VILLAGE BURNED BY ENEMIES 1673

PAUL LE JEUNE

INTRODUCTION

We have already met Father Paul Le Jeune several times, for he was founder and, after 1632, historian of the Huron mission. He was born at Châlons-sur-Marne in 1591, of Calvinist parents. At the age of sixteen he was converted to Catholicism, and six years later, September 22, 1613, he entered the Jesuit novitiate at Rouen. After three years of philosophy at La Flèche, he was appointed teacher of the fifth form at Rennes; then he was sent to Bourges to take charge of the third form. The next year he advanced to the second form with his class. He studied theology at the Collège de Clermont in Paris and taught rhetoric for two years at Nevers before making his tertianship under the direction of Father Louis Lallemant at Rouen from 1628 to 1629. His appointment as teacher at Caen was followed by that of preacher and superior of the residence at Dieppe. From Dieppe he went to Canada, although he had never volunteered for the missions.

We have also seen his great ability for conceiving and bringing to fruition extensive plans for the apostolate. At the same time, however, he was careful of the least details in administering the material needs of the mission. In a letter to his provincial in France, he outlined his plans for the men under his charge and followed this with suggestions for the different products he wished to see cultivated, for the livestock to be cared for, and for the building program he intended to undertake (cf. Thw. 6:28, 70–74). Although he was attentive to these minutiae, it was his great missionary projects that carried him forward and enlivened his zeal. There is no question that in the beginning he had entertained numerous illusions about the possibilities of seeing some tangible results rapidly accomplished. For example, in his first *Relation* of 1632, he wrote:

> [The Jesuit missioners] harvested great fruits in the East Indies and in South America, although they found in these countries not only numerous vices but also strange superstitions to which the people clung more closely than to their own lives. In New France there are no serious vices, but only sins to be destroyed, and these are few in number. These poor people, so far from all pleasures, have not abandoned themselves to many sinful habits. Superstitions and false religions, if they exist anywhere, are few in number and are not very widespread. The sole thought of the Canadians is gaining their livelihood and avenging themselves on their enemies. They are not attached to the cult of any divinity. They are allowed to have several wives; in general, however, they have only one. I have heard of but one man who had two, and he was reproached for it. I am sure that when I know their language I can handle them as I please (Thw. 5:32–34).

He was soon disillusioned. Thereafter the thought of the other missions, instead of permitting him to affirm the superiority of Canada, served him as an argument to justify the delays he experienced. He stated:

> I fear only one thing in these delays, namely, that Old France will become weary of helping the New. The harvest is so slow in maturing. Only let our friends at home remember that although the pumpkin ripens in a single night, it takes years to develop the fruit of the palm tree. I have heard that it was thirty-eight years before any results were seen in Brazil. How long did the missionaries stand outside the gates of China? We will enter when God wills. Those who run

too fast and become heated only grow weary, without making much progress (Thw. 6:22–24).

It seems rather that it was not the French of France whom Le Jeune sought to persuade, but himself, impatient like all great founders (cf. Thw. 6:38). He repeats for his own sake as well as for that of his readers: "Great results are not ordinarily accomplished in a short time" (Thw. 9:88); or again, "Well, give us patience in doing God's work! 'They patiently bear fruit' (Lk 8:15). The most precipitate affairs are not the most perfect. He who runs too fast is soon out of breath" (Thw. 9:92).

These words reveal to us that from that time on, his spirit would be limited only by his strength and endurance. He continually took on new enterprises; he tried to establish a seminary; he began to stabilize the savages around the colony; he made appeals to congregations of women religious to come and take care of the little girls and to found a hospital; he corresponded with Marie de l'Incarnation, since he perceived what a great support she would be for the mission.[1] However, he found great difficulty in understanding the mind of the Indians. He loved them—there is no doubt of that. He was eager to devote himself completely to them, but, French to the marrow of his bones, he could not grasp the fact that he was confronting a cultural complexity totally different from his own. He obstinately persisted in his desire to send the children to France. He was disconcerted by the failure of the seminary, unable to see why the boys invariably ran away to return to the woods and lakes.

---

[1] Marie de l'Incarnation, *Écrits* 3:95.

Brébeuf, who had neither the literary gifts nor the eagle eye of Le Jeune, but who was equally gifted in his broad views as well as in his attention to small details, proceeded much further in penetrating the Indian soul. In this respect, it was characteristic of Le Jeune to attribute a prime importance—and sometimes an exclusive one—to the study of their language. Even though he was the superior of the mission, he spent a winter among the Algonquins in his efforts to master their tongue. He thought he would convert them immediately upon learning to address them in their own admirable language (cf. Thw. 5:116). He even asked to be relieved of his superiorship in order to have more time to study (cf. Thw. 6:60). Humanist to the core, he believed in the decisive virtue of language, the mastery of which in missionary countries cannot be underestimated. But he did not sufficiently realize that a knowledge of the language could be accompanied by a certain lack of understanding of the civilization that the language expresses.

The superiors did not err in leaving Le Jeune at this central post from which he could direct and inspire the others, for in this he excelled. They were equally correct in having him write the *Relation de la Nouvelle-France,* even after he had given up the superiorship. In this work, as is evident from the extracts that follow, he manifested all of his talent. Without ever lapsing into edifying platitudes, he reminded his reader of the apostolic purpose of these trips and the religious inspiration that sustains all efforts of the missionary. He was a sprightly storyteller; he knew how to play on the humorous and the serious with the same skill; he excelled in his stories by adding the "punch line" that would touch or would cause a smile. He could raise his voice when necessary and take from his heart the note that subdued his hearer. After three centuries, those pages have lost nothing of their youth, and it is surprising to see a man, burdened with multiple tasks, without leisure, without repose of spirit, succeed in writing what others could not have produced in peace and quiet.

For Le Jeune, the mastery of the language was joined to the winning of the person. He could speak of events that happened to him without betraying the fact that he was talking about himself, nor did he ever seek to place himself in the foreground. His goodness toward those about whom he was writing and even toward those of whom he was making fun is always evident. He was full of sympathy for those who surrounded him. He spoke of his fellow workers with respect and understanding, and sometimes even with affection. His esteem for them was a source of great happiness for him. On every page he reveals himself as a man profoundly detached, whose heart was free. He did not go out of his way to seek difficulties, but he accepted those that were sent him. The heroic note so constantly present in him during his stay in the Huron mission is difficult to reconcile with his personality. He did not volunteer for the missions; he definitely did not desire martyrdom, because he knew how weak he was. However, he was undauntedly willing to go wherever God willed to lead him. Moved by the goodness of the provincial in France, who took so much care of him and his mission, he exclaimed: "O what heart! What love! What good will our Reverend Father has for us! I do not know how to respond to it except to say, 'Here I am, here I am, completely in your hands, for Canada, for France, and for the whole world. *Ad majorem Dei gloriam!*' In everything I see myself so weak and God so powerful that I can no longer desire anything, nor refuse anything" (Thw. 6:34). None of the other Canadian missioners used such language, not because they were less obedient, but because they had the certainty of having been called by God to live and die in this far-off land. This dedication to the missions was not the vocation of Le Jeune, who was more sensitive to the universal needs of the Church. He was never able totally and completely to immerse his strength, his intelligence, and his soul in this particular place where he was working at the moment.

Nevertheless, he knew, as did the others, the comfort of God's visits in times of extreme pain and the mysterious sustenance of the Lord in time of destitution. Referring to the winter of 1633, Le Jeune wrote:

> Hunger had planned to kill us, but God is so manifestly present in these difficulties that the time of famine seemed to me to be a time of abundance. If I were not afraid of exaggerating I would tell you, Reverend Father, of the sentiments that God gives at a time like that. I admit that sometimes I knew hunger and that often these words came to my lips: "Give us this day our daily bread"; but I never dared pronounce them without adding this condition: "if such be your good pleasure" (Mt 11:26). Sometimes I used to say—with a fair amount of sincerity—these words of Saint Xavier: "Lord, do not take me away from these sufferings unless you are preserving me for greater ones" (MHSJ, *Ep. Xav.* 1:394). Then I was consoled, even in my sleep; but that was to be expected, for God was acting in me at those times. Here is the sort of person I am: as soon as we were helped by creatures, I became sick in body and in soul. God thus showed me what he is and what I am. I was impatient, disgusted, and sought solitude in our tiny house. I tried hard to stop this state of misery, but since my passions are completely vitiated, I was staggering under every blow and brought back from this trip nothing but my faults (Thw. 6:38–40).

This page is the only one on which Le Jeune has left us something of his most secret life. In the others, one strongly suspects a man favored by God, very much aware, through his own experience, of divine help, the predisposition to the action of grace, and the laws of the spiritual life. However, Le Jeune never describes directly the ways he followed. In the letters he wrote[2] after his return to France in 1649, he hid his inner self behind the advice he gave; he always maintained a certain aloofness, dominating events and persons by the detachment of his heart as much as by the power of his spirit. As a good superior, free and detached, sometimes even incisive, he urges his readers to put themselves at the service of our Lord Jesus Christ without regard for preferences or tastes.

After fulfilling the offices of procurator for the missions in Canada, then of preacher and of director of souls, he died at Paris in 1664.

---

[2] *Lettres spirituelles* (Paris: Palmé, 1875). Father Le Jeune also wrote after his return to France *La Solitude de dix jours sur les solides vérités et maximes de l'Evangile* (Paris, 1664).

A BRIEF ACCOUNT OF
THE VOYAGE TO NEW FRANCE

Reverend and dear Father:

When your letter, which came on the last day of March, informed me that I should embark as soon as possible at Havre de Grâce and sail directly to New France, the joy and happiness that filled my soul was so great that I believe I have never experienced anything like it for twenty years. Never has any letter been so welcome to me! I left Dieppe the next day for Rouen, where I joined Father de Nouë and our Brother Gilbert. While at Havre, we went to pay our respects to M. du Pont, nephew of the cardinal, who gave us a passport, signed by his own hand, saying that it was the wish of the cardinal that we go to New France. We are under special obligations to the kindness of the Curé of Havre and of the Ursuline Mothers. Our departure had not been foreseen, and if Father Charles Lalemant of Rouen and these good people in Havre had not assisted us in our hasty preparations, we would certainly have fared very badly. From Havre we went to Honfleur, and on Low Sunday, April 18, we set sail.

At first we had very fine weather and made about six hundred leagues in ten days. The next thirty-three days, however, we scarcely covered two hundred. After the fine weather, we had little but storms and contrary winds, except

---

French title, *Brève Relation du voyage de la Nouvelle-France*, and text in Thw. 5:10–20. These are the first pages of the *Relation* of 1632.

for a few pleasant hours from time to time. I had often seen the angry sea from the windows of our little house at Dieppe, but watching the fury of the ocean from the shore is quite different from tossing about on its waves. For three or four days we were close-reefed, as the sailors say, with our helm fastened down. The vessel was left to the will of the waves and of the billows, which bore it at times upon high mountains of water, then suddenly plunged it into the depths of the sea. The winds were unchained against us, to use a poetic expression. Every moment we feared that they would snap our masts or that the ship would spring a leak. In fact, there was a leak, which, as I heard later, would have caused us to sink if it had been farther down. It is one thing to reflect on death in one's cell, before the image of the Crucified; but it is quite another to think of it in the midst of a tempest and in the actual presence of the "Grim Reaper". But I say honestly that, although nature longs for its preservation, nevertheless, in the depths of my soul I felt quite as much inclination to death as to life—or even more. I kept constantly before me the thought that he who had brought me upon the sea had some good purpose and that he must be allowed to do as he pleases. I dared not ask of him anything for myself except to offer up my life for all on the ship. When I realized that within a few hours I might see myself in the midst of the waves—and that, perhaps, in the blackest night—I found some consolation in the thought that where there was less of the creature there would be more of the Creator, and that I really would be dying by his hand. But my weakness makes me fear that perhaps, if it really had happened, my thoughts and inclinations might have been very different.

But let us turn to other things. We found winter in summer on this trip. In the month of May and a part of June, the winds and the fogs chilled us. Besides this, I had pains in my head and in my heart that scarcely left me at all during the first month. We suffered also because we ate nothing but salted food, and there was no fresh drinking water on our vessel. We had such magnificent cabins that we could not stand upright, kneel, or sit down; and to make matters worse, when it rained, water dripped down on my face. All these discomforts were shared by the others, but the poor sailors suffered many more. But now all that is past, thank God. Still, I would not wish to be in France. All these little afflictions have not as yet, I believe, caused us the least sadness over our departure. God never lets himself be outdone in generosity. If you give him mites, he will give you gold mines. It seems to me, however, that I get along better than Father de Noué, who for quite a long time has not been able to eat. As to our Brother, he is like the amphibious animals, just as much at home on the sea as on land.

On Pentecost Sunday, just as I was starting to preach, as I usually did on Sundays and big feast days, one of our sailors began to cry out, "Codfish! Codfish!" He had thrown in his line and brought out a big one. For several days we had had our lines over the rails but had caught very little. On that day we drew in as many as we liked. It was really a pleasure to see so great a slaughter and so much codfish blood on the deck of the ship. Fresh fish was very welcome after so much salted and dried food.

On the following Tuesday, June 1, we sighted land. It was still covered with snow, for the winter, always severe in this country, was extremely so this year. Some days before, namely, on the fifteenth and the eighteenth of May, while we were still about two hundred leagues from land, we had met two enormous icebergs floating in the sea. They were longer than our ship and higher than our masts. When the sun shone on them, they looked like cathedrals—or rather, mountains of crystal. I would hardly have believed it if I had not seen it. No wonder that when a ship is caught among a number of them it is soon completely crushed.

On Thursday, June 3, we entered the country by one of the most beautiful rivers in the world. The large island of Newfoundland intercepts the river at its mouth, leaving two openings by which it can empty into the sea, one to the north and the other to the south. We sailed in through the latter, which is about thirteen or fourteen leagues wide. As soon as you go in, you find a gulf about one hundred fifty leagues wide; as you go still farther up, it narrows to about thirty-seven leagues wide. Where we are, at Quebec, about two hundred leagues from its mouth, it is still half a league wide.

At the entrance of this gulf we saw two rocks, one round, the other square. It looks as if God threw them into the midst of the waters like two dovecotes, as a retreat for the birds that roost there in such multitudes that you almost step on them. If you do not have a firm footing, they almost knock you over, because they swarm up in such numbers. When the weather permits an approach to these islands, named Bird Island by the French, boats or little skiffs are filled with birds and brought back to the ships. Large vessels also come into this gulf on whaling expeditions, as do a great many who come fishing for cod. Here, too, I saw a number of seals, some of which our people killed. In this remarkable river, called the Saint Lawrence, white porpoises are found, but nowhere else. The English call them white whales because they are much larger than other porpoises; they are found as far up as Quebec.

On Trinity Sunday we were compelled to stop at Gaspé, a large bay extending into the coast. Here we touched land for the first time since our departure. Never did man, after a long voyage, return to his country with more joy than we entered ours—that is what we call these wretched lands. There were two ships here, one from Honfleur and the other from Biscay, the latter one having come to fish for cod. We begged the people from Honfleur to raise an altar for us, that we might celebrate Holy Mass in their cabin. They vied with each other as to who should work on it, they were so pleased. So I said to them, laughingly, that when they built their cabin they did not think they were building a chapel. The Gospel appointed for the Mass of that day, the first that I had read in these lands, surprised me with these words of the Son of God to his disciples: "Absolute authority in heaven and on earth has been conferred upon me. Go, therefore, and initiate all nations in discipleship: baptize them in the name of the Father", and so forth. "And mark that I am with you at all times", it continued. I took these words as a good omen, although I saw clearly that they were not addressed to so poor a person as I. However, it is my opinion that I came here like the pioneers, those who go ahead to dig the trenches; after them come brave soldiers who besiege and take the citadel.

HARDSHIPS WE MUST BE READY TO ENDURE WHEN WINTERING WITH THE SAVAGES

Epictetus says that he who intends to visit the public baths must previously consider all the improprieties that will be committed there, so that, when he finds himself surrounded by the derision of a mob of scoundrels who would rather wash his head than his feet, he may lose none of the gravity and modesty of a wise man. I might say the same to those in whom God inspires the thought and desire to cross the seas and seek out the savages to instruct them. It is for their sakes that I am writing this chapter, so that, knowing the enemy they will encounter, they may not fail to fortify themselves with the weapons necessary for the combat. They will need especially a patience of iron or of bronze, or rather, a patience entirely of gold, to bear bravely and lovingly the great trials they will have to endure among these people. Let us begin by describing the house in which they will have to live if they wish to work among the Indians.

In order to have some concept of the beauty of this edifice we must describe its construction. I speak from firsthand knowledge, for I have often helped to build one. As soon as we arrived at the place where we were to camp, the women, armed with axes, went here and there in the huge forests, cutting the framework of the mansion in which we

---

French title, *De ce qu'il faut souffrir hivernant chez les sauvages,* and text taken from chapter 12 of the *Relation* of 1634 (cf. Thw. 7:34–64). Le Jeune left in October 1633 to learn the Algonquin language. The next year he knew enough to teach the other missionaries. Cf. Rochemonteix, 1:236.

were to live. In the meantime, the men, having drawn up the plan, cleared away the snow with their snowshoes or with shovels that they make and carry expressly for this purpose. Imagine, then, a large circle or square in the snow two, three, or four feet deep, according to the weather or the place where they encamp. This makes a white wall surrounding us on all sides except at that end where the men break through to form the door. Twenty or thirty poles, more or less, according to the size of the cabin, are brought for the framework. These are set up, not on the ground, but on the snow. Then, on these poles, which converge a little at the top, the men fasten two or three rolls of bark sewn together, beginning at the bottom, and lo! the house is finished. The Indians then cover the ground and the wall of snow, which extends all around the cabin, with little branches of fir. As a final decoration, a mangy skin is fastened to two poles to serve as a door, the doorposts being the snow itself. Now let us examine in detail all the comforts of this North American Louvre.

You cannot stand upright in this house, as much on account of its low roof as because of the suffocating smoke. Consequently, you must always either sit flat on the ground—the usual posture of the savages—or lie down. When you go out, the cold, the snow, and the danger of getting lost in these immense woods drive you in again more quickly than the wind and keep you prisoner in a dungeon that has neither lock nor key.

This prison, in addition to the uncomfortable position you are forced to take, has four other major discomforts: cold, heat, smoke, and dogs. As to the cold, you have the snow at your head, protected only by a pine branch or, quite often, only by your hat. The winds are free to enter in a thousand places. Do not imagine that these pieces of bark are joined as tightly as paper glued and fitted to a window frame. They are more like Saint John's wort,[1] except that their holes and their openings are a little larger. Even if there were only the opening at the top, which serves both as window and chimney, the coldest winter in France could come in there every day without any trouble. When I lie down at night, through this hole I can study the stars and the moon as easily as if I were in the open fields.

Nevertheless, the cold did not annoy me as much as the heat from the fire. A place as small as an Indian cabin is easily heated by a good fire. Sometimes I was roasted and broiled on all sides. The cabin was so narrow that I could not protect myself against the heat. You cannot move to right or left, because the savages, your neighbors, are at your elbows. You cannot withdraw to the rear, for you bump into the wall of snow or the bark of the cabin that hems you in. I never knew what position to take. If I stretched myself out, the place was so narrow that my legs would be halfway in the fire. If I rolled myself up into a ball and crouched up like the Indians, I could not retain that position as long as they could because my muscles would cramp. My clothes were all scorched and burned. Perhaps you will ask if the snow at our backs did not melt under so much heat. It did not, and if sometimes the heat did soften it the least bit, the cold immediately turned it into ice. However, both the cold and the heat are endurable, and some relief can be found for these two discomforts.

But, as to the smoke, that is a martyrdom. It almost killed me, and made me weep continually, although I had neither grief nor sadness in my heart. It sometimes grounded all of

---

[1] Hypericum, a plant that grows in moist areas. It often has yellow flowers and transparent areas on its leaves.

us who were in the cabin; that is, it caused us to place our mouths against the earth in order to breathe. For, although the savages were accustomed to this torment, yet occasionally it became so dense that they, as well as I, were compelled to prostrate themselves, and, as it were, to eat the earth so as not to drink the smoke. Sometimes I stayed in this position for several hours, especially during the most severe cold and when it snowed. It was then that the smoke assailed us with the greatest fury, seizing us by the throat, nose, and eyes. How bitter that drink is! How strong its odor! How painful to the eyes are its fumes! Sometimes I thought I was going blind. My eyes burned like fire; they watered and spilled forth drops as copiously as a still. I could no longer see anything distinctly; I was like the good man in the Gospel who said: "I see the people; they look to me like trees that move about" (Mk 8:24). I recited the Psalms of my breviary as best I could, knowing them half by heart, and waited until the pain might relax a little to read the lessons; and when I did read them, they seemed to be written in letters of fire, or of scarlet. I have often closed my book, seeing things so confusedly that it hurt my eyes.

Perhaps someone will say that I ought to have gone out from this smoky hole to get some fresh air. My answer is that the air was usually so cold at those times that the trees, which have a harder skin and a more solid body than men, could not withstand it. They split even to the core, making a noise like the report of a shotgun. Nevertheless, I occasionally emerged from this den, fleeing the pain of the smoke, only to place myself at the mercy of the cold. I tried to protect myself against it by wrapping up in my blanket like an Irishman, and in this garb, sitting in the snow or on a fallen tree, I recited my Hours. The trouble was, the snow had no more pity on my eyes than did the smoke.

As for the dogs, which I have mentioned as one of the discomforts in the homes of the savages, I am really not sure if I should blame them, for they have sometimes rendered me good service. True, they exacted from me the same courtesy they gave, so that we reciprocally aided each other, illustrating in a new way the motto *mutuum auxilium*. These poor beasts, not being able to live outdoors, came and lay down sometimes on my shoulders, sometimes on my feet. I had only one blanket to serve both as covering and mattress, so I was not sorry for this protection, willingly restoring to them a part of the heat that I drew from them. It is true that, being large and numerous, they occasionally crowded and annoyed me so, that in giving me a little heat they robbed me of my sleep. As a result, I very often drove them away. One night when I did this, a little incident occurred that caused some confusion and laughter. A savage lay down on me while I slept. I thought it was one of the dogs, and seizing a club, I hit him, crying out: "*Ache! Ache!*" the words they use to drive away the dogs. My man woke up greatly astonished, thinking he had met his end. When he discovered where the blows were coming from, he said to me: "You have no sense. It is not a dog, it is I!" At these words, I do not know which of us two was more astonished. I gently dropped my club, very sorry to have found it so near me.

Let us return to our dogs. These animals are famished, having nothing to eat any more than we do. They do nothing but run back and forth, gnawing at everything in the cabin. Now, since we were as often lying down as sitting up in these bark houses, they frequently walked over our faces and stomachs. They did this so often and so persistently that, being tired of shouting at them and driving them away, I would sometimes cover my face, giving them liberty to go where they wanted. If anyone happened to throw them a bone, there was an immediate race for it, and all whom they encountered sitting, unless they held themselves firmly, were turned over. They have often overturned my bark dish and all its contents into my cassock. I was amused whenever there was a quarrel among them while we were eating, for every one of us, with both hands, held down his plate to the ground—our table, chair, and bed for men and dogs alike. Because we had no table, we experienced much annoyance from these animals, who thrust their noses into our bark plates even before we ourselves could get our hands in. But now I have said enough about the inconvenience of the savages' houses; let us speak of their food.

When first I went to live with them I could not eat their mixtures, as they salt neither their soup nor their meat, and filth itself presides over their cooking. I contented myself in those days with a few sea biscuits and smoked eels. At last my host took me to task because I ate so little, saying that I would starve even before the famine overtook us. Meanwhile, our savages had feasts every day so that soon we were without bread, flour, or eels, with no means of helping ourselves. We were very far into the woods, where we would have died a thousand times before we reached the French settlement. Besides this, we were wintering on the other side of the great river, which cannot be crossed during this season because of the large masses of ice that are continuously floating about in it and that would crush not only a small boat but even a large ship. Hunting elk was not profitable either, because in comparison with other years the snow was not very deep, and the large animals went elsewhere to feed. The Indians did, however, capture a few beaver and porcupines. Even then, this was so seldom and the number so few that they merely kept us from dying rather than helped us to live.

My host said to me during this scarcity: "*Chibine*, harden your soul, resist your hunger; sometimes you will go two, or even three or four days, without food. Do not let yourself be downcast. Take courage. When the snow comes, we shall eat." It was not Our Lord's will that they should be long without capturing anything. Ordinarily, we ate once every two days. For example, we very often would have a beaver in the morning and the next evening a porcupine as big as a suckling pig. This was not much for nineteen of us, it is true, but this little sufficed to keep us alive. When our supply of food ran out, if I could have the skin of an eel for my day's fare, I considered that I had breakfasted, dined, and supped very well.

In the beginning I had used one of these eel skins to patch my cloth cassock, as I had forgotten to bring some patches with me. But when hunger pressed too hard, I ate my patches. I assure you that if the whole cassock had been made of the same stuff, I would have brought it home much shorter than it was. Indeed, I ate old moose skins, which are much tougher than eel skins. I went about through the woods biting the ends of the branches and gnawing the more tender bark, as I shall relate in my diary of the trip.

Our neighboring savages suffered still more than we did. Some of them came to see us and told us that their comrades had died of hunger. I saw some who had eaten only once in five days, and who considered themselves very well off if they found something at the end of two days. They were reduced to skeletons, being little more than skin and bones. Occasionally we had some good meals, but for every good dinner we went three times without supper. When a young savage was dying of hunger in our cabin, as I shall relate in the following chapter, the Indians often asked me if I was not afraid, if I had no fear of death. Seeing me quite calm, they were astonished, especially at those times when they were close to despair. When they reached this point, they adopted the attitude of every man for himself, so to speak; they threw away their bark and their baggage, deserted each other, and abandoned all interest in the common welfare. Each one would then strive to find something for himself. When this happened, the children, the women—in a word, all those who could not hunt—died of cold and hunger. If we ever had reached this extremity, I am sure that I would have been among the first to die.

These are the things that we must be prepared for before deciding to live with the Indians. Even though they do not suffer from famine every year, still the risk of not having any—or very little—food threatens unless there are heavy snowfalls and a great many moose.

Now if you were to ask me how I felt in the presence of these terrors of death—death so lingering as that which comes from hunger—I have to say that I can hardly tell. Nevertheless, in order that those who read this may not dread coming over to our assistance, I can truly say that the time of famine was for me one of abundance. When I realized that we were beginning to hover between the hope of life and the fear of death, I made up my mind that God had condemned me to die of starvation for my sins. A thousand times I kissed the hand that had written my sentence, and I awaited the execution of it with a peace and joy that can be experienced but not described. I acknowledge that one suffers and that he must reconcile himself to the cross; but God glories in helping a soul when it is no longer aided by creatures. Let us continue our account.

After this famine, we had some good days. The snow, which was only deep enough to be cold but too slight for hunting moose, greatly increased toward the end of January. Our hunters then captured some moose, which they dried. Now, either because of my lack of moderation, or because this meat, dried as hard as wood and as dirty as the street, did not agree with my stomach, I fell sick early in February. Thus, here I was, obliged to lie on the cold ground. This did not help to cure me of the severe cramps that tormented me and compelled me to go out at all hours of the day and night, plunging me every time in snow up to my knees, and sometimes almost up to my waist, especially when we had first begun our encampment in any one place. These severe attacks lasted about eight or ten days and were accompanied by a pain in the stomach and a weakness in the heart that spread throughout my whole body. I recovered somewhat from this sickness, but not entirely. I was still dragging myself around at mid-Lent, when I was again assailed by the disease. I recount this to show how little help may be expected from the savages when a person is sick. One day I was very thirsty and asked for a little water. They said there was none, but they would give me some melted snow if I wanted it. As this drink was bad for my disease, I made my host understand that I had seen a lake not far from our cabin and that I would like very much to have some of that water. He pretended not to hear, because the road was somewhat bad. This was not the only time it happened like this; it was the same any time the river or brook was a little distance from our cabin. We had to drink the snow melted in a kettle whose copper was not as thick as the dirt. If anyone would like to know how bitter this drink is, let him take some water from a kettle just out of the smoke and taste it.

The savages divide their food with the sick just as with the well. When they have fresh meat they give him his share if he wants it, but if he does not eat it then, no one will take the trouble to keep a little piece for him to eat when he feels better. They will give him some of what they happen to have at the time in the cabin, namely, smoked meat, and nothing better, for they keep the best for their feasts. So a poor invalid among them is often obliged to eat what would horrify him even in good health if he were in France. A soul very thirsty for the Son of God, that is, for suffering, would find enough here to satisfy him.

I must still speak of their conversation in order to give a complete picture of what is to be suffered among these people. I had gone with my host and the Renegade[2] on condition that we should not pass the winter with the Sorcerer, whom I knew to be a very wicked man. They had yielded to my conditions but were faithless and kept none of their promises. This involved me in trouble with the pretended magician, as I shall reveal later. This wretched man and the smoke were the two greatest trials I endured among these barbarians. The cold, the heat, the annoyance of the dogs, sleeping in the open air or upon the bare ground, the position I had to assume in their cabins, rolling myself up into a ball, crouching down, sitting without a chair or a cushion, hunger, thirst, the poverty and filth of their smoked meats, sickness—all these things were merely play to me in comparison to the smoke and to the malice of the Sorcerer,

---

[2] An Indian named Pierre who had been taken to France by the Recollets but who, on his return, had resumed his former way of life. The Sorcerer was his brother. Cf. Rochemonteix, 1:233–35.

with whom I have always been on very bad terms, for the following reasons:

First, because when he invited me to winter with him, I refused. He resented this very much, especially when he saw that I cared more for my host, his younger brother, than I did for him.

Secondly, because I could not gratify his covetousness. I had nothing that he did not ask for, often taking my mantle off my shoulders to put it on his own. Since I could not satisfy all his demands, he looked on me with an evil eye. Indeed, even if I had given him all the little I had, I could not have gained his friendship, because we were at odds on other subjects.

In the third place, seeing that he acted the prophet, amusing these people by a thousand absurdities that he invented, in my opinion, every day, I did not lose any opportunity of convincing them of his nonsense and childishness. I exposed the senselessness of his superstitions. This was like tearing his soul out of his body. He was no longer able to hunt, so he acted the prophet and magician more than ever before, in order to maintain his prestige and thus to obtain delicacies. When I thus shook his authority, which was diminishing daily, I touched the apple of his eye and wrested from him the delights of his paradise, the pleasures of his palate.

In the fourth place, wishing to make sport at my expense, he sometimes made me write vulgar things in his language. He would assure me there was nothing wrong in them and make me pronounce these shameful words, which I did not understand, in the presence of the other savages. Some of the women warned me of this trick, so I told him I would no longer soil my paper or my lips with those vile words. He insisted, however, that I should read before all those in the cabin and some other savages who had come there something he had dictated to me. I answered that if the Apostate[3] would interpret them for me, I would read them. The Renegade refused to do this, so I refused to read. At this the Sorcerer commanded me imperiously, that is, in very strong words. At first I begged him gently to excuse me, but he did not wish to be thwarted before the savages. He continued to urge me and had my host, who pretended to be vexed, urge me also. Finally, aware that my excuses were of no avail, I spoke to him peremptorily, and after reproaching him for his lewdness, I said to him: "You have me in your power. You can murder me if you like. But you cannot force me to repeat indecent words." "They are not bad", he said. "Why, then," I replied, "will no one interpret them for me?" He emerged from this conflict very much exasperated.

In the fifth place, seeing that my host was greatly attached to me, the Sorcerer was afraid that this friendliness might deprive him of some choice morsel. I tried to relieve him of this apprehension by stating publicly that I did not live to eat, but that I ate to live, and it mattered little what they gave me, provided it was enough to keep me alive. He retorted sharply that he did not feel like that, but made a profession of being a gourmet; that he was fond of delicacies and was very much pleased when people gave them to him. Now, although my host gave him no cause for fear in this matter, he attacked me at almost every meal as if he were afraid of losing his preeminence. This apprehension increased his hatred toward me.

In the sixth place, he saw that the savages of the other cabins also showed me some respect. He realized that I was

---

[3] The Renegade.

a great enemy of his impostures and that if I gained influence among his flock, I should ruin him completely. He did all he could to destroy me and to make me appear ridiculous in the eyes of the other savages.

In the seventh place, add to all the above-mentioned things the aversion that he and all the savages of Tadoussac had at this time against the French, aroused and enkindled by the Indians' trading with the English. You can then judge what treatment I might have received from those barbarians who adore this miserable Sorcerer, against whom I was generally in a state of open warfare. A hundred times I thought I would emerge from this conflict only through the gate of death. He treated me shamefully, it is true; but I am surprised that he did not act worse, seeing that he was a devotee of those superstitions that I was fighting with all my might. To relate in detail all his attacks, gibes, sneers, and contempt, I should have to write a book instead of a mere chapter. Suffice it to say that he sometimes even attacked God to displease me and that he tried to make me the laughingstock of the great and small, abusing me in the other cabins as well as in our own. He never had, however, the satisfaction of arousing our neighboring savages against me. They merely hung their heads when they heard the blessings he showered on me. The servants, instigated by his example and supported by his authority, continually heaped upon me a thousand taunts and a thousand insults. I was reduced to such a state that, in order not to irritate them or give them any occasion to become angry, I passed whole days without saying a word. Believe me, if I have brought back no other fruits from my stay with the savages, I have at least learned many of the insulting words in their language. They would say to me at every turn: "*Eca titou, eca titou; nama khitirinisin* (Shut up, shut up; you have no sense);

achineou (he is proud); *moucachtechiou* (he is a parasite); *sasegau* (he is haughty); *cou attimou* (he looks like a dog); *cou mascoua* (he looks like a bear); *cou ouabouchou ouichtoui* (he has a beard like a hare); *attimonai oukhimau* (he is the lead dog of the team); *cou oucousimas ouchtigouan* (he has a head like a pumpkin); *matchiriniou* (he is deformed; he is ugly); *khichcouebeon* (he is drunk)." These are the colors in which they paint me, plus a multitude of others that I will omit. The best part of it was that they sometimes thought I did not understand them, then seeing me smile, they were embarrassed—at least, those who sang these songs only to please the Sorcerer. The children were very troublesome, playing numerous tricks on me and imposing silence when I wanted to talk. When my host was at home I had some relief, and when the Sorcerer was absent I was in smooth water, managing both children and adults just as I wished.

This is a good sampling of the difficulties that must be endured among these people. These difficulties really should not frighten anyone. Good soldiers are encouraged by the sight of their blood and their wounds. God is greater than our hearts. We do not always have a famine; we do not even frequently meet a sorcerer or a magician with such a bad temper. In a word, if we could understand their language and reduce it to rules, there would be no need of living with these barbarians. As to the stationary tribes, from which we expect the greatest fruit, we can have our cabins apart and consequently be freed from many of these inconveniences. But let us finish this chapter; otherwise I see myself in danger of becoming as troublesome as that impostor whom I recommend to the prayers of all who read this. In the following chapter, I will set down some conversations I had with him when we were enjoying a truce.

DIARY OF THE TRIP

As soon as we had set foot on land, my host took a shotgun he had bought from the English and went out to look for supper. Meanwhile, the women began to build the house where we were to live. Now the Apostate, noticing that everyone was busy, returned to the boat that was lying at anchor, took the keg of wine, and drank from it to such excess that, being drunk as a lord, he fell into the water and nearly drowned. He finally got out after much scrambling and started for the place where they were putting up the cabin. Screaming and howling like a demon, he snatched the poles and beat on the bark, trying to break everything to pieces. When the women saw his frenzy, they fled to the woods, some here, some there. My savage, whom I usually call my host, was stewing in a kettle some birds he had killed. This drunken fellow, coming on the scene, broke the tripod and upset everything into the ashes. No one seemed to get angry at all this, but then, it is foolish to fight with a madman. My host gathered up his little birds, went to wash them in the river, refilled his kettle, and placed it once more over the fire. The madman was running hither and thither on the shores of the island, foaming like one possessed. The women, seeing this, ran quickly to get their bark and take it to a safe place, lest he should tear it to pieces as he had started to do. They scarcely had time to roll it up when he came toward them completely infuriated. He did not know upon what to vent his fury, for they

---

Extract from chapter 13 of the *Relation* of 1634, where Le Jeune gives the diary of this same trip among the Algonquins in 1633 to 1634. French title, *Journal de voyage*, and text taken from Thw. 7:72–94.

had all suddenly disappeared, thanks to the darkness that had fallen and that concealed us. He approached the fire, which he could see in the dark, and was about to overthrow the kettle again when my host, his brother, quicker than he, seized it and threw the water, boiling as it was, into his face. I leave you to imagine how this poor man looked, finding himself thus deluged with hot water. Never was he so well washed. The color of his skin, of his face and his whole chest, changed. Would to God that his soul had changed as well as his body. He redoubled his howls and pulled up the rest of the poles that were still standing. My host has told me since that he asked for an ax with which to kill me. I do not know if he really did ask for one because I did not understand his language, but I do know very well that when I went up to him and tried to stop him, he said to me in French: "Go away. It is not you I am after; let me alone." Then, pulling on my cassock, he said: "Come, let us embark in a canoe; let us return to your house. You do not know these people here. All they do is for their stomachs; they do not care for you but for your food." To this I answered in an undertone and to myself, "*In vino veritas!*"

As the night was coming on rapidly, I retired into the woods to escape annoyance from this drunkard and to get a little rest. While I was saying my prayers near a tree, the woman who managed the household of my host came to see me. She gathered some fallen leaves and then said to me, "Lie down there and make no noise." She gave me a piece of bark for a cover and then left. So this was my first resting place, my open-air inn, which I named "The Sign of the Moon", and as if acknowledging this honor, she shone brightly on me from all sides. Here I was, an accomplished horseman on the first day I entered the riding academy! A little before midnight, it began to rain. I was afraid I would get wet, but before I decided how I could protect myself, it stopped. The next morning I came to the conclusion that, although my bed had not been made up fresh since the dawn of creation, it was not too hard to keep me from sleeping.

The next day I wanted to throw the rest of the wine, keg and all, into the river. I had told the savages that I would do this if anyone abused it. But my host, seizing me around the waist, cried out: "*Eca toute, eca toute!* Don't do that, don't do that! Don't you see that Petrichtich (this is what they call the Renegade in derision) doesn't know anything? That he is a dog? I promise you that we will never touch the barrel unless you are present." I yielded and made up my mind to distribute it liberally in order to rid myself of the fear that a little wine might make us all drink a great deal of water, for if they were to get drunk while we were in the canoe, we should all drown.

We intended to leave this island in the morning, but the tide ebbed sooner than we expected and stranded our boat. Therefore, we had to wait for the evening tide. We embarked then and sailed away with the aid of the moon as well as that of the wind. We reached another island, called *Ca ouapascounagate*. As we arrived there about midnight, our people did not take the trouble to make a cabin. I lodged at the same inn, "The Sign of the Moon", and slept in the same bed as the night before—under the shelter of the trees and of the sky.

The next day we left this island to go to another one, called *Ca chibariouachcate*. We might have called it the Island of the White Geese, for I saw more than a thousand of them in one flock.

The following day we tried to leave, but the bad weather compelled us to land again at the end of the same island. It is deserted, like all this country; that is, it has only temporary inhabitants, for these Indians have no fixed place of residence. The island is bordered by rocks so huge, so lofty, so craggy, yet covered so picturesquely with cedars and pines, that a painter would consider himself fortunate to view it. He would be greatly inspired by this desert, frightful in its precipices, yet pleasing in the variety and number of its trees, which seem to have been planted by the hand of Art rather than by that of Nature. As it is indented by bays full of silt, such a quantity and variety of wild game are covert here as I have never seen in France. One must truly see them to believe it.

We left the island of game and sailed all day. Toward nightfall we landed at a small island called *Atisamoucanich etagoukhi*, that is, the place where dyes are found. I am inclined to think that our people gave it that name because they found there some little red berries and roots that they use in dyeing their *matachias* (ornaments of shell, beads, and the like). I would like to call it the Island of Misfortune, for we suffered a great deal there during the eight days that the storms held us prisoners. It was night when we disembarked. The rain and the heat assaulted us. In the meantime, we could scarcely find five or six poles to serve as beams for our house, which for such weather as this was so small, so narrow, and so exposed that in trying to avoid one discomfort, we fell into two others. We had to shorten ourselves, roll up like hedgehogs, so that we would not scorch half of our bodies. For our supper, which was also our dinner because we had eaten nothing since early morning, my host threw to each one a piece of the biscuit I had given him. He told us that we were not to drink anything with our food, as the water in this great river began to be salty in this area. The next day we collected some rain water, which had fallen into dirty rocks, and drank it with as much enjoyment as if it were the wine of Ay.

The Indians had left our shallop at anchor in a strong tidal current. I told them it was not safe and that it ought to be placed under shelter behind the island; but, as we were only waiting for a good breeze in order to set out, they did not heed me. During the night the storm increased. It seemed as if the winds were uprooting the island. Our host, foreseeing what might occur, roused the Apostate and urged him to come and help him save our shallop, which threatened to go all to pieces. Now either this wretch was lazy or he was afraid of the billows, for he did not even try to get up. He gave as his only reason that he was tired. During this delay, the wind broke the fastening, or cable, of the anchor and in an instant carried away our shallop. My host, seeing this happy outcome, came and said to me, "Nicanis, my well beloved, the shallop is lost. The winds that have torn it loose will break it into pieces against the rocks that surround us on all sides." Who would not have been vexed at that Renegade, whose negligence caused us untold trials, considering that we had a number of packages among our baggage and several children to carry as well. Yet my host, barbarian and savage that he is, was not at all troubled at this accident, but fearing it might discourage me, he said, "Nicanis, my well beloved, are you angry at this loss, which will cause us so many difficulties?" "I am certainly not very happy over it", I answered. "Do not be cast down," he replied, "for anger brings on sadness, and sadness leads to sickness. Petrichtich has no sense. If he had tried to help me, this misfortune would not have happened." And these were the only reproaches he made. Truly, it humiliates me that considerations of health should check the anger and vexation of a barbarian and that the law of God, his good pleasure, the hope of his great rewards, the fear of his chastisements, our own peace and comfort, cannot check the impatience and anger of a Christian.

The above misfortune was soon followed by another. In addition to the shallop, we had a little bark canoe. The tide, rising higher than usual because of the strong wind, robbed us of that, too. There we were, prisoners more than ever. I neither saw any tears nor heard any complaints, not even among the women, upon whose shoulders this disaster fell most heavily because, like beasts of burden, they usually carried the baggage. On the contrary, everyone began to laugh.

When morning came—for the tempest committed this theft during the night—we all ran along the edge of the river to learn firsthand some news of our poor shallop and our canoes. We saw both of them stranded a long distance away, the shallop among the rocks and the canoe along the edge of the woods of the mainland. Everyone thought they were all in pieces. As soon as the sea had receded, some ran toward the shallop and others toward the canoe. Wonderful to tell, nothing was harmed! I was amazed, for out of a hundred ships, even if they were made of wood as hard as bronze, scarcely one would have been saved in those violent blasts of wind upon these rocks.

While the wind held us prisoners on this unhappy island, a number of our people went to visit some savages who were five or six leagues distant from us, so that there remained in our cabin only the women and children and the Iroquois. During the night, a woman who had gone out returned terribly frightened. She cried out that she had heard the *Manitou*, or devil. At once all the camp was in a state of alarm, and everyone, filled with fear, maintained a profound silence. I asked what was the matter, for I had not heard what the woman had said. "*Eca titou, eca titou*", they told me. "*Manitou!* keep still, it is the devil." I began to laugh and, rising to my feet, went out of the cabin. To reassure them I called, in their language, the *Manitou*. I shouted in a loud voice that I was not afraid; I dared him to come near me. Then, having made a few turns on our island, I reentered and said to them, "Do not be afraid; the devil will not harm you as long as I am with you, for he fears those who believe in God. If you will believe in God, the devil will flee from you also." They were greatly astonished and asked me if I was not afraid of him at all. I answered, to relieve them of their fears, that I was not afraid of a hundred of them. They began to laugh and were gradually reassured. Now I noticed that they had thrown some eels on the fire. I asked them why. "Keep still", they replied. "We are giving the devil something to eat so that he will not harm us."

I arranged a few prayers in their language, with the help of the Apostate. Since the Sorcerer had not yet returned, I recited them in the morning and before our meals. The Indians themselves reminded me of them and took pleasure in hearing them. If the wretched magician had not come with us, these barbarians would have taken great pleasure in listening to me. My host asked me a thousand questions—why we died, where our souls went, if night was universal all over the world, and many other such things—and was most attentive to my answers. But let us now proceed to other matters.

I noticed here that the young women did not eat from the same dish as their husbands. When I asked the reason, the Renegade told me that the young unmarried women and the women who had no children took no part in the management of affairs and were treated like children. That is why his own wife said to me one day, "Tell my husband to give me plenty to eat, but do not tell him that I asked you to do so."

One night when everyone had sunk into a deep sleep, I began to talk to this poor miserable Renegade. I showed him that while he was in our house, he had lacked for nothing of whatever we had; that he might have spent his life there peacefully; that in forsaking God he had rushed into the life of a brute, which would finally end in Hell if he did not open his eyes; that eternity was very long and to be a companion of devils forever was a long term. "I see clearly", he replied, "that I am not doing right, but it is my misfortune that I do not have a will strong enough to remain firm in my determination. I believe everything anyone tells me. When I was with the English, I allowed myself to be influenced by their talk; when I am with the savages, I do as they do; when I am with you, it seems to me your belief is the true one. Would to God I had died when I was sick in France. I would now be saved. As long as I have any relatives, I will never do anything of any account, for when I want to stay with you, my brothers tell me I will rot, always staying in one place like that. That is why I leave you to follow them."

I presented all the arguments and made all the offers I could to strengthen him, but his brother, the Sorcerer, who will soon be with us again, will upset all my plans. He does whatever he wishes with this poor apostate.

On October 30 we left this wretched island, and toward nightfall we disembarked at another island that had a name almost as long as itself, for it was not half a league in circumference. This is what our savages tell me it is called: *Ca pacoucahtechokhi chaghagou achiganikhi, Ca pakhitaouananiouihi.* I believe they make up these names on the spot. This island is nothing but a big, frightful rock. There was no spring of fresh water, so we had to drink very dirty rain water that we collected in the bogs and on the rocks. The sail of our shallop was thrown over some poles to form our shelter. Our beds were white and green. There were so few pine branches under us that in several places we touched the snow, which three days before had begun to cover the earth with a white mantle.

Here we found the cabin of a savage named *Ekhennabamate*, whom our host had been seeking. This man told us that the Sorcerer had passed by here a short time before and that, having the wind against him, he could not have gone far. Our host did not wait until broad daylight to follow him. His canoe, paddled by three men, went like the wind. In short, on the beautiful Feast of All Saints, he brought back this demon, the Sorcerer. I was very much surprised when I saw him, for I did not expect him. I thought my host had been hunting. Would that he had, and that this miserable prey had escaped from his hands.

As soon as he came, there was nothing but feasting in our cabins. We had only a little food left, but these barbarians ate it with as much calmness and confidence as if the game they were to hunt was shut up in a stable.

One day when my host was having a feast, the guests made signs to me that I should address them in their language. They wanted to laugh, for I pronounce their language as a German pronounces French. Wishing to please them, I began to talk, and they burst out laughing. They were well pleased to make sport of me, while I was very glad to learn to talk. In conclusion I told them that I was a child and that children made their fathers laugh with their stammerings, but that in a few years I would grow up and that then, when I knew their language, I would make them see that they themselves were children in many things, ignorant of beautiful truths of which I would speak to them.

Immediately I asked them if the moon was as high in the heavens as the stars; if it was in the same sky; where did the sun go when it left us; what was the form of the earth. (If I had known their language perfectly, I would always have proposed some natural truth before speaking to them of the truths of our belief, for I have observed that these phenomena make them more attentive.) To keep me on the subject of my discourse, one of them, after frankly confessing that they could not answer these questions, asked me, "But how can you know these things, since we do not know them?" Right away I took out a little compass that I had in my pocket, opened it, and, placing it in his hand, said to him, "We are now in the darkness of night. The sun no longer shines over us. Tell me, then, while you look at what I have given you, in what part of the world the sun is at this time. Show me the place where it must rise tomorrow, where it will set, where it will be at noon. Point out the places in the sky where it will never be." My man answered with his eyes, staring at me without saying a word. I took the compass and explained to him all the things I had just asked him. Then I added, "Well, now, how is it that I know these things and you do not know them? I have still greater truths to tell you when I know how to talk." "You are intelligent", they responded. "You will soon know our language." But they were mistaken.

My host had invited all the neighboring savages to a feast. When they had come and seated themselves around the fire and the kettle, waiting for the banquet to begin, the Sorcerer, who had been lying down opposite me, suddenly arose. He had not said a word since the arrival of the guests. He seemed to be in a diabolic fury. He threw himself upon one of the poles of the cabin to tear it out; he broke it in two and rolled his eyes around in his head, looking here and there like a man out of his senses. Then he faced those present and said to them: "*Iriniticou nama Nitirinisin.* O men, I have lost my mind. I do not know where I am. Take the hatchets and javelins away from me, for I am completely mad." At these words all the savages lowered their eyes to the ground and I raised mine to heaven, from where I expected help. I imagined that this man was acting the madman in order to take revenge on me, to take my life, or at least to frighten me. Then he could reproach me afterwards that my God had failed me in time of need and would proclaim among his people that I, who had so often testified that I did not fear their *Manitou*, who makes them tremble, had turned pale before a man. So far was I from being seized by fear of this man—I who ordinarily recoil at the thought of death in any form—that, on the contrary, I faced this maniac with as much assurance as if I had had an army at my side. I knew that the God I adored could bind the arms of fools and madmen as well as those of demons. Besides, if his Majesty wished to open to me the portals of death by the hands of a man who was acting the devil, his providence was always loving and kind. This Thraso[1] redoubled his furies. He did a thousand foolish actions of a

---

[1] Thraso is the name of a braggart soldier in Terence's *Eunuchus*. The Greek word *thrasos* means bold, inclined to brag, blustering.

lunatic or of one bewitched. Sometimes he shouted at the top of his voice and then would suddenly stop short, as if frightened. He pretended to cry and then burst into laughter like a wanton devil. He sang without tune or rhythm; he hissed like a serpent; he howled like a wolf or a dog; he screeched like an owl or a nighthawk. He would roll his eyes around in his head and strike a thousand poses, always seeming to be looking for something to throw. At every moment I was waiting for him to pull up one of the poles to strike me down, or to throw himself upon me. But in order to show him that I was not at all astonished at these devilish acts, I continued, in my usual way, to read, to write, and to say my little prayers. When my hour for retiring came, I lay down and rested peacefully through his orgies, as I would have done in a profound stillness. I was already accustomed to go to sleep in the midst of his shouts and the sound of his drum, as a child falls asleep to the songs of his nurse.

The next evening, at the same hour, he seemed disposed to enter into the same infuriated state and again to alarm the camp, saying that he was losing his mind. Seeing him already half-mad, it occurred to me that he might be suffering from some violent fever. I went up to him and took hold of his arm to feel the artery. He gave me a frightful look, seeming to be astonished. He acted as if I had brought him news from another world, rolling his eyes here and there like one possessed. Having touched his pulse and his forehead, I found him as cool as a fish and as far from a fever as I was from France. This confirmed me in my suspicion that he was acting the madman to frighten me and to draw down upon himself the compassion of all our people, who of their little were still giving him the best they had.

VARIOUS THOUGHTS AND FEELINGS OF THE FATHERS IN NEW FRANCE
(*Taken from their last letters of* 1635)

1. Truly New France is a region where one learns perfectly to seek God alone, to desire God alone, to have one's intentions sincerely directed toward God, and to trust and rely closely upon his fatherly providence. This is rich treasure for the soul, impossible to estimate.

2. To live in New France means truly to live in the bosom of God and to breathe only the air of his divine guidance. The sweetness of that air can be realized only by actually inhaling it.

3. It is not fitting that everyone should know how agreeable it is in the sacred awe of these forests and how much heavenly light one finds in the thick darkness of this barbarism. We should have too many persons wishing to come here, and our settlements could not accommodate so many. What confounds us is that God has chosen us to share in this mercy when there are many of our Fathers in France who would do better than we.

4. The joy that a priest feels when he has baptized a savage who dies soon afterward and flies directly to Heaven to become an angel[1] is certainly one that surpasses anything that can be imagined. No longer does he remember the sea, or the seasickness, or the horrors of past tempests. He longs for the sufferings of ten thousand tempests to help

---

French title, *Divers sentiments et avis des Pères qui sont en la Nouvelle-France*, and text in Thw. 8:168–92. We cite these pages because they were published at the end of the *Relation* of 1635, edited by Le Jeune. Cf. *Lettres du Bas-Canada*, June 1961, p. 80.

[1] The terminology here is, of course, popular rather than theological.

save one soul, since Jesus Christ for a single soul would willingly have shed all of his Precious Blood.

5. The greatest contest we had among ourselves was to see which one could be lucky enough to be chosen to go to the Hurons. God let the lot fall upon those it pleased him to choose. They are going to these barbarous nations as if to a terrestrial paradise. Once a person has tasted fully the sweetness of the Cross of Jesus Christ, he prefers it to all the empires of the earth.

6. Lately we were in a tempest so furious that the whole ocean seemed to be in a turmoil. We were told that we were the cause of this horrible storm. This surprised us at first, as it was said by people of good faith. When we asked why, they told us that with so furious and raging a tempest, it must be that Hell was enraged at seeing us go to New France to convert the infidels and to diminish its infernal power. For revenge it raised up all the elements against us and was trying to sink the fleet with all its component parts. But we said to them very gently: "Remember, gentlemen, that God is more powerful to defend us than Lucifer is to persecute us. The sea may rise as high as it will, yet God will still be its Master." "Mightier far than heaving waves, mightier far than seething sea, aye, mighty is the Lord on high!" (Ps 92:4). Indeed, we fear the anger of God against our faithlessness far more than that of the sea against our human weakness.

7. In Europe there is a saying that whoever wants to learn to pray to God should go to sea; but it is quite a different thing to be there than to talk about it. Lately we were more than two days and two nights in continual danger of being engulfed by the ocean. It seemed that every moment must be our last. We saw mountains coming toward us which seemed about to swallow us up. Both of us were down on

our knees, praying to God with earnest hearts. Our greatest fear was that some might die without confession. In situations like this, one can make many ejaculatory prayers as he looks hopefully toward Heaven. But it is very difficult to believe in the power of grace and the strong assurance that God gives to his servants in the midst of the most fearful tempests and despair.

8. I have never understood what it is to reach such a point of virtue that it would require a miracle to advance still further. Yet how true it is that a person sometimes finds himself so far plunged into either suffering or danger or desertion by his fellow creatures that nothing is left to him but God. He, however, is always found at the end of Jacob's ladder, with arms and heart wide open to embrace the angels and the souls that fly straight to him. It is wonderful how God takes pleasure in communicating himself so abundantly to souls who have abandoned all and given themselves to him completely. To lose all in order to find God is a sweet loss and a holy usury.

9. The heart grows in proportion as its works for Jesus Christ increase. New France is the most suitable country in the world in which to understand the literal meaning of these beautiful words: "As the Father has made me his ambassador, so I am making you my ambassadors" (Jn 20:21); "Listen! I am sending you like sheep among a pack of wolves" (Mt 10:16). In the midst of these forests, at the sight of these savages, what can we poor foreigners and servants of God expect but to feel their teeth and some of the effects of their natural barbarism? He who truly fears God can fear nothing more in this world.

10. There is no doubt that to travel nine hundred leagues on the waves of the sea and to endure hundreds of encounters with Turks, icebergs, reefs, and horrible storms can appall

human nature and cause our hearts to throb. In such circumstances one experiences what David meant: "Imperiled is my life at every step, yet I do not forget your law" (Ps 118 [119]:109). I am very happy that I can so frequently make a precious sacrifice of myself. The infusion of God into our hearts and the relief he pours into our souls exceed all our ills. I confess that I have learned better on the sea than on land what the infusion of God into a well-disposed soul can mean.

11. When we see these savages, well formed, strong, of good mien, endowed with natural good sense; when we realize that only a drop of water is needed to make them children of God and that Jesus Christ has shed all of his Blood for them, we feel an incredible ardor to attract them to God and to the Church. And it is true that we should prefer the conversion of one of these poor savages to the conquest of a whole empire. The trouble we take to accomplish this is so pleasant that we do not even consider it trouble but a truly extraordinary favor of Heaven. "Love for Christ impels us" (2 Cor 5:14). How true it is that charity presses our hearts!

12. When we were pursued by the Turks on leaving the English Channel, I spent twenty-four hours expecting nothing else than to fall into their hands, to be loaded with chains, and to live in slavery. In the midst of these natural fears, a strong thought took possession of my heart: "Ah, how good it would be to be able to imitate Saint Paul and to see myself in fetters for the love of Jesus, who was bound for me, treated like a slave, and was the King of Thieves." This sweet thought prevailed so strongly in my soul that I desired those chains more than I feared captivity.

13. Three forceful thoughts console a good heart that is in the infinite forests of New France or among the Hurons.

The first is: "I am in the place where God has sent me, where he has led me by the hand, where he is with me, and where I can seek him alone." The second is, in the words of David: "When worries throng my heart, your consolations are my soul's delight" (Ps 93 [94]:19). The third is that we never find crosses, nails, or thorns in the midst of which, if we look closely, we do not find Jesus Christ. Now, can any person be evil when he is in the company of the Son of the living God?

14. When I saw myself surrounded by murderous waves, by infinite forests, and by a thousand dangers, there came to my mind that precious saying of Saint Ignatius the Martyr: "Today I begin to be the disciple of Christ." For what do so many exercises, so many fervent meditations, so many eager desires avail? All these are nothing but wind if we do not put them into practice. Thus, Old France is fitted to conceive noble desires, but New France is adapted to their execution. What one desires in Old France he has in the New.

15. I do not know what the country of the Hurons is, to which God in his infinite mercy is sending me, but I do know that I would rather go there than to an earthly paradise, since I see that God has so ordained. How strange it is! The more crosses I see prepared for me there, the more my heart rejoices and flies thither! What happiness it is for me to see nothing but savages, crosses, and Jesus Christ. Never in my life in France have I understood what it was to distrust self entirely and to trust in God alone—really alone, without the presence of any creature. "God is greater than our conscience, and knows everything" (Jn 3:20). This is very evident in New France, and it is an unutterable consolation that when we find nothing else we immediately encounter God, who communicates himself most fully to hearts that are well disposed.

16. My consolation among the Hurons is that I can confess every day and then say Mass as if it were my last; I receive Holy Communion as if it were Viaticum and I were to die that very day. I do not think that a person can live better nor live with more satisfaction and courage—and even merit—than to live in a place where he expects every day to die. The motto of Saint Paul, "Day after day I face death" (1 Cor 15:31), is truly applicable to me.

17. To convert the savages, not so much knowledge is necessary as goodness and sound virtue. The four qualities requisite for an apostle in New France are affability, humility, patience, and a generous charity. A zeal too ardent scorches more than it warms and thus ruins everything. Great magnanimity and adaptability are necessary to attract these savages, little by little. Our theology is difficult for them to understand, but they comprehend perfectly our humility and friendliness, and through these they are won.

18. The Huron nation is disposed to receive the light of the Gospel, and inestimable good is to be hoped for in all these regions. However, two kinds of persons are needed to accomplish this: those in Old France, assisting by their holy prayers and their charity; and those in the New, working with great gentleness and tirelessness. The conversion of many thousands of souls, for each one of whom Jesus Christ has shed his Precious Blood, depends on the goodness of God and on this sweet harmony.

19. If a small seminary of a dozen little Hurons could be founded at Quebec, within a few years it would lend incredible assistance to the conversion of their fathers and in the establishment of a flourishing church in the Huron nations. Alas! How many thoughtless and frivolous people in Europe lose in three casts of the dice more money than it would take to convert a world!

20. One of the thoughts that weighs most heavily upon those who are so fortunate as to serve God in these forests is their unworthiness of so exalted an apostolic calling and that they have so few of the virtues needed for so noble a work. He who sees New France only through his natural bodily eyes sees only forests and difficulties; but he who looks upon these with the eyes of grace and of his noble vocation sees only God, virtues, and graces. He finds therein so many and such strong consolations that if I were able to buy New France by giving in exchange for it an earthly paradise, I should certainly buy it. How good it is to be in the place where God has put us by his grace! Truly I have found here what I had hoped for: a heart in harmony with God's heart, a heart that seeks God alone.

21. It is said that the pioneers who found churches are usually saints. This thought so melts my heart that, although I see that I am not of much use here in this pleasant New France, yet I must confess that I cannot forbid one thought that presses upon my heart: "I will most gladly spend myself and be spent to the limit for the sake of your souls" (2 Cor 12:15). Poor New France! I desire to sacrifice myself for your welfare, and even if it cost me a thousand lives to assist in the salvation of a single soul, I should be very happy to offer them and should consider all of them well spent.

22. I do not know what it is to enter paradise, but I do know that in this world it is difficult to find a greater and fuller joy than I experienced on entering New France and saying my first Mass here on the Feast of the Visitation. It was a Visitation in every sense of the word. Through the goodness of God and of Our Lady, it seemed more like Christmas. I felt that I was being reborn to a completely new life, a life in God.

23. The seasickness that had caused me so much discomfort on the ocean was soon effaced by a clear sky and the joy that God poured into my soul when we landed at Cape Breton. When I met our Fathers, I felt as if I were embracing angels from paradise. I could not refrain from exclaiming: "Ah, what will it be like to enter paradise when God and the angels receive a beautiful soul released from the tempests of our wretched earthly life!"

24. I used to think it required miracles to convert these nomad savages, but I was mistaken. The real miracles of New France are to do much good and endure many pains; to complain to God alone; to realize our unworthiness and uselessness. Whoever practices these virtues will perform miracles greater than miracles and will become a saint. Indeed, to humiliate oneself deeply before God and man, to annihilate oneself completely, is harder than to raise the dead. That takes only a word if we have the gift of miracles. But to humiliate ourselves as we ought requires a man's whole life.

25. We were greatly astonished and infinitely glad to observe that in our little cabins and in our settlements, religious discipline is as strictly observed as it is in the largest houses of France and that the interior fervor is in inverse proportion to the exterior diversions. In his infinite goodness, God ordinarily multiplies the gift of his graces according to our needs; and, indeed, to the same extent that a servant of God submits to his holy guidance, Our Lord pours forth in great measure the precious shower of his graces.

26. These untutored barbarians call all the priests "patriarchs" and show great respect for men of integrity. They promise to bring us for baptism their children when they are sick unto death; in fact, some have been baptized shortly before they expired. Unquestionably these are the

elect, so blessed as to go forth from barbarism directly into paradise. If I never do anything else, what happiness it is to have been instrumental in placing these little souls among the elect!

27. Sometimes we meet men so devoid of every notion of religion that we cannot find a name to make them understand God. We have to call him the great "Captain of Men", "He Who Feeds All the World", "He Who Lives on High", and so forth. We do all we can to help them understand. What an obligation they owe to those who instruct them and who try to make them know God and serve him as well as they can. To win these uneducated savages, no deep learning is needed—only profound humility, unconquerable patience, and apostolic charity. In all other respects, these people have good common sense. Once we begin to win them, the fruit will be incalculable.

28. A thousand times the thought of Saint Francis Xavier comes to our minds and encourages us greatly. If, in order to have beaver skins and codfish and all sorts of other commodities, the men of the world fear neither storms at sea nor savages on land, nor even death itself, how dreadful will be the confusion of God's servants who tremble at these things or shun a few little hardships in their efforts to win souls ransomed by the Precious Blood of Jesus Christ and empurpled by his Precious Blood? On the day of judgment, these petty traders and fishers of cod will rise up to condemn us if they take more pains to gain a little money than we do to help save the savages. This thought stimulates our courage so vehemently that we do not even feel our sufferings, or if we do feel them, we dare not complain of them.

29. There are many persons in France who are completely idle and have nothing to do. They are educated people

but are of no use to the Church or to God. In New France these men would be apostles if they wanted to come and use their talents here. Less learning and more humility and zeal would perform miracles in this land. It is possible that in New France such dedicated souls would gain more in a year than they will in a lifetime in Old France.

30. Experience shows that those men of the Society who come to New France should be impelled by a special and very forcible call. They should be persons who are dead to themselves and to the world; men truly apostolic, who seek God alone and the salvation of souls; who love with real love the cross and mortification of self; who do not spare themselves; who can endure the hardships of the sea and of the land and who desire the conversion of the savages more than to rule all Europe; who have God-like hearts, all filled with the Holy Spirit; who are like little John the Baptists, crying through these deserts and forests like voices from God that summon all these graceless savages to acknowledge Jesus Christ—in sum, let them be men whose sole satisfaction is in God and to whom suffering is the greatest delight. That is what experience shows us every day. But it is also true that it seems as if God sheds the dew of his grace much more abundantly upon this New France than upon the Old. Interior consolations and divine infusions are much stronger here, and hearts are on fire. "The Lord knows who are his" (2 Tim 2:19). But it is God alone who chooses those he will use and whom he favors by taking them to New France to make saints of them.

Saint Francis Xavier said that there was an island in the Orient that could cause a person to lose his sight by tears of excessive joy. I do not know if our New France resembles this island, but we have learned that if anyone here gives himself up in earnest to God, he runs the risk of losing his sight, his life, his all, and this with the greatest joy, yet by dint of hard work. Those who are here and who enjoy God can speak from experience.

31. We clearly recognize that it is Heaven alone that will convert this land of New France and that we are not sufficiently strong of ourselves. We fear nothing so much as that our imperfections may prevent the conversion of these miserable savages; that is why we have all been minded to have constant recourse to Heaven and to the most holy Virgin, Mother of God, through whom God is accustomed to do what seems impossible and to convert the hearts of the most abandoned and profligate sinners. To accomplish this, we have resolved to make a very solemn vow, whose content will be something like this:

> My God and my Savior, Jesus Christ, although our sins ought to banish us from your presence, yet, inspired with a desire to honor you and your most holy Mother and urged by a wish to see ourselves corresponding most faithfully to your inspirations and your graces, as you desire your servants to do, and wishing also to see you acknowledged and adored by these wretched people, we promise and solemnly vow to you and to your most holy Mother, the Virgin Mary, and to her glorious spouse Saint Joseph, to celebrate twelve times in twelve succeeding months the Sacrifice of the Holy Mass, those of us who are priests; and for the others, to say twelve times the Crown or Chaplet of the Virgin, in honor of and in thanksgiving for her Immaculate Conception. We promise to fast on the day before this festival, and promise further that if a permanent church or chapel is erected in this country within this specified time, we will have it dedicated to God under the title of the Immaculate Conception if this be in our power. All this we promise in order to secure by the goodness of Our Lord the conversion of these

peoples through the mediation of Mary, his Mother, and of her holy spouse. In the meantime, receive, O Queen of Angels and of Men, the hearts of these poor abandoned barbarians that we present to you through the hands of your glorious spouse and of your faithful servants Saint Ignatius and Saint Francis Xavier and of all the guardian angels of these wretched countries. Offer them to your Son, that he may give them knowledge of himself and apply to them the efficacy of his Precious Blood. Amen.

May God in his infinite goodness render us worthy of this noble calling and grant that we may cooperate wholeheartedly with his grace for the welfare of these poor savages.

ENEMOND MASSÉ

INTRODUCTION

With Father Enemond Massé we seem to turn backward, since he was, with Father Biard, the first Jesuit to penetrate the land of Canada. But he was also part of the group of missionaries who worked there after 1632 under the direction of Father Le Jeune.

Born at Lyons in 1574, Massé entered the Jesuit novitiate in 1594. He taught grammar at Tournon from 1597 to 1600, then did his theology and was ordained priest in 1603. He remained at Lyons after his third year of probation until 1608. It is from there that he wrote to the general of the Society the first of the two letters that we translate on the following pages.

Massé did not have the gifts for writing equal to those we recognize in several of his friends. As soon as he takes up his pen, he becomes a stammerer like Jeremiah and is able to do nothing but jump from one scriptural quotation to another to indicate the zeal that is burning within him but that he is incapable of expressing in a personal way.

Father [Lucien] Campeau, engaged in the study of the mission of Acadia and intending to publish the sources of its history, wrote to us that there was in Massé a "certain affability and a certain tact that attracted to him the affection and confidence of simple people. At Port Royal, a locality quite hostile to the Jesuits, the men were more drawn to him than to Father Biard. When the sailors of Saint-Sauveur, defeated by the English, returned to France and were offered the opportunity of choosing the priest who was to share their risks, they spontaneously and unanimously chose Father Massé, though they had known him only a month and Father Quentin had been with them much longer."

In 1609 Massé was sent as companion to Father Coton, at that time Court Preacher at the palace of Henri IV. Massé was soon afterward appointed to New France but had to wait until 1611 before he could embark for Acadia. As has already been mentioned above in the general introduction (pp. 21ff.), he was forced to return to France with Father Biard in 1614. He was then sent to Paris and later spent ten years at the college of La Flèche. Here he met Anne de Nouë, Charles Lalemant, Paul Le Jeune, Barthélemy Vimont, and Paul Ragueneau, along with many other future missioners of Canada. In 1625 it became possible for him to embark a second time.

Four years later the missionaries were again expelled by the English. Father Massé went first to La Flèche, then to Rouen in 1631 and to Pontoise in 1632.

The following year he took up for the third time the route for Canada, where he was to die in 1646. During this whole period, he was occupied especially with the material organization of the mission and did not leave Quebec. In his letter of 1634 to the provincial in France, Father Le Jeune had written: "Father Massé, whom I sometimes jokingly call 'Father Useful', is well known to you, Reverend Father. He takes care of managing the household and all our livestock. He has been very successful at it." Active, industrious, a good organizer, he knew how to take care of the place to which he had been assigned so as to give others greater freedom for their work.

The vivacity of his temperament never manifested itself except by charity and good humor, a quality that rendered him very attractive. His profound humility led him to spend his energies in the untiring service of others and to consecrate the impetuosity of his character to the Passion and the Cross.

LETTER TO
REVEREND FATHER GENERAL

December 8, 1608

Very Reverend Father:

Pax Christi!

Now, at last, in the fear of God, my lips have pronounced the vows of a formed Spiritual Coadjutor. The ceremony took place on the Feast of Saint Luke[1] in the public church and in the presence of the Fathers, Brothers, and of all the people. Your desires, my God, are now part of me. What return shall I make to you? "Ah, ah, ah, Lord God: behold I cannot speak" (Jer 1:6). "I am a man of unclean lips" (Is 6:5). Where shall I, small as I am, find a hymn suitable to God, who is without equal; and where, Reverend Father, shall I find thanks suitable to your paternal kindness, which, through God, is without equal? Up until now "I kept dumb and silent; I refrained from rash speech" (Ps 38:3 [39:2]), stupefied as I was at the greatness of this unexpected kindness. I still do not know how to repay you or which way to

---

The original of this letter, a copy of which was obligingly sent to us along with the following note (2) by Father Campeau, is kept in the archives of the Society of Jesus in Rome, *Indipetae* 752:20, doc. 13. Father Massé had already requested to be sent to the missions of Canada earlier in the year 1608.

[1] *Lucalibus*: this is an expression peculiar to the Jesuits, who thus designated the day for the formal opening of classes in the schools on October 18, the Feast of Saint Luke. It is the day on which Father Massé pronounced his holy vows.

turn. "So I bethought myself to solve this riddle, and oh, how difficult it seemed to me until I pierced the holy mind of God" (Ps 72:16 [73:16–17]). But if I continue to hesitate and to postpone taking up my pen, this delay will in the end cause me the shame of ingratitude. Should I volunteer to do but little, this minimum, all out of proportion to the immensity of the gift, will make me ashamed of myself; if I seek to do much, my limited capacity, my useless prolixity, will indicate my imprudence. There are difficulties, assuredly, in every alternative. I know what I should do; and though I hesitate to speak of it, still I am ashamed to put it off. I hope that to this modest beginning I shall be able to give an immense conclusion, an infinite termination; still, I am overwhelmed. For it is not a childish hymn of praise but an awed silence that is inspired by the munificence of God's gifts and your own kindly concern for me, Reverend Father.

So—"with God's help we will bravely act" (Ps 107:14 [108:13])—with all my heart I offer these vows taken so recently to God and to you, Father. Freed by them from natural ties, I am able very joyfully to sacrifice myself as a hymn of praise not only by my voice but also by my actions even to death, if necessary—if, "among the Gentiles to voice his glory; in all the tribes, his wondrous deeds" (Ps 95 [96]:3)—I may be a missionary in Canada. "Therefore my heart is glad, my soul exults: and so my body, too, will rest secure" (Ps 15 [16]:9). May this, then, be my joy next March.[2] I not only wish but implore this favor from you, Reverend

---

[2] The boats for Canada left in spring. On the date that this letter was written, the Visitor, Father Christopher Baltasar, had already chosen Father Biard, who was teaching in the same college at Lyons, for the missions in Canada and had sent him to Bordeaux to wait for an opportunity to embark. However, he did not leave until three years later, when he and Father Massé together set out for New France.

Father. Please include me, unworthy as I am, in your prayers and your Holy Masses.

Your son and servant in Christ,

Enemond Massé

Lyons, the Feast of the Immaculate Conception, 1608

LETTER TO
REVEREND FATHER GENERAL

June 10, 1611

Very Reverend Father:

Pax Christi!

If my letter of October 13 caused you pleasure, Reverend Father, I felt a great deal more joy and honor in receiving yours of December 7, especially since I was privileged to be that member of the Society to whom your first letter to Canada was addressed. I take this as a happy omen and accept it as coming from Heaven to encourage me "to run so that I will surely win the prize" (1 Cor 9:24) and to merit and receive the "prize in store for those who have received from above God's call in Jesus Christ" (Phil 3:14). I am moved to sacrifice myself more promptly and more completely for the salvation of these people.

I must tell you that because of your letter, I said frankly to God: "'Here I am' (Heb 10:7); if you 'chose what the world holds foolish, to put to shame the wise, and what the world holds weak ... to put the mighty to shame, and what the world holds ignoble and despicable, and what counts for nought' (1 Cor 27:28), you have surely found all of this in Enemond. Here I am; send me and make my words and

---

This letter was written at Acadia during the time of Father Massé's first stay in Canada. The text we give here is from the Latin.

my speech intelligible, so that I may not be a barbarian to those who hear me."

I am sure that your prayers will not be fruitless. Our arrival here on the Feast of Pentecost seems to have special significance. "We are weak in him", but I hope with him "we shall live ... through the power of God" (2 Cor 13:4). I earnestly beg you, Reverend Father, by your prayers and Holy Masses to prevail upon the Lord to accomplish all these things in us.

> Your unworthy son of the Society,
> in Jesus Christ,
>
> Enemond Massé

Port Royal, New France, June 10, 1611

SPIRITUAL NOTES

If Jacob was content to serve fourteen years in order to win Rachel, how much more eagerly should I serve my dear Master twice seven years for New France—my dear Canada[1]—beautified with a great variety of most lovable and adorable crosses! So great a blessing, so lofty an occupation, so sublime a vocation—in a word—Canada and its delights, which are the cross, can be obtained only through a frame of mind conformed to the cross. For this reason I must resolve to observe inviolably these points:

1. Never to lie down except on bare ground, that is, without sheets, without mattress, without straw bed; however, I must keep some of these in my room for the sake of appearances.
2. To wear no linen except about my neck.
3. Never to say Holy Mass without wearing a hair shirt. That armor will remind me of the Passion of my Master, the Passion of which this Sacrifice is the great memorial.
4. To take the discipline every day.
5. If ever I omit making my examination of conscience before I go to meals, no matter how circumstances may hinder me from doing so, I will eat only a dessert, as one may do at collation on fast days.[2]

---

[1] This phrase leads us to believe that these notes were written shortly before 1625. At that date it was more than seven years since Father Massé had been forced to return to France. Cf. *Relation* of 1646, Thw. 29:32–34.

[2] Collation was a very light meal, and this dessert would probably have been only fruit and cheese.—ED.

6. I will never yield to the cravings of my sense of taste.
7. I will fast three times a week, but in such a way that no one will notice it except him who should know it. As I usually take my meals only at second table,[3] I can easily conceal these little mortifications.
8. If I permit any word, however slight, against charity to escape my lips, I will gather up secretly with my tongue the spittle and phlegm from the mouths of others.

---

[3] Father Massé, as procurator at the college at La Flèche, often took his meals after the community had finished.

SAINT JEAN DE BRÉBEUF

INTRODUCTION

The Indians, to whom hunchbacks, the lame, and persons crippled in any way at all were unknown and who made fun of the deformities sometimes found among the French, had unbounded admiration for the stature, strength, and bodily proportions of Jean de Brébeuf. They were quite surprised, then, to see that this handsome giant never used his strength for violence. His gestures and words were always as gentle as those of a child. However, as we shall see, these were merely the external signs of the paradoxical dynamism of this saint. His spirit was so impregnated with divine power and gentleness that in his presence one felt a sort of veneration, almost piety.

Brébeuf was born on March 25, 1593, at Condé-sur-Vire in Basse-Normandie, and he entered the Society of Jesus at Rouen on November 8, 1617. He had already finished his studies in the humanities and in philosophy before joining the Jesuits, so that at the end of his novitiate in 1619, he was appointed instructor of the sixth form at the college of Rouen. During the course of the following year, he fell gravely ill, but after a period of rest he was able, with the help of one of the Fathers, to pursue his theological studies and to be ordained priest at Pontoise in February 1622. He

---

In his *Étude sur les écrits de saint Jean de Brébeuf*, Father Latourelle not only gives an exhaustive list of all the saint's writings, but he includes the unpublished works and comments on the whole corpus. The two-volume documentation is as convenient as it is exact.

remained at the college of Rouen as teacher and procurator, that is, in charge of the finances, until his departure for New France in 1624. At first he was sent to the Montaignais and then to the Hurons, but the fall of Quebec in 1629 forced him to return to France with the other Jesuit missioners. He returned to Rouen, then went to the college at Eu, where he spent four years of hidden apostolic impatience, convinced that his sins were the only reason for his separation from Canada.

Brébeuf returned to his missionary labors in 1633 and was appointed superior of the Huron mission the following year. Here he devoted himself to the systematic study of the language of his people, and in spite of innumerable difficulties, which he described in the documents quoted in our collection, he succeeded in setting up a dictionary and a grammar, then in translating a catechism for the use of the Indians. As the political situation in New France became more stabilized, additional missionaries arrived and new houses were founded. Unfortunately, however, the Indians considered the Fathers responsible for the contagious illnesses that ravaged the region, and Brébeuf prepared himself and his companions for the death that threatened them. He drew up his will and sent it to his superior. This document reveals both the sadness aroused at seeing his apostolic work jeopardized, and an intense eagerness for his approaching martyrdom. The latter feeling by no means indicates temerity, but for a man whose life was based solely on the Cross, in which he had found great happiness and peace, it was impossible to repress a desire for the supreme identification with Christ Crucified. Brébeuf's will, one of the strongest and most beautiful of all the documents written by any of the Jesuits in New France, reminds us of the testimonies of the first generations of Christians. Like them, he met similar perils with equal courage. His spiritual journal reechoes their apostolic confidence, unshaken in the face of persecution.

In 1638 Brébeuf was replaced as superior by Father Jérôme Lalemant, who changed the underlying principles and the methods of the apostolate by substituting for the individual residences a single center from which the missionaries were to radiate to their various fields of activity. This change, although a contradiction of the system initiated by Brébeuf, did not disturb the saint. Indeed, he even praised the new superior and supported him with all his knowledge of the language and customs of the country. Never was anyone less attached to his own views or more ready to devote his energies to the tasks indicated by obedience. It is interesting to note that the innovations of Lalemant were not successful and that he later reverted to the original plan.

After a stay in the Neutral nation, where he and his companion Father Chaumonot received only insults and outrages, Brébeuf was removed from the mission because it seemed to him that his mere presence provoked the tribe to hatred. His personality was so dynamic that the Indians attributed to him, as to a sorcerer, an extraordinary evil power, and as a consequence, the primary source of all their misfortunes. Another reason for his leaving the Neutral country was an unfortunate fall on the ice. He broke his left shoulder blade and for two years could not use his arm. Father Chaumonot describes the incident thus:

> To complete the difficulties of this trip, on which it took him two whole days to cross a lake, burdened as he was with the provisions that he had to carry on his shoulders because there were no hostels on the way, he fell on the ice with such force that for a long time he was unable to

move, much less to get up. Finally, one of his companions helped him to his feet. He had broken one of his shoulder blades—an injury that he did not mention to a surgeon until two years later. Besides this, he had so completely severed the nerves that he could not lift his feet from the ground. For the remaining twelve leagues of the journey, he had to drag his feet, one after the other, in order to walk on the flat, level places. When he came to the mountains, he crawled on hands and knees through the snow on the way up, and to go down he sat down in the snow and helped himself with his hands to slide to the bottom. Several times his companions offered to help him, to pull him the rest of the way, but he always declined (*MS de 1652*, pp. 218–19).

Brébeuf returned to the Hurons in 1644 and worked among them for five more years. On March 16, 1649, he was martyred, put to death by the Iroquois, who were devastating the land.

Rare are the missionaries of the Gospel who in their hearts or bodies suffered more than this saint; rare also are those upon whom God has heaped riches of nature and grace more than on him. Father Ragueneau, Brébeuf's superior during his last years and also his biographer (cf. Thw. 34:138–94), understood thoroughly the complexity of his character, the strong contrasts in his personality. Brébeuf was a mystic, called to the highest spiritual favors, yet also an excellent organizer and practical financier; a daring but prudent superior, he attacked zealously the extensive problems of the mission, yet was attentive to the smallest financial details. A linguist of the first order, he mastered the Huron language and, as the Indians themselves testified, spoke it better than they did; an ethnologist superior to most of his contemporaries, he discerned the degradations effected by magic upon the most primitive traditions. With all these gifts, however, his only desire was to be forgotten and to submit his judgment to that of others.

Even though he was often enraptured by the love of God, Brébeuf remained convinced that his innumerable sins deserved the worst chastisements. His countenance revealed a striking benignity and tranquillity, a total absence of worry or disquietude, despite his having endured all types of suffering. Very few men in this "valley of tears" have been afflicted as he, but his expression by its calmness reminded one of an angel. Ragueneau, describing his gentleness, says:

> In him this virtue seemed to exceed all others and was constant in all situations throughout the twelve years that I knew him as superior, inferior, equal; in temporal affairs, in the labors and fatigues of the missions, in dealing with savage Christians, infidels, enemies; in sufferings, persecutions, and calumnies; never have I seen him angry nor even the slightest bit indignant. Sometimes a person would goad him on a sensitive point in an attempt to surprise him into some show of discomposure, but his look was always kindly, his words gentle, and his heart calm (Thw. 34:184).

Father Jogues, in contrast, resembled an interior sea, always ready to be stirred; Brébeuf was comparable to an ocean without a ripple, on whose surface the sun is reflected but that conceals monsters in its depths.

Monsters? Yes, indeed. For the composure of this saint was frequently threatened, not by movements of a fragile, delicate sensitiveness, but by demons who assailed him under a thousand forms and whose strangeness is revealed in the saint's spiritual journal. God, who invested him, as he himself said, "with forbearance, kindness, and charity", permitted him to be "as a secure fort" when he was besieged by the infernal spirits. At one time these would take on the appearance of a Spaniard; at another, that of a serpent; at still another, that of an old woman who had come to embrace him. For years Brébeuf carried on this monstrous struggle against the invisible forces that try to dominate humanity. It seems probable that this continuous struggle prevented his natural and supernatural kindness from degenerating into a servile compliance. His calmness under all circumstances, even the most trying, can be nothing but the triumph of Jesus Christ and of his love. Only once does Brébeuf's journal give forth a faint echo of an "extreme fear and fright"; this is on the occasion when, seeing in vision the head of a Jesuit turned into a river crab, he feared that this was a warning sent to himself. On all other occasions, it was enough for him to make the Sign of the Cross to ward off all fear or even the slightest tendency to take fright.

Through what half-open door or by what interior weakness was the devil able to make his way into this soul? Brébeuf accounted for his torments as the tricks of an adversary who came to sow weeds in the field of the father of a family, basing his explanation on the fact that these visions took place during the time that the mission was seriously threatened. But there must have been something else: Brébeuf the strong, Brébeuf the fearless, the gentle Brébeuf, keenly perceived the absolute vanity of earthly things. He frequently felt an acute disgust with himself for his too terrestrial attitudes and longings. When in 1630, after having considered his sins, he cried out: "O shame! O baseness and deformity of my life!"; when, later, he thought he should take his place "in the Society as a beggar admitted as a favor"; when he affirmed that "all our justice is like soiled linen", it is easily perceived that only the divine protection was capable of delivering him from the despair that threatened to submerge him.

Quite frequently it happens that vigorous men whose success and serenity are admired by all around them have within the depths of their being, far from the eyes of the curious, a breach through which the serpents can glide, as into the holes of walls that have resisted centuries. So it was with Brébeuf. This saint, so pure, so luminous, aided by nature and by grace, searched out the abscess hidden in every human soul and strove to eradicate it. That is why, it seems, that by means of his visions, he experienced such an astonishingly rapid passage from the marvelous to the horrible, from the ravishing to the grotesque. If we again contrast this saint with Jogues, we see that the latter's dreams and revelations were transmuted into beauty. Brébeuf, conversely, whose psychological receptivity was both more extensive and more intensive than that of his fellow martyr, and who never took fright at any form of the real, was able to support the unveiling of these monsters in his spirit. His perfect tranquillity held them enchained.

Was it this same intensity of feeling that caused Brébeuf to flee the responsibilities of the duties and offices that he foresaw? When, in the course of his novitiate, he asked to be a Coadjutor Brother; when, in the full flower of his missionary labor, he repeated that he seemed "not fit for anything except to take care of the door, to attend to the refectory, to prepare the meals", was he prompted only by humility and a desire to serve his companions? Was there not also present here a subtle temptation, hidden perhaps even from himself, to seek an outlet for the self-scorn that gnawed at him? Was he searching out a place or a human situation on a level with his self-disgust? In the so-called "low and humiliating" occupations of the household, did he think he would be less conscious of the distance between these menial tasks and the grandiose work he felt that God was imposing upon him? Was it in this way that he sought to appease the duality that racked him? This humble solution to his problem attracted him all the more, for his virtues of sweetness, patience, and charity moved in a similar direction where they could develop easily, undisturbed by his obligations to make difficult decisions, to impose necessary burdens on others, and to remind his brothers in the Society of the exigencies of their duties.

But this temptation, which drove Brébeuf to seek refuge in the lowest, most hidden, and most menial occupations, had its counterpart in another, which sprang from the same source but that impelled him to raise his soul to the heights. "I feel within me", he wrote, "a strong desire to die in order to enjoy God. I feel an intense aversion for all the created things we must leave behind at death." Here again he is longing for rest, turning aside from the created toward unlimited contemplation of God. This is not, as formerly, a longing for a lower place, but a flight to a higher one, a place that would permit him to escape the reality that constantly reminded him of his painful condition. As a mystic, he had tasted divine love in his transports. He realized that terrestrial concerns were restraining him; he wished to rid himself of them in order to attain eternal tranquillity and bliss. He forced himself to "live in God with the single loving desire to reject every creature". He wished to "fly toward the contemplation of heavenly things", and he saw himself impeded by attachments to the things of earth. This temptation—this attempt to separate God from his creatures—can be seen throughout the whole history of pagan mysticism and is still typical of souls well advanced in the complete divestment of the senses and the spirit.

Since Brébeuf could not find the true God in this way, and since "he was agitated by divers distractions and filled with temptations", the correct solution became clear to him: he heard an interior voice say: "Turn toward Jesus Crucified, and from now on let him be the base and foundation of all your contemplations." By means of the cross, he would attain to love and would receive peace of soul from the unction of the Holy Spirit. No longer would he need to reject earthly things, since on the wood of the cross, he would meet the most faithful image of God, visible even under the aspect of a leper, and an exact representation of what he truly is. By means of the cross, which during the succeeding weeks penetrated still further into his life, he was delivered from his other temptation also. No longer did he seek a solitary corner or an obscure duty to appease his self-scorn. His sufferings, and then his martyrdom, fulfilled all his dearest wishes and aspirations for nothingness. By the cross, not only in tracing its sign, but also through experiencing its bitterness, he found himself totally protected from the demon whose presence he could not forget.

The few notes that Brébeuf left us make it possible to attempt a description of his spiritual development. He had promised his service and sealed it with his blood in May 1630. Father Latourelle says of this: "This is already a martyrdom welcomed in advance; there is nothing precipitate in the work of grace. Today a promise of service; later, the wish for martyrdom; finally, the desire for the highest perfection" (*Étude* 2:215). Here are, indeed, the three decisive moments in Brébeuf's total oblation of himself to God, which furnish the means of reconstructing his interior journey.

In 1630 Brébeuf was already profoundly purified, since he said he no longer had the slightest inclination toward even venial sin. However, he was overwhelmed with the weight of his innumerable sins; he was thoroughly convinced that he was only a dead tree, deserving to be cut down by God. That is why, in the course of the retreat for that year, he thought of Christ essentially as the Redeemer who had personally ransomed him. His response to this inspiration was to pour out his life in the service of God alone. The year 1637 marked a decisive turning point: he was assailed by demons, and he found the answer to the double temptation mentioned above in the total acceptance of the cross. He mounted the next step of his spiritual ladder by making a vow "never to avoid any occasion of death". In the course of the next few years, he experienced visions of demons alternating with visions of the Cross. The "sacred wood" often appeared in the light of love and under the protection of Our Lady of Sorrows. This was a period of definitive purification during which the face of the leprous Crucified delivered him forever from all that could remain either in his psychology or in his soul of any connivance with Satan, of any false humility, or of any contemplative aspirations that might still be egotistical.

Ten years after the promise of service, in the middle of the month of May, 1640, the apparitions of infernal powers disappeared. A new period then began, in which images of light became more and more frequent; he saw the Blessed Virgin, no longer transpierced with three lances, but in glory on the holy mountain; he saw angelic figures, the Cross, the royal road to paradise. Only then did he understand and acquire perfect humility—humility that suggests in him, as in all his Jesuit companions, the absence of every worldly good. In one of his visions, he saw bloodstains on the clothing of his fellow missioners as well as on his own. He interpreted this by recalling a quotation from Isaiah: "All our justices are like soiled linen" (64:5), for God alone "hath clothed me with the garments of salvation and with the robe of justice he hath covered me" (Is 61:10). No longer did he seek the annihilation of self through the fear of punishment, no longer did he try to find refuge in humble works; he now realized man's basic powerlessness to gain the least merit. Brébeuf was ready, then, in the following year, 1645, to pronounce the vow that would attach him definitively to love: "I vow to perform", he wrote, "all that I recognize as being for the greater glory of God and for his greater service."

It is somewhat surprising at first that through a maxim so strict, so cold, so juridical, Brébeuf accomplished an extraordinary mystical ascent. This vow, however, surpassed in contemplative quality all the visions and all the raptures that had preceded it. In it the power of love and its unforeseeable liberty joined the numerous distinctions of morality to the exacting demands of God's law. Brébeuf's will no longer tended toward anything save becoming a slave of God. It forged chains that prevented the saint from ever separating himself from God's good pleasure by even the least self-consideration. Thus, as in God the spontaneity of love, answerable only to itself, is necessarily identified with his nature, incapable of anything but love, so man at the summit of perfection and under the impulse of divine charity imposes upon himself an unbreakable law that expresses, more surely than either the passing or more lasting transports, his decision to belong no longer to himself in anything. Brébeuf, in his supreme humility, adapted this rule of asceticism to a form that would take into account our human weakness, always inclined toward sin, as well as the hierarchy of values that his actions would hold in the service of God and of his Church. After having made this vow, Jean de Brébeuf could keep silent. His love was sealed by the complete privation of images, visions, and raptures.

We need not question the graces that God gave him between 1645 and 1649, the date of his martyrdom, for by their help he brought to its full flowering that serene nature, sweet and noble, which "was going to suffer like a rock" because it "reposed in God".[1]

The description of Brébeuf's spiritual itinerary presents only one facet of his sanctity, for this mystic is essentially an apostle, and there is a direct correspondence between his interior progress and the exterior circumstances by which God led him. In 1630 his fear for his salvation sprang from his having to leave Canada and return to France. The extraordinary aspects of this seemingly independent and most exterior situation, however, are summed up in his dialogue with God. It was not the English, as historians would say, who unjustly chased the French from Quebec and consequently Brébeuf from the Hurons; it was the sins of this Jesuit; it was his lack of response to the graces granted him by God that separated him from this mission field. The blame lay

---

[1] Can we not compare the mystical ascent of Saint Jean de Brébeuf to the path marked out by the *Spiritual Exercises*? In his spiritual journal, we find included in the entries for the year 1630 the consciousness of sin and merited punishment, the certainty of being redeemed by the death of Christ, the request "Lord, teach me to do what you will"—all of which recall the First Week and especially the colloquy of the First Exercise. From 1637 to 1639, by the apparitions of crowds of demons, Brébeuf engages in the spiritual combat of the Two Standards; by the vow of martyrdom, he chooses deliberately the third degree of humility, seeking always the greater glory of God. Until May 1640, his soul shares in the burdens of the Cross of Christ, with the help of the Virgin of Sorrows, as in the Third Week. In August 1640, there is the echo of the Fourth Week. On December 13 the "body of sin" of Brébeuf, which he has put to death in the course of the preceding period, separates itself from him in the form of a cadaver; he is then with the angels and is happy. Finally, his vow always to seek the most perfect recalls to us the soul stripped of all earthly attachments and the total gift of the *Sume et suscipe*.

completely on him. Consequently, he promised to reform his life and to offer to God every drop of his blood. Thus do those saints act who judge themselves the cause of all evil but at the same time affirm that their sanctity would bring salvation.[2]

In 1637, when a troop of demons appeared to him for the first time, he had returned to the country he so strongly desired to evangelize. This period was also marked for him by the terrible persecution he suffered from those Christians he himself had baptized and who were now abandoning the Faith. His vow of martyrdom, then, was inspired neither by temerity nor by routine; it was the answer to a very real threat. Moreover, the gift of himself to God was increased by the fact that he was certain God was speaking to him about them.

The demons reappeared, as we have seen, during the first five months of the year 1640. Brébeuf was at that time at *Teanostaiae*, a Huron village, where he had founded a post two years before. Hence, "it was in this ministry that Brébeuf, with Father Chastelain, had to suffer the harshest persecutions of his career" (Latourelle, *Étude* 2:25). To make matters worse, he saw a portion of his Christians abandon the Faith, just as they had done in 1637. For this missionary, Satan took on a very special form: he was the demon of infidelity. That is why, no doubt, he tempted Brébeuf only interiorly and disturbed him psychologically. His satanic force did not attack the saint's purity or arouse to violence his strong nature or tempt him to idolatry. His tool was discouragement at the sight of his protégés turning away from grace. During his stay in the Neutral nation, Brébeuf, along

---

[2] See, for example, the *Dialogues* of Saint Catherine of Siena.

with Father Chaumonot, met with equally violent persecutions; these, however, were not accompanied by internal trials—he wrote in his spiritual notes—since the Neutrals were pagans. They were as children to Brébeuf, children whom he had brought forth in Jesus Christ. They could hurt him only superficially, while the apostasy of the Hurons wounded not only his priestly heart but, as it were, penetrated to the very roots of his soul, as if he himself were experiencing the same heinous rejection of Christ that his Christian Hurons were guilty of. "I felt an extreme fear and fright at the thought that I was that miserable Jesuit in whom such a terrible change had to take place."[3] This seems to be the ultimate meaning of the diabolical visitations recounted in the spiritual journal of Brébeuf. The vision of March 11, 1640, is interpreted in this way, and that of March 21 clearly revealed to him that "certain terrestrial affections prevented him from reaching the One toward whom he was tending". During the vision of March 30, it seemed to him that a hand was anointing his heart and soothing his whole interior, as if he had surmounted all obstacles. From that moment on, the demons were no longer able to trouble him even for an instant or to challenge his love for God by taking the appearance of an old woman who wished to embrace him. His soul was now re-created to its very depths, and Satan was unable to find the least weakness, the least breach through which he could penetrate it.

From his stay in Quebec, which lasted from the spring of 1641 to September 1644, Brébeuf's journal does not include a single entry. He was at that time procurator of the mission and bore all the hardships that ceaselessly poured

---

[3] This vision is that of March 11, 1640, when he was still among the Hurons.

down upon it. After returning to the Huron country, he seemed to think of martyrdom no longer. He had not interpreted the stains of blood on his own clothing and that of his companions in this sense but saw them only as an indication of complete misery. Perhaps, at this stage, he had already advanced beyond the desire for martyrdom and all else that bordered on the romantic, to substitute a limitless abandonment to God, a peace that nothing could destroy and that would constantly nourish his zeal.

His vow to seek the most perfect was not that of a pure contemplative but that of an apostle, careful to choose in the concrete actions of his life, in his service of God and his fellows, what would give the most glory to God. When he wrote to the Father General in 1648 a long letter in which he spoke of the divers problems of the mission, he closed it thus: "What I wish is not my own will, and I wish it only in proportion as it contributes to the greater glory of God" (Latourelle, *Étude* 2:130). Certainly this is a formula that any Jesuit at all could sign, but it is also one that expresses the summit of Brébeuf's spiritual ascent: a power of decision perfectly controlled. His vow to act always in the more perfect way resulted immediately in his receiving an increase of divine love. Brébeuf, at the end of his interior pilgrimage, an end he was able to attain through extraordinary graces, simply carries the very essence of his vocation as a Jesuit to its fulfillment: to will *in affectu et in effectu* whatever reveals the glory of God most completely.

We know very little about Gabriel Lalemant, Brébeuf's companion in martyrdom and consequently associated with him in our thoughts. He was born in 1610 and entered the Society in 1630. He taught at Moulins after his novitiate, at La Flèche after his theology, again at Moulins from 1641 to

1644, and finally at Bourges. On June 13, 1646, he embarked for Canada, remained two years at Quebec, Silléry, and Three Rivers, and arrived at Sainte-Marie in Huronia in September, 1648. He was martyred there about six months later, on March 17, 1649.

In describing Lalemant's martyrdom, Father Ragueneau took advantage of the opportunity to cite some of his spiritual notes. Unfortunately, the letters that the saint wrote to his Carmelite sister are lost.[4]

---

[4] It seems that Father de Rochemonteix saw them (cf. 2:87, n. 1).

IMPORTANT ADVICE FOR THOSE WHOM IT SHALL PLEASE GOD TO CALL TO NEW FRANCE, ESPECIALLY TO THE COUNTRY OF THE HURONS

We have learned that the salvation of many innocent souls, washed and whitened in the Blood of the Son of God, is stirring deeply the hearts of many men, inflaming them with fresh desires to leave Old France and come to the New. May God be forever blessed! By this means he has showed us that he has finally opened up to these tribes the depths of his infinite mercy. Far be it from me to chill the ardor of the generous resolutions of those noble souls who aspire to become missionaries. Theirs are hearts according to God's own, and we are eagerly waiting for them. I wish to give them only one word of advice.

It is true that "love is strong as death" (Song 8:6), that the love of God has power to do what death does—that is, to detach us entirely from creatures and even from ourselves! These impulses we feel to work for the salvation of infidels, however, are not always a sure sign of that pure love. There may be sometimes a little self-esteem and self-seeking in them if we look only to the blessing and satisfaction to be reaped from putting souls in Heaven and do not maturely consider the pains, labors, and difficulties inseparable from all evangelical activities.

French title: *Avertissement d'importance pour ceux qu'il plairait à Dieu d'appeler en la Nouvelle-France, et principalement au pays des Hurons*. This title and the text are taken from chapter 3 of the *Relation* of 1636 for the Huron missions, Thw. 10:86–114.

To prevent anyone from being mistaken on this point, "I myself will show him how much he must suffer for my name" (Acts 9:10). It is true that those two most recently arrived, Fathers Mercier and Pijart, did not have nearly as much discomfort on their journey as those of us who came here last year. They did not have to paddle at all; their men were not sick, as ours were; they did not have to bear the heavy portages. Yet, no matter how easy a trip through the lands of the savages may be, there is always hardship enough to cast into dejection a heart not well under subjection. The adaptability of the savages does not shorten the road or smooth down the rocks, or remove any of the other dangers. Nor does it matter with whom you travel; you must expect to be at least three or four weeks on the road; to have as companions persons you have never seen before; to be cramped into a bark canoe in an uncomfortable position; to be not free to turn yourself to one side or the other; to be in danger of capsizing or of being cast upon the rocks a minimum of fifty times a day. During the day the sun burns you; during the night you are consumed by mosquitoes. Sometimes you must ascend as many as five or six rapids in a single day, and for your evening meal you have only a little corn crushed between two stones and cooked in clear, fresh water. Your only bed is the earth—quite frequently only rough, uneven rocks; usually your only roof is the stars. Furthermore, you suffer all this in perpetual silence. Should you accidentally hurt yourself or fall sick, do not expect any help from these barbarians, for where would they get it? Should your illness prove serious and you are far from a village—they are very scattered in this region—I would not like to promise that they would not abandon you unless you were able to help yourself sufficiently to keep up with them.

When you reach the land of the Hurons, you will indeed find our hearts full of love. We will receive you with open arms as we would an angel from paradise. We would have all the best intentions in the world to make you comfortable, but it is impossible for us to do much. We shall receive you in a hut so miserable that I know of none in France sufficiently wretched to enable me to say to you: This is how you will be lodged. Completely exhausted as you will be, we shall be able to give you nothing but a poor mat, or at most a skin, to serve you as a bed. Besides, you will arrive at a season when those annoying little insects that we call here *taouhac*, and, in good French, *puces* [and, in good English, *fleas*], will prevent you from closing an eye all night long, for in these regions they are incomparably more irksome than in France. The dust in the cabin nourishes them; the savages transfer them to us; we even go to their houses to get these pests! This petty martyrdom, not to speak of the stings of mosquitoes, sandflies, and other like vermin, usually lasts the three or four months of the summer season.

You may have been a famous professor or an outstanding theologian in France, but here you will be merely a student and—God be praised!—with what teachers!—women, little children, all the savages. You will constantly be exposed to their ridicule. The Huron language will be your Saint Thomas and your Aristotle, and—clever man that you are, speaking glibly among learned and capable persons—you must make up your mind to be for quite some time mute in the company of these barbarians. It will be quite an achievement if, at the end of a considerable time, you begin to stammer even a little.

And then, how do you think you would spend the winter here? You have probably heard about all that must be endured in wintering among the Montaignais savages. Our life with the Hurons is just about the same. I am not exaggerating when I say that the five or six months of the winter season are spent in almost continuous discomforts—excessive cold, smoke, the annoying habits of the savages. Our cabin is built of bark, but it is so well jointed that we have to send someone outside to learn what kind of weather it is. The smoke is very often so thick, so annoying, and so persistent that for five or six days at a time, if you are not completely immune to it, about all you can do is recognize a few words in your breviary. And as if that were not enough, from morning to evening our fireplace is practically besieged by savages. They never miss mealtime. If you happen to have something more than usual, no matter how little it may be, you must count most of these gentlemen as your guests. If you do not share with them, you are considered stingy. In general, the food is not too bad. We are usually satisfied with a little corn or a piece of dry smoked fish or some fruits, which I shall describe later on.

For the rest—well, so far our life has been a bed of roses. Our real troubles are these: we have Christians in almost every village, so we must plan on making our rounds through the villages at all seasons of the year and plan on staying at one or another, if necessary, for two or three whole weeks, in the midst of indescribable annoyances. Besides all this, our lives hang by a thread, and if anywhere in the world we can expect death at any and every hour and should be prepared for it, this is particularly true here. Our cabin is only straw, so to speak, and may catch fire at any moment despite all our care to prevent accidents. The malice of the savages causes almost perpetual fear in this respect. Some malcontent may set fire to your house or cleave open your head in some lonely spot. You are entirely responsible for the sterility or the fecundity of the earth under penalty of your life; you are the cause of droughts; if you cannot make it rain, the Indians talk most casually about doing away with you. I will pass over the dangers that threaten from our enemies; it is enough to say that on the thirteenth of this month of June, they killed twelve of our Hurons near the village of *Contarrea*, only a day's journey from us. A short time before this, about four leagues from our village, some Iroquois were discovered lying in ambush in the fields, only waiting to strike a blow at some unwary passerby. Our Huron tribe is very fearful and timid. The men make no effort to prepare arms or to enclose their villages with palisades; their usual recourse, especially when the enemy is powerful, is in flight. So, amid these alarms prevailing throughout the whole country, I will leave you to imagine whether or not we have any grounds for a feeling of safety.

After all, if we had here the exterior attractions of piety that are found in France, all this might still be tolerable. There the great number of Christians with their good example, their solemn celebration of feasts, the majesty of the churches decorated so magnificently—all these preach piety to you. In the houses of our Society, the fervor of our brothers, their modesty, the noble virtues that shine forth in all their actions are so many powerful voices always urging you to "look at them and model your conduct on them" (Lk 10:37). You have the consolation of celebrating Holy Mass every day. In a word, you are almost entirely out of danger of falling, and if you do, the falls are insignificant, with help immediately at hand. Here we have nothing, it seems, to incite us toward good. We are among peoples who are astonished when you speak to them of God and who often have nothing but horrible blasphemies on their lips. Frequently you are forced to deprive yourself of the Holy Sacrifice of the Mass. When you do have the opportunity of celebrating it, your chapel is a little corner of the cabin that the smoke, the snow, or the rain prevents you from decorating and beautifying, even if you had the means. I pass over the slight opportunity for recollection you have among these barbarians, who almost never leave you and who do not know what it is to speak in a low tone. Most of all, I hesitate to speak of the danger there is of losing your soul in the midst of their impurities, should your heart not be sufficiently anchored in God so as to resist this poison. But I have said enough; the rest you will learn from experience.

"But is that all?" some one of you may exclaim. "Do you think these arguments can dampen the fire that consumes me or lessen ever so little the zeal I have for the conversion of these heathens? I declare that these hardships have served only to strengthen me all the more in my determination. I feel myself more than ever carried away by my affection for New France, and I bear a holy jealousy toward those already enduring all these sufferings. All these labors seem to be a mere nothing in comparison with what I am willing to suffer for God. If I knew a place under Heaven where there was still more to be suffered, I would go there." Ah! Whoever you are to whom God gives such feelings and such light, come, come, my dear brother! It is workers like you that we need here; it is to souls like yours that God has appointed the conquest of so many others whom the devil still holds in his power. Anticipate no difficulties—you will have none, since your whole consolation is to see yourself crucified with the Son of God. Silence will be sweet to you, since you have learned to commune with God and to converse in Heaven with the saints and angels. The food would be quite insipid if the gall endured for our Lord did not render it sweeter and more savory to you than the most delicious viands of the world. What satisfaction to pass these rapids and to climb these rocks for him who has before his eyes our loving Savior, harassed by his tormentors and ascending Calvary laden with his Cross. For him who thus considers the Crucified One constantly, the discomfort of the canoe is very easy to bear. What consolation! (I must use such terms, since that is the only way I can give you pleasure.) What consolation it is to see yourself abandoned on the road by the savages, languishing with sickness and untended by anyone, even dying from hunger in the woods, and so being able to say to God: "My God, it is to do your holy will that I am reduced to the state in which you see me." Above all, you can then consider yourself like that God-man who, as he was expiring on the Cross, cried to his Father: "My God, my God, why do you abandon me?" (Mt 27:46). And if, in the midst of all these hardships, God should preserve you in health, no doubt you will arrive happily in the Huron country with these holy thoughts. "He whom the grace of God carries, travels sweetly."

And now, in regard to a place of abode, food, and beds, shall I dare to say to a heart so generous, one that mocks at all I have already described, that truly, even though we have hardly more of those necessities than the savages have, in some way or another the divine Goodness makes every difficult circumstance easy. Each and every one of us finds that the external details of daily life differ very little from those in France. The sleep we get lying on our mats seems as sweet as that we enjoyed in a good bed. The food of the country does not disgust us, although there is scarcely any other seasoning than that which God has put into it. In spite of the cold, long winter, lasting nearly six months, spent in the shelter of a bark cabin open to the daylight, we have yet to experience any evil effects. No one complains of his head or his stomach; we do not know what diarrhea, colds, or catarrh are. This leads me to say that in France delicate persons do not know how to protect themselves from the cold; those well-carpeted floors, those well-fitted doors and carefully closed windows only make its effects more keenly felt; it is an enemy from whom one wins more by holding out his hands to him than by waging a cruel war upon him. About our food, I would like to add this, that God has shown us his providence very clearly; in one week we have obtained a whole year's supply of corn, without taking a single step outside our cabin. The Indians have brought us so much dried fish that we had to refuse some of it. It would seem that God in his all-knowing solicitude for our being here only for his service wishes to be our generous provider. This same loving care gives us fresh fish from time to time as a change of provisions. We live on the shore of a great lake that supplies us with fish as delicious as any I have ever eaten in France. We do not ordinarily have them, it is true, and still less frequently do we have meat. We have fruits according to the season, provided the year be favorable: strawberries, raspberries, and blackberries are to be found in almost incredible quantities. We gather plenty of grapes, which are fairly good; the squashes last sometimes four and five months and are so abundant that they can be had for almost nothing, and they are so good that, when roasted over the coals of our fire, we eat them as they do apples in France. The only grain the country produces is sufficient nourishment after you become somewhat accustomed to it. The savages prepare it in more than twenty different ways and yet use only fire and water. Consequently, to tell the truth, the change in diet from that in

France is not very great. The best sauce, of course, is the appetite we bring to it.

As for the dangers of the soul, to speak frankly, there are none for him who brings the fear and love of God with him to the country of the Hurons. On the contrary, I find unparalleled opportunities for acquiring perfection. Is it not a great deal to have no other attraction in your food, clothing, and sleep than that of satisfying your simplest needs? Is it not a glorious opportunity to unite your soul with God there, where no creature whatsoever gives you reason to spend your affection upon it, and when your exercises of devotion lead you gently to interior contemplation? Besides your spiritual exercises, you have no other duties than the study of the language and conversation with the savages. Ah! how much pleasure there is for a person whose heart is devoted to God to make himself the pupil of a savage, even of a little child, in order to gain his teachers for God and to make of them in turn disciples of Our Lord! How willingly and how liberally God communicates himself to a soul practicing such heroic acts of humility for love of him! The words he learns are so many treasures stored up, so many spoils carried off from the common enemy of the human race, so that he has reason to say a hundred times a day: "I am delighted with your oracles as when a man finds rich spoils" (Ps 118 [119]:162). Seen in this light, the visits of the savages, however frequent, cannot be a source of annoyance to him. God teaches him the same beautiful lesson that he once taught Saint Catherine of Siena, that he should make his heart into a room or temple for him, where he will never fail to find him each and every time he withdraws into it; moreover, if he meets savages there, they do not interfere with his prayers but only make him more fervent, for he then takes occasion to present these poor wretches to the Sovereign Goodness and to entreat him warmly for their conversion.

It is true that we do not have here the exterior solemnity of worship that awakens and sustains devotion. The only external sign of our holy religion that we have is the Blessed Sacrament of the Altar. To its marvels we must open the eyes of our faith without the aid of any sensible mark of its grandeur, like the Magi of old in the stable. It seems, moreover, that God supplies what we lack and rewards us with grace for having transported the Holy Sacrament beyond so many seas and having found an abode for it in these poor cabins. He seems to delight in crowning us in the midst of these infidels with the same blessings that he is accustomed to bestow upon persecuted Catholics in the countries of the heretics. These good people hardly ever see either church or altar, but the little they do see is doubly worth what they would be able to perceive in full liberty. Can you imagine the consolation there is in prostrating yourself once in a while before a cross that has been erected in the midst of this barbarism? Can you conceive the comfort you receive in the midst of even the most trifling domestic occupations when you turn your eyes toward the tabernacle or enter the room that the Son of God has been pleased to take for his own in our tiny dwelling? Is this not living in paradise day and night, being separated from this Well-Beloved of Nations only by a piece of bark or a branch of a tree? "Behold he standeth behind our wall" (Song 2:9); "I sat down under his shadow whom I desired" (Song 2:3).

So much for the inside. If we go outside our cabin, Heaven is open to us. No huge buildings, which in large cities lift their heads to the clouds, conceal the celestial dome from our view. Thus, we can pray in full liberty before the noble oratory that Saint Francis Xavier loved better than any other.

If your questions concern the fundamental virtues, in my reply all I can say is that I glory not in myself but in the lot that has fallen to me. I acknowledge humbly in the presence of the cross, which Our Lord by his grace grants us to bear after him, that the exercise of these virtues is easy for us. There is no doubt that this country and our work here is much better fitted to feed the soul with the fruits of Heaven than with the fruits of earth.

I may be deceiving myself, but I imagine that here we have a powerful means for increasing faith, hope, and charity in our souls. Can we plant the seeds of the Faith in others without profiting by them ourselves? Can we put our confidence anywhere but in God in a region where, from a purely natural point of view, everything is lacking to us? Can we wish for a more fruitful opportunity to practice charity than the one we have here, with all its roughness and discomfort? These, too, are unquestionably conditions natural to a country that is still new, where no human art or industry has provided any conveniences; still, this fact does not detract from their efficacy. We live here for one reason only: to bring to God men who so little resemble men that we live in daily expectation of dying by their hand, if they should take such a notion, or have a dream suggesting it, or if we should fail to control the rains or droughts as they wish or to provide whatever weather they desire at the moment. They always hold us responsible for the weather. And so, if God does not inspire us or if we cannot work miracles by faith, we are continually in danger—according to their threats—of being attacked, innocent as we are of any wrong. Indeed, if he who is Truth itself had not declared that there is no greater love than to lay down one's life once and for all for one's friends, I should conceive it equally noble, or even more so, to do what the Apostle Paul said to the Corinthians: "I swear, brothers, by the very pride I take in Christ Jesus our Lord, that day after day I face death" (1 Cor 15:31).

It is unquestionably much more difficult to drag out a life full of misery amid the frequent and continued dangers of sudden death from those whom you hope to save. Occasionally I call to mind what Saint Francis Xavier once wrote to Father Simon, and hope that it may please God to bring it about that at least the same thing may be said or written one day even of us, unworthy though we are. Here is what he said: "We receive excellent news from the Moluccas; John Beira and his companions are in very great trials and perpetual dangers in their efforts to make progress in our Christian religion" (MHSJ, *Ep. Xav.* 2:77).

There seems to be one thing here that might give cause for apprehension in a son of the Society, and that is to see himself in the midst of a brutal and sensual people whose example might tarnish the luster of the most delicate of all the virtues unless special care be taken—I mean chastity.

To reassure anyone thus troubled, I make bold to say that if there is any place in the world where this so-precious virtue is safe, especially for one who is on his guard, it is here. "Unless the Lord protects the city, in vain is the watch of the guards" (Ps 126 [127]:1); "And as I knew that I could not otherwise be continent except God gave it, and this also was a point of wisdom, to know whose gift it was" (Wis 8:21). It is said that the victories this heavenly virtue gains over her enemies are gained by flight. But I believe that it is God and no one else who puts to rout the attacks of the flesh and the devil in his deadly encounters. His divine strength and providence are especially effective for those who, fearing nothing so much as these temptations, with bowed heads and hearts full of confidence in his goodness, go where his glory calls them. And where should we seek this glory? I would say that we find it most fully purified and disentangled from our own interests in a place where there is nothing more to be hoped for than the reward of having left all for the love of him of whom Saint Paul has said: "For I know whom I believed" (2 Tim 1:12).

Do you remember the plant named "the fear of God", with which it is said that our Fathers in the early days of the Society charmed away the spirit of impurity? It does not grow in the land of the Hurons, but it falls here abundantly from Heaven if we take only a little care to cultivate it. Barbarism, ignorance, poverty, misery—which render the life of these savages more deplorable than death—are a continual reminder to us to mourn Adam's fall and to submit ourselves entirely to him who still, after so many centuries and in so manifest a fashion, chastises disobedience in his children. Saint Teresa once said that her meditations were never more profitable than when she contemplated the mysteries in which she found Our Lord apart and alone, for example, in the Garden of Olives. She called this a part of her simplicity. You may consider this one of my idiosyncrasies if you like, but it seems to me that we have here so much leisure to caress, so to speak, and to entertain our Lord with an open heart in these uninhabited lands because there are so few people here who trouble themselves about him. And, grateful for this favor, we boldly say: "No evil shall I fear because you are with me" (Ps 22 [23]:4). In short, I imagine that all the guardian angels of these neglected and abandoned nations are continually watching and working to protect us from all dangers. They know well that if there were anything in the world that ought to give us wings to fly back from whence we came—the two wings of our obedience and our own holy desires—it would be the misfortune of a lapse from virtue. We depend on the protection of Heaven to shield us from this calamity. That is why the guardian spirits procure for us the means to safeguard this virtue, namely, that they may not lose the brightest hope they have ever had of the conversion of these peoples through the grace of God.

My final thought as I close this discourse is this: if, at the sight of the difficulties and crosses that are here prepared for us, anyone should feel so fortified from above that he can say it is too little, or exclaim like Saint Francis Xavier: *Amplius, amplius*,[1] I hope that our Lord will also draw from his lips this other exclamation in regard to his consolations, that they are too much for him, that he cannot endure more: *Satis est. Domine, satis est.*[2]

---

[1] "More, more." These words are recorded by Simon Rodriguez. Cf. Schurhammer, *Franz-Xaver* (Freiburg: Herder, 1955), p. 698.

[2] "It is enough, Lord, it is enough." These words are attributed to Saint Francis Xavier. Cf. MHSJ, *Ep. Xav.* 1:175, n. 39.

INSTRUCTIONS FOR THE FATHERS OF OUR SOCIETY WHO WILL BE SENT TO THE HURONS

The Fathers and Brothers whom God shall call to the holy mission of the Hurons ought to exercise careful foresight in regard to all the hardships, annoyances, and perils that must be encountered in making this journey in order to be prepared for all emergencies that may arise.

We must have a sincere affection for the savages, looking upon them as ransomed by the Blood of the Son of God and as our brothers, with whom we are to spend the rest of our lives.

In order not to annoy the savages, we must take care never to make them wait for us to embark.

We must provide ourselves with a tinderbox or with a magnifying lens or both, to furnish them with fire in the daytime to light their pipes and in the evening to light their campfires. These little services win their hearts.

We must try to eat their *sagamite* or *salmagundi* as they prepare it, although it may be dirty, half-cooked, and quite tasteless. As to the other numerous inconveniences, we must endure them for the love of God, without complaint or even seeming to notice them.

It is well at first to take everything they offer even though we are unable to eat it all, because once we become accustomed to it, there is never too much.

Father Le Jeune inserted into the *Relation* of 1637 this note, which had been sent to him by Father de Brébeuf.

We must try to eat at daybreak unless we can take our meal with us in the canoe, for the day is very long, especially if we have to spend it without eating. The barbarians eat only at sunrise and at sunset when they are on their journeys.

We must be prompt in embarking and disembarking and tuck up our cassocks so that they do not get wet and thus drip water and sand into the canoe. To be properly dressed, we must keep our feet and legs bare, except when crossing the rapids and on the long portages, when we can wear shoes and even leggings.

We must behave at all times so as not to be a burden to even one of the savages.

It is not good to ask too many questions or yield to our desire to learn the language or even make aimless remarks on the journey. We must spare our fellow travelers this annoyance, especially since they cannot give us much attention while they are working. Silence is our best contribution to the tasks at hand when we are in the canoe.

We must bear with the imperfections of the Indians without saying a word—yes, without even seeming to notice them. Should it become necessary to criticize anything, it must be done quietly and humbly, with words and gestures that indicate love and helpfulness, not aversion. In short, we must always try to appear, and really to be, cheerful.

Each Father coming to the missions should be provided with a half gross of awls, two or three dozen pocketknives, a hundred fishhooks, and some beads of plain and colored glass to exchange for fish or other articles. These supplies are also very useful when the different tribes happen to meet each other, or to use as rewards for the savages. It is well to say to them: "Here is something for you to buy fish." At the portages, each of us should carry some little thing according to his strength. No matter how little we carry, even if it is only a kettle, the natives are greatly pleased.

We must not be ceremonious with the savages but accept whatever comforts they offer us, such as a good place in the cabin. Even the greatest conveniences are still quite inconvenient, and standing on ceremony often offends the Indians.

Another point to watch is that we do not annoy anyone in the canoe with our hat. It is better to wear a nightcap. There is no sense of impropriety among the savages.

Further, we must not undertake any task unless we intend to continue it. For example, it is not wise to begin to paddle unless we wish to continue paddling. This is also true of our place in the canoe; there will be no opportunity to change. We should not lend the natives our clothing unless we are willing to do without it during the whole journey. It is much easier to refuse at first than to ask for it to be returned or exchanged afterward.

Finally, we must understand that the savages will maintain the same estimate of us when they are in their own country that they will have formed on the journey, and one who has shown himself an irritable and troublesome person will have considerable difficulty later in changing this opinion. We have to deal not only with the men in our own canoe but also with those of the whole nation. We meet some today and others tomorrow, and our new acquaintances do not hesitate to ask those who brought us what sort of men we are. The way they observe and remember even the slightest fault is almost incredible. When we first journey with the savages, we cannot yet greet them with kind words since we do not know their language, but we can at least show them a cheerful face and thus prove ourselves able to endure uncomplainingly the fatigues of the trip. In this way we not only profit personally by overcoming ourselves, but we also advance considerably in gaining the esteem and affection of the barbarians.

This lesson is very easy to understand but very difficult to put into practice. Having left a highly civilized society, we are now in the midst of a barbarous people who care nothing for our philosophical and theological education. All the fine qualities that make us admired and respected in France are like pearls trampled under the feet of swine, or rather, mules, which despise us utterly when they see that we are not such good pack animals as they. If we could go naked and carry on our backs the load that a horse carries, then we would be wise according to their views and would be recognized as great men, otherwise not. Jesus Christ is our true greatness; it is he alone and his crosses that should be sought in ministering to these people. If we seek for anything else, we will find nothing but bodily and spiritual afflictions. But if we have found Jesus Christ in his Cross, we have found the roses among the thorns, sweetness in bitterness, all in nothing.

LETTER TO
REVEREND FATHER LE JEUNE

October 28, 1637

Reverend and dear Father:

Pax Christi!

We are, perhaps, on the point of shedding our blood and sacrificing our lives in the service of our good Master, Jesus Christ. It seems that he in his goodness consents to accept this sacrifice from me for the expiation of my great and innumerable sins, and in this hour to crown any past services as well as the sincere, ardent desires of all of our Fathers here.

There are two reasons why I think that this will not happen. One is the excess of my past wickedness, which renders me utterly unworthy of so precious a favor. The other is that I do not believe his goodness will permit the death of his workmen, since through his grace there are still some good souls eager to receive the seed of the Gospel in spite of the calumnies and all manner of persecutions inflicted on us. And yet I fear that divine Justice, seeing the obstinacy with which the majority of these barbarians cling to their superstitions, may very justly permit them to take away the life of the body from those who, with all their hearts,

---

Letter inserted into the *Relation* of 1638 (Thw. 15:60–64).

desire and procure for these same heathens the life of their souls.

Be this as it may, all our Fathers await the outcome of this affair with great calmness and contentment of spirit. For myself, I can tell you, Reverend Father, with all sincerity, that I have not yet had the least apprehension or fear of death from such a cause. This one thing we all regret, namely, that these poor barbarians through their own malice are closing their doors against the Gospel and God's grace. Whatever conclusion they reach, and no matter what treatment they give us, we will try, as long as God sustains us, to endure it patiently for his service. It is indeed an eminent favor that his goodness extends to us in letting us endure something for his love. It is only now that we consider ourselves truly members of his Society. May he be forever blessed for having appointed us to this country, for having chosen us from so many others much more deserving than we to aid him in bearing his Cross. In all things, may his holy will be done! If it is his holy will that at this hour we should die—oh, fortunate hour for us! And still, if it is his will to reserve us for other labors—may he also be blessed! If you should hear that God has crowned our insignificant labors, or rather, our desires, help us to bless him, for it is only for his sake that we desire to live and to die. It is only he who can give us the grace to accomplish this. If any of the other Fathers survive, I have left instructions as to all they are to do. I felt it advisable for our Fathers and other members of our household to withdraw to the houses of those they regard as their best friends. I have arranged for them to carry to the house of Pierre, our first Christian, all that belongs to the sacristy—above all, to be especially careful to put our dictionary and all other materials concerning the Huron language in a safe place. As for me, if God grants me the grace to go to Heaven, I will pray to him for them, my poor Hurons—and I will certainly not forget you, Reverend Father.

And finally, we beg you, Father, and all the other priests of the Society not to forget us in your Holy Masses and prayers, so that, in life and after death, he may grant us mercy. We are all, here and in eternity, Reverend Father,

Your very humble and affectionate servants in the Lord,

Jean de Brébeuf
François Joseph le Mercier
Pierre Chastelain
Charles Garnier
Paul Ragueneau

La Conception at *Ossossane*, October 28

I have left Fathers Pierre Pijart and Isaac Jogues at the house of Saint Joseph, sharing our sentiments in all respects.

GRACES, VISIONS, ILLUSTRATIONS, AND COMMENTS EXCERPTED FROM THE WRITINGS OF FATHER JEAN DE BRÉBEUF

In January 1630[1] I felt within me an overpowering desire to suffer something for Christ. I feared for my salvation because so far he had dealt much too kindly with me, especially since I might have very grievously offended his divine Majesty. It is only when occasions of suffering present themselves that I have a firm hope for my salvation.

January 11. Having considered how grave and how numerous my sins are, I still seemed to see the divine Mercy extending his arms to me to embrace me sweetly and, furthermore, pardoning me for all my past sins through a divine amnesty,

---

The title, *Quelques grâces, visions, illustrations, et autres remarques, extraites des manuscrits du Père Jean de Brébeuf*, is found in the *Manuscrit de 1652*, p. 220. The text of Brébeuf's journal, however, does not begin until p. 224, and ends on p. 240. These notes are written for the most part in Latin and were gathered together by Father Ragueneau. The portions that are written in French are indicated here by a double slash (//). [The statement "Quae sequuntur ex manuscriptis P. Joannis de Brébeuf excerpta sunt. Paulus Ragueneau" heads this section of the *Manuscrit*.—TRANS.]

We have also attempted to follow a chronological order in our presentation; therefore, we have transferred to their supposed place the text of the vow of 1645, which was found among the notes for the year 1637, and other authentic fragments of the year 1640, not included in the *Manuscrit*. These changes are indicated by a single slash (/).

The historical notes are those of Father Latourelle, but we have made a completely new translation. On the spiritual interpretation of the journal, see our introduction to the texts of Brébeuf.

[1] Brébeuf was at that time in Rouen. He had had to leave Canada after the fall of Quebec. From January 10 to 19 he made his retreat preparatory to taking his final vows.

thus bringing to life again my good works—performed in charity but killed by sin—and moreover, calling me to himself in sublime friendship, saying to me as he had said to Saint Paul: "For this man is my chosen instrument, to carry my name among nations" (Acts 9:15). Accordingly, I gave thanks and offered myself to him with these words: "Make of me, Lord, a 'man after your own heart' (Acts 13:22); teach me what you want me to do."[2] Nothing in the future will "separate me from your charity—not nakedness, nor the sword, nor death" (cf. Rom 8:35). I, who am a son in a most holy Society; I, who would have been an apostle in Canada if I had responded wholeheartedly to you; I, to whom, certainly, the gift of tongues has not been granted, but who at least have a great aptitude for them—have I, until now, been entirely forgetful of self? Oh, the wickedness, the baseness, the ugliness of my life!

I have never perceived in myself any disposition toward venial sin, that is, any pleasure I would take in committing venial sin.

Lest God cut me down as an unfruitful tree, I have prayed that he should pass me by this one year more so that I may bring forth better fruit.[3]

February 9. It seemed to me that I was completely severed from all my senses and united to God in total rapture.

---

[2] Cf. Acts 22:10. Ragueneau wrote: "One day, speaking to our Lord and saying to him, 'Lord, what do you wish me to do?' he heard this response, which Jesus Christ had made to Saint Paul: 'Go to Ananias, and he will tell you what you must do.' And after that experience, he was so strong in his resolutions that he never sought any other conduct except that of obedience, which virtue, I can truly say, was perfect in him" (*MS de 1652*, p. 199).

[3] Ragueneau adds the word *promisi* (*MS de 1652*, p. 210), which is not found in the notes cited as coming directly from the hand of Brébeuf on p. 225.

However, this ravishment was only momentary and was attended by a slight physical disturbance.

On March 25, 1630, I shall be thirty-seven years old. I was born in the year of our Lord 1593, on the Feast of the Annunciation.

On January 20, 1630, I pronounced the vows of a Formed Coadjutor in the chapel of the college at Rouen and placed them in the hands of Reverend Father Jacques Bertrix, Rector.[4]

I had received the subdeaconate at Lisieux in the month of September, 1621; in December of the same year, I received the diaconate at Bayeux; the following year, 1622, I was raised to the priesthood at Pontoise at the beginning of Lent, and on the Feast of the Annunciation[5] I offered the Holy Sacrifice of the Mass to God for the first time, at Rouen.

During the annual retreat, begun on May 12, 1630.

Lord Jesus Christ, my Redeemer, you have redeemed me by your Blood and most precious death; I, in turn, promise that I will serve you all my life in the Society of Jesus and will serve no one else unless for you and because of you. This promise I have signed with my own hand and my blood, being ready to pour out my whole life as willingly as this one drop of blood.[6]

---

[4] Jogues also speaks of Father Bertrix, who was rector at the colleges in Bourges and Rouen.

[5] In 1622, March 25 fell on Good Friday. The Annunciation was therefore transferred to Monday of Quasimodo, April 4. Brébeuf, ordained priest at the beginning of Lent, that is, in February, did not say his first Mass until April 4, the day of the solemnity of the Feast of the Annunciation.

[6] This promise prepares the way for the vow of martyrdom (1637) and that of always doing what is most perfect (1645).

/ I feel deep in my heart a great desire to die in order to be happy with God. I also feel a great aversion for all the created things that must be left behind at death. It is in God alone that my heart reposes, and aside from him all is as nothing to me if it is not for him.[7] /

September 4, 1636, during the Exercises.

God in his goodness has given me gentleness, benignity, and charity toward everyone, indifference to whatever may happen, and patience in suffering adversity. His divine benevolence desires me, thus endowed, to reach perfection and eternal life. This, then, shall be the subject of my particular examen: that I use as I should the gifts that God has given to me.

1637.[8] On August 21 (or, possibly, 22 or 23), during the evening examen of conscience and the Litany of the Blessed Virgin, I had a vision—either real or imagined—in which I saw a vast throng of demons coming toward me in order to devour me, or, at least, to bite me. But not one was able to harm me. Those who came first resembled huge horses, but their manes were long and curly, like rams or goats. I do not remember the forms of the others, but I know that they had numerous and divers shapes, more frightening than any I had ever seen before. This vision lasted about as long as a *Miserere*. I do not recall being frightened, but placing

---

[7] This text, cited by Ragueneau (*MS de 1652*, p. 211) is not included in the excerpts of Brébeuf. It would have been written more than fifteen years before the saint's death, that is, about 1633.

[8] This is the year of the revolt of the Hurons against the missionaries, who were held responsible for the diseases that were ravaging the country. See above (pp. 157ff.) the letter of Brébeuf to Father Le Jeune, dated October 28, 1637.

my confidence in God, I said: "Do all that God permits you to do; you will not pluck a single hair from my head without his assent and his command" (cf. Mt 10:29–30; Lk 21:18).

/ I realize that I have no special abilities except that I am ready to obey. It seems to me that I am suited only to act as porter, to take care of the refectory, or to work in the kitchen. I shall conduct myself in the Society as if I were a beggar, admitted to it as by a special favor, and I shall consider all that is done for me as performed through charity alone.[9] /

/My Lord Jesus, "how then shall I requite (you) for all that (you) have granted me? In thanks for health received, I take the cup and will invoke the name of the Lord" (Ps 115:3–4 [116:12–13]). This I vow, in the presence of your Eternal Father and of the Holy Spirit, in the presence of your most holy Mother and of her most chaste spouse, Saint Joseph; before the angels, the apostles, and the martyrs; before my blessed Fathers Saint Ignatius and Saint Francis Xavier—this I vow, I repeat, my Lord Jesus, that if you most generously offer me the grace of martyrdom, me, your unworthy servant, I will never reject this favor. Never will I permit myself either to avoid the occasions of death that may present themselves (at least insofar as I judge these to be for the greater glory of God) or to withhold a joyful acceptance of the blow when it is struck. And so, my Lord Jesus, beginning with today, I joyfully offer you my body, my blood, my spirit, so that—if such be your holy will—I may die for you, who have deigned to die for me. Help me to live in such a way that you

---

[9] Ragueneau dates this text 1639 (cf. *MS de 1652*, p. 199). Thw. 34:178, then, is in error in referring it to 1631.

will allow me thus to die. Yes, Lord, I take the cup and will invoke your name: Jesus, Jesus, Jesus![10] /

During the annual retreat, 1640.

On the eve of my retreat, after examen, while I was making my confession and later as I was saying my penance, two suns appeared, shining with the utmost brilliance, and in between them was a cross. All four arms of the cross seemed to be of the same length and width, but I did not see what it was made of. On the upper portion there seemed, if I am not mistaken, to be a likeness of our Lord Jesus Christ. Later I wondered if perhaps it was a representation of the Blessed Virgin. It was then that I realized in my soul that I was called particularly to the cross and to mortification.[11]

The next day, February 12, the opening day of the Exercises, while I was forcing myself to live in God with no

---

[10] This text, which is quoted by Ragueneau (*MS de 1652*, pp. 189–91) both in Latin and in French, is not contained among the notes found on pp. 224–40. It dates from the period of persecution lasting from 1637 to 1640. Father Latourelle calls attention to the fact that if it had been written in 1640 or 1641, it would have been dated along with the other fragments of Brébeuf's notebook for this period. It is logical to consider this vow the reaction of his soul to the threats of 1637. Ragueneau (*MS de 1652*, p. 188) refers to the vow always to perform the most perfect action, and dates it "plus de douze ans avant sa mort", that is, 1637, while in reality, it dates from 1645. Did he possibly confuse it with the vow of martyrdom, which he quotes on the same page?

The scriptural quotation is from Psalm 115:4 [116:13], which the priest recites at Mass before partaking of the Precious Blood.

[11] According to Father Latourelle, it is very likely that Brébeuf received at this time a directive from his spiritual director or from his superior to write, as Ragueneau (*MS de 1652*, p. 187) says, "the extraordinary experiences that he was undergoing, at least those that he could easily recall, for they were very frequent, and his activities for the salvation of his neighbor hardly gave him any time at all to record them." Brébeuf once more found himself in a period of persecutions.

other thought but love and was trying to drive from my mind all earthly things, the result was that I was troubled by various distractions and filled with unrest. I seemed to hear a voice within me say: "Turn to Jesus Crucified, and let him be both the basis and source of your contemplation." Thereupon I felt myself drawn to Christ as to a magnet.

On that same day, a terrifying face appeared to me, a face just like the lion's head that is, I think, in the picture of Father Joseph Anchieta,[12] but much larger and gradually becoming larger still. I thought it was a demon. However, I was not frightened and quietly said: "Do whatever God permits you to do." I think I made the Sign of the Cross, and at once the image vanished.

On the fourteenth, during the time of meditation, it seemed to me that I saw Christ our Lord hanging on the Cross and coming toward me as if to remove the burden from himself and place it on my shoulders. I willingly offered my body, but I do not know what happened. I know only that I saw, as it were, a corpse snatched from the Cross, but it no longer had the same appearance as before. It was completely covered with leprosy, "having neither beauty nor comeliness". Nevertheless, I know it was the body of Christ our Lord, because the wounds in the hands were quite evident. My thought then was that in our meditations Christ Crucified should not be considered as he is usually represented, but as a "leper; there is no beauty in him, nor comeliness" (Is 53:4, 2).

Toward evening on that same day, when I was preparing to meditate on Christ's perfections and on the many

---

[12] Blessed Joseph Anchieta was a Spanish Jesuit sent to Brazil in 1553 and to whom was attributed a remarkable power over wild animals.

different relationships that he had with me and that I, miserable wretch, had with him, the thought came to me that all the aspects of his extraordinary love for us should be referred to this charity as to a central point. At once I seemed to see an immense rose window, a huge multicolored stained glass circle, breathtaking not only for its size but also for its variety, yet even more because all its beauty seemed to emanate from its center.

Also during this retreat, on February 18, I seemed to see the Blessed Virgin as if in a blue cloud, holding the Child Jesus. Through different sections of the cloud, there burst forth golden rays, dazzling in their beauty. I was hoping that the Blessed Virgin would present me to Christ, but she did not do so.

On February 23, during the time of the evening examen, it seemed that I saw a face like that of a Spaniard with a crenate ruff and a Spanish hat. At once I realized that this was the devil, hiding under this form, seeking to distract me from prayer. Immediately I forced my attention to the matter of my examen.

On the twenty-sixth of the same month, as soon as I started reciting my rosary in the evening, it seemed to me that I saw the tabernacle of our house at Sainte-Marie, on which are painted seven angels, and I felt urged to pray more devoutly. Then it seemed that I was in the church and, shortly after, in the chapel. I saw all the relics that are kept there and so I was inspired to invoke all those saints.

On March 9, when, after examen, I was reading a spiritual book by the hearth, I saw near the house of Sainte-Marie a huge serpent of various colors coming, as it were, out of the river and gliding toward the house. It seemed to be about eight or nine feet long. Then, as it drew near the house, it stood erect and jumped on one of the Frenchmen. It seemed to pull him by the hair. One of the Fathers, I do not know which, running up from behind and seizing it by the back, threw it to the ground. As everyone jumped on it, suddenly this vision disappeared.

Then I saw // behind the gable of the little house of Sainte-Marie // four dogs of marvelous size // with drooping ears. They were sitting on their haunches, looking toward the cabin. Two had gray coats, and two were of a brown-violet color. That was all I saw. //

On March 11, when I was beginning my morning examen in the presence of the Blessed Sacrament, I saw a Jesuit whom I did not recognize raised up in the air, the way our Fathers are usually painted, // a bust // surrounded by a bright light. Then, a little later, from the head of this Jesuit, there sprouted two horns like those of a crab, and finally his whole head was turned into a freshwater crab and he grew a number of claws // hanging down toward the earth //. This vision did not last long, but I felt a profound fear and trembling that I might be that unhappy Jesuit in whom such a terrible change took place.

On March 21, 1640, while I was at the residence of Saint-Joseph,[13] during evening prayer, I saw approaching from the top of the altar a fantastic being with a human face. It had huge wings, and by waving them up and down, it

---

[13] The residence of Saint-Joseph was at *Teanaostaiae*, where Brébeuf had to suffer many persecutions from apostate Christians. Sainte-Marie was the central residence of the Huron mission.

balanced itself, keeping itself up in the air. It could not advance very far because it was restrained by a cord or some other force from behind. When it first began to appear and to fly around me, I thought it had four wings. Then I noticed it had only two. I interpreted this vision as meaning that I or someone else who was striving very hard to fly toward heavenly contemplation was held back from reaching that goal by certain earthly affections.

On March 30, when after Mass I was interiorly recollecting myself so that I might hear Christ speaking within me, I seemed to feel a hand anointing my heart and my whole interior with some sort of ointment. This vision brought the utmost peace and tranquillity to my soul.

On the eleventh of April, an Indian revolt broke out near the residence of Saint-Joseph. In the fray Pierre Boucher was wounded in the arm, and Father Chaumonot and I were beaten. All sorts of insults and outrages were heaped upon us, and we were quite fearful because Ondihoahorea[14] and other leaders of the village had ordered us to leave. Later, when I was offering thanks to God for all these afflictions and, despite my uneasiness and distress, was striving to conform my will to his, I seemed to see the Blessed Virgin as she is represented as Our Lady of Sorrows—grieving, and her heart pierced with three swords. I felt interiorly as if she were telling me that even when she, the holy Mother of God, was most sorely afflicted, she was nevertheless always perfectly conformed to the divine will and thus ought to be an example to me in my adversities.

---

[14] Ondihoahorea was a very influential apostate.

On May 9, when I was in the village of Saint-Joseph, I was, as it were, ravished in God by powerful acts of love, and I seemed to be impelled by God to embrace him. Then there appeared something that looked like an old woman. First she embraced me, then she struck my head so hard against hers that it hurt. Suspecting that this old woman was really the devil, I made the Sign of the Cross to protect my forehead. After this, the old hag stepped back, not daring to approach closer to me.

The whole time I was at *Teanaostaiae*, I was often overcome by movements of love for God.

// On May 17, while I was praying to God during the day, I felt myself lifted up in spirit to consider a cross like the one at Sainte-Marie, in which there are some relics of the Holy Land. This cross is shaped like a star. The vision lasted a long time, and throughout its whole extent, I had no other thought but that God wished to send me some new cross. //[15]

// On the fourth of August, having returned from the burial of our Christian firebrand,[16] I had several visions during the evening examen. I remember nothing at all of the first one. The second seemed to show me a sort of tent or dome that descended from Heaven and placed itself on the grave

---

[15] A few days later, Brébeuf left *Teanaostaiae* for the residence of Sainte-Marie. He remained at the mission of the Neutrals from November 2, 1640, to March 17, 1641.

[16] The "Christian firebrand" was Joseph Chiwatenwa, to whom Brébeuf refers in the following vision. Chiwatenwa was baptized when he was in danger of death on August 16, 1637, and after he recovered his health, he became a pillar of the Huron church. He was killed by two Iroquois, attacking him from ambush, on August 2, 1640.

of our Christian. Then it seemed that someone turned up the two ends of the tent and lifted it on high, as if to carry it to Heaven. However, I did not see how it was raised or the persons who lifted it. The vision ended here, having lasted quite a long time. I felt that God wished to make me understand the state of the soul of this good Christian. //

// On August 12 or 13 I seemed to see a high mountain all covered with saints. I do not know if there were a great number of them, but it clearly seemed that there were saints only. They were arranged on this mountain as if in an amphitheater, so that from the foot of the mountain to its peak, the saints diminished in size until they were reduced to a single one, Our Lady, who was seated on the crest of the hill. // Then I thought of our Joseph Chiwatenwa, but I could not identify him on that hill. I felt that the vision signified the preeminence of the Blessed Virgin over all the other saints.

On August 27, while saying the litanies in the evening, I saw a man's form hanging in midair, but upside down, so that the feet were above and the head below. The man's feet did not seem to be attached to anything; he was suspended in the air in this position. At first I could not recognize the man. But quite soon I saw and identified distinctly a certain person. However, I am not sure whether it was he from the first or whether originally it had been the form of someone else. This man was sitting down and had his face turned toward the ground. He was completely covered with large pustules like those of certain contagious diseases, large blisters, not unlike those of smallpox.[17] Not only were his

---

[17] An epidemic of smallpox was raging among the Hurons at that time.

face and his whole body covered with this leprosy or pox, but even the air around him was polluted with it. // I think there was someone a short distance from him who was already infected by this same contagion. // I thought this vision represented the contagious condition of that unfortunate soul and his communication of that hideous pestilence to those who came in contact with him.

//On August 31, during the evening litanies and examen, I saw a woman's robe, unusually beautiful because of its rich material as well as its decorations—the embroidery of gold and pearls that were on it. This garment was worn by a woman who I doubt not at all was Our Lady, but I did not see her face, and my spirit was completely engrossed and enraptured at the sight and inspection of this robe, which was extremely wide and ample. Finally I asked myself why I hesitated to look this lady in the face; then in spirit I raised my eyes and seemed to see a tall, venerable statue, covered with a veil and crowned, in the customary fashion of representing our glorious Virgin. This vision was short-lived and not very clear.

In addition to this, alongside Our Lady, something like a huge sphere was opening up, the inside of which contained many beautiful objects, so surprising and so ravishing that I could never have imagined them, nor do I know how to describe them. There was no lamp, yet everything gleamed with light. I have never seen anything like it, nor even read of it. The first idea that came to me when the globe was opened was that this was the same vision I had had of a clock with innumerable springs. But this was entirely different. The feelings I then experienced were admiration and love of God, but also fear of being deceived. //

// On November 17 I was en route to the Neutral nation. On the evening before our arrival, while I was saying my prayers, // I seemed to see many, many angelic forms before me.

// On December 13 I was at *Andachkhroeh Chenusohahissen*. During my examen, if I remember rightly, I saw as it were a skeleton that fled from me. // I do not know if it was coming from me or if it had approached me from some other direction. One thing I do know: when I saw it, it was quite close to me, and it vanished immediately.

// January 16, 1641. // During my sleep, I thought I was with Father Coton,[18] who told me that on the next day he was to plead his cause before the judges. I told him that I, too, was to be tried within the next few days but as yet had given no thought as to how I would defend myself. When I awoke, I was sure that the holy Father Coton would be a successful advocate in pleading my cause.

// February 7. // I saw as it were two hands joined in sign of alliance. I also saw what seemed to be half of the globe. At this moment also, I think, or a few days later, during evening prayers, I seemed to see many crosses, all of which I very gladly embraced. On the following night, while at prayer, forcing myself to conform to the will of God in my regard and saying to him, "Lord, may your will be done", I heard a voice say to me: "Take and read." The next morning, I took up the precious little book the *Imitation of Christ*

---

[18] Father Coton was preacher and confessor of Henri IV, and, later, provincial of France. It was he who sent Brébeuf to Canada in 1625. Several times Coton had had to defend himself against the attacks of the pamphleteers.

and happened to open it at the chapter "The Royal Road of the Holy Cross" (2:12). From that time on, I felt in my soul a great peace and tranquillity despite my present sufferings.

On October 8, 1644, in the chapel of Sainte-Marie des Hurons, during evening prayers before supper, I seemed to see bloodstains or purple spots on the clothes of all our Fathers and on my own, too. This filled me with surprise, but then there came to mind that saying of Isaiah (64:6) that "all our justices are like soiled linen".[19]

During the annual retreat, 1645.[20] August 18. Every day from now on, with the permission of the superior, at the time of Holy Communion, I will vow to do whatever I know is for the greater glory of God and for his greater service.

The conditions of this vow are twofold: (1) I myself, when the matter appears properly, clearly, and without doubt, will judge an action to be for the greater glory of God or not; (2) if there should be some doubt, I will consult the superior or the spiritual Father, if this is possible.

To make this vow explicit, note first of all: I vow to do all that has been commanded, so that what would be a mortal sin according to the precept will also be a sacrilege by virtue of the vow; however, should it be a venial sin according to the precept, it shall remain a venial sin according to the vow. Secondly, regarding a matter that is only of counsel and not of precept, yet may be very important and

---

[19] Brébeuf does not interpret this vision as a prefiguration of his martyrdom.
[20] This vow is found in the *Manuscrit de 1652*, p. 228, immediately after the vision of August 21, 1637.

exceedingly fruitful for the glory of God, I shall be held to act under pain of mortal sin; but in a matter not too important, I shall be held only under venial sin. Thirdly, so that I may be bound under venial sin by force of my vow in a matter of no great significance, it must be clearly evident to me, with no possible doubt, that the affair advances the greater glory of God, whether I myself judge it to be so according to the divine law as a result of my election during the Spiritual Exercises, from the dictates of reason, or through the grace of God, or whether the superior or the spiritual Father so judge the matter.

/ O my God, may you be known! May this barbarous country be completely converted to you! May its sins be abolished! May you be loved! Yes, my God, if all the torments that the captives endure in these regions, if all their cruel afflictions shall fall upon me, I offer myself with all my heart to suffer them alone! /[21]

---

[21] Ragueneau quotes this text (*MS de 1652*, p. 207), saying that it was written "a short time before his death".

THE HOLY DEATHS OF FATHER JEAN DE BRÉBEUF AND FATHER GABRIEL LALEMANT

We had been informed by some escaped captives of the certain deaths of Fathers Jean de Brébeuf and Gabriel Lalemant. The next morning, as soon as we were assured that the enemy had departed, we sent one of our Fathers and seven other Frenchmen to seek their bodies at the place of torture. There they found a spectacle of horror—the remains of cruelty personified—or, rather, the testimony of the love of God, which alone triumphs in the death of martyrs.

If I were so allowed, I would gladly call them by that glorious name because, of their own free will, motivated solely by the love of God and the salvation of their neighbor, these men exposed themselves to death, and to an extremely cruel death, if ever in the world there was one. They could easily and without sin have put their lives in safety had they not been filled with love for God rather than for themselves. A much stronger reason for this title of martyr, however, is that despite their charitable dispositions, hatred for the Faith and contempt for the name of God were among the most powerful incentives influencing the minds of the barbarians to exercise upon them cruelties as racking as ever the rage of tyrants obliged the early martyrs to endure—martyrs who, at the climax of their tortures, triumphed over both life and death.

Title, *De l'heureuse mort du Père Jean de Brébeuf et du Père Gabriel Lallemant*, and the text are those of Ragueneau, taken from the *Manuscrit de 1652*, pp. 169–83.

As soon as the Fathers were taken captive, they were stripped naked and some of their nails torn out. The welcome they received upon entering the village of Saint-Ignace was a hailstorm of blows with clubs on their shoulders, their loins, their legs, their chests, their abdomens, and their faces—no part of their bodies escaped suffering its own torment.

Father Jean de Brébeuf, overwhelmed by the burden of these blows, did not for all that disregard the care of his flock. Seeing himself surrounded by Christians whom he himself had instructed and who were now suffering captivity with him, he encouraged them thus: "My children, let us raise our eyes to Heaven in the midst of our unutterable afflictions; let us remember that God is witness to our sufferings and that he will soon be our glorious reward. Let us die in this faith and let us hope from his goodness the fulfillment of his promises. I feel much more pity for you than for myself. Bear with courage the few remaining torments. They will end with our lives, but the glory that follows them will never end." "*Echon*," (this is the name the Hurons gave to Father Brébeuf) they replied, "our spirits will be in Heaven while our bodies are still suffering on earth. Pray to God for us, that he may show us his mercy; we will invoke him until death."

Some Huron infidels—former captives of the Iroquois and now naturalized among them, long-standing enemies of the Faith—were annoyed by these words and by the fact that the Fathers, though their captives, did not hold their tongues captive. The infidels cut off the hands of one Father and pierced the other Father's hands with sharp awls and iron points. They applied hatchets heated red in the fire to their armpits and to their loins. They placed a necklace of these glowing ax heads about their necks in such a way that any motion of their bodies produced a new torture. If they attempted to lean forward, the red-hot iron hanging behind them burned their shoulders, and if they thought they could avoid that pain by bending back a little, their chests and stomachs suffered a similar torment. If they stood upright, without leaning to one side or the other, these glowing hatchets touched them on all sides and were an intolerable torment to them. Their persecutors fastened on them belts of bark filled with pitch and resin, then set them afire and thus burned the entire body of their poor victims.

At the height of these torments, Father Gabriel Lalemant raised his eyes to Heaven, clasped his hands several times, and sent prolonged sighs to God, begging his aid. Father Jean de Brébeuf suffered like a rock, insensible to the fires and the flames, not uttering a single cry, but keeping a profound silence. This restraint thoroughly astonished his tormentors. No doubt the heart of the sufferer was already reposing in his God. Then, as if returning to himself, he preached to those infidels, his torturers. He had more encouragement, however, for the many good Christian captives who felt a deep sympathy for him.

Father de Brébeuf's persecutors then became indignant at his zeal, and to hinder him from speaking further of God, they gouged out circles around his mouth, cut off his nose, and tore off his lips. His blood then spoke more loudly than his lips had done. Since his heart was not yet torn out, his tongue did not fail to serve him until his last sigh, blessing God for all these torments and exhorting his Christians more vigorously than ever.

In derision of holy baptism, which these good Fathers had so charitably administered even during the attack and in the heat of the fight, those wretched enemies of the Faith devised the plan of baptizing the Fathers with boiling water.

Their charred bodies were completely bathed in it, not only once, but two or three times, and even more, with biting insults to accompany these torments. "We baptize you," announced these heathens, "so that you may be blessed in Heaven, for without proper baptism you cannot be saved." Others mockingly added: "We treat you as a friend, since we are the cause of your greatest happiness in Heaven. Thank us for our kind services, for the more you suffer the more your God will reward you."

Most of these tormentors were apostate Hurons who had been captives among the Iroquois for a long period and were longtime enemies of the Faith. They had had sufficient instruction for their salvation but had impiously abused it. Truly their cruelty did serve for the glory of the Fathers, but it is much to be feared that it was also for their own ignominy.

The more their torments were increased, the more the Fathers entreated God that their sins should not be the cause of the wickedness of these poor blind souls whom they pardoned with all their heart. How truly they can now say: "Through fire and water we have passed; but now relief you granted us" (Ps 65 [66]:12).

When they were fastened to the post where they suffered these tortures and where they were to die, they knelt down, embraced it with joy, and kissed it piously as being the object of their desires and their love and as a sure and final pledge of their salvation. They spent some time in prayer, a much longer time than their executioners were willing to allow them.

Their tortures were not of the same duration. Father Jean de Brébeuf was at the height of his agony at about three o'clock on the same day he was captured, March 16. He rendered up his soul about four o'clock in the evening.

Father Gabriel Lalemant suffered longer, from six o'clock in the evening until about nine o'clock the next morning, March 17.

Before they died, both of them had their hearts torn out by means of an opening above the breast. Those inhuman barbarians feasted on these organs, drinking the blood of their victims while it was still quite warm, drawing it from its source with sacrilegious hands. While the Fathers were living and still conscious, pieces of flesh were removed from their thighs and from the calves of their legs. These morsels their executioners placed on coals to roast and then ate them in the sight of their captives.

The torturers had slashed the holy bodies of the Fathers in various places, and, in order to increase their pain, had thrust red-hot hatchets into their wounds.

Father Jean de Brébeuf had had the covering of his skull torn away; his feet were cut off and the flesh torn from his thighs all the way down to the bone. A hatchet blow had split one of his jaws.

Father Gabriel Lalemant had received a hatchet blow on the left ear, driving it all the way into his brain and clearly exposing this latter organ. We could find no part of his body, from his feet to his head, which had not been broiled and scorched while he was still alive—even his eyes, into which those impious wretches had thrust burning coals.

They had broiled the tongues of both saints, repeatedly thrusting flaming firebrands and burning pieces of bark into their mouths to prevent them from invoking, even while dying, him for whom they were suffering and who could never die in their hearts. I have learned all these details from persons worthy of credence. They saw it and reported it to me firsthand. These men had been the fellow captives of our Fathers but, having been reserved for death at a later date, had managed to escape.

But let us leave these objects of horror, these monsters of cruelty. Someday, all those tortured members of our Fathers will be endowed with immortal glory. The magnitude of their torments will be the measure of their happiness, and from this time on, they are living in the repose of the saints, where they will continue to dwell forever.

We buried the precious relics on Sunday, March 22, with so much consolation and such tender feelings of devotion in all those present at the obsequies that I know of none who did not long for a similar death, rather than fear it, and who did not regard himself as blessed to stand in a place where, possibly within a few days, God would grant him the grace of shedding both his blood and his life in a like manner. Not one of us could prevail upon himself to pray to God for them, as if they had any need of it. Our spirits were instead directed toward Heaven, where we had no doubt that their souls were reposing. Be this as it may, I beg God to fulfill in us his holy will, even to death, as he has done in the persons of our companions of the Society.

Father Gabriel Lalemant was the last to come to the combat and yet fortunately bore away one of the first crowns. He was the latest to arrive at our Huron mission, having come only six months ago, yet he has been chosen by God as one of the first victims to be sacrificed to the pagan hatred of the Christian name and Faith.

For several years, he had been begging God with tears and sighs to be sent to this mission at the end of the world, notwithstanding his very delicate constitution and the fact that his body had no strength except what the spirit of God and the desire of suffering for his name could give him. I cannot refrain from making public a personal note concerning the motives that prompted him to desire so ardently to work in these missions. It was written in his own hand, and I found it after his death. Here are his words:

1. My God and my Savior, it is my duty to requite the obligations I have toward you. You put aside your satisfactions, honors, comfort, joys—indeed, your very life—in order to save me, a wretched creature. Is it not, then, only reasonable that I should follow your example and abandon all these things for the salvation of souls that you claim as yours, souls that have cost you your Blood, which you have loved even to death, and of which you have said, "Inasmuch as you did this to one of these least brethren of mine, you did it to me" (Mt 25:40)?

2. Indeed, even though I were not moved by a spirit of gratitude to make to you this holocaust of myself, I would do so with all my heart in consideration of the grandeur of your adorable Majesty and of your infinite goodness, which deserves that a man sacrifice himself in your service and generously lose himself in the faithful accomplishment of what he judges to be your will concerning him, through the special inspirations that it pleases you to give him for your greater glory.

3. Since in my wickedness I have so greatly offended your goodness, O my Jesus, it is only right for me to make amends to you by extraordinary efforts. Therefore, I must walk before your face the rest of my life, with my heart humbled and contrite, enduring the pains that you first suffered for me.

4. I am indebted to my relatives—to my mother and my brothers—and I must draw down on them the effects of your mercies. My God, never permit that any of our family, which you love so much, perish in your presence or be of the number of those who blaspheme you eternally. Let me

be the victim for them, for I am ready for suffering; burn and cut me now, so that you may spare me in eternity.

5. Yes, my Jesus and my love, it is necessary for your Blood, shed for the barbarians as well as for us, to be applied efficaciously to their salvation. It is in this that I wish to cooperate with your grace and to sacrifice myself for these pagan souls.

6. It is also necessary that your name be adored, that your Kingdom be spread through all the nations of the world, and that I devote my whole life to withdrawing from the hands of your enemy, Satan, these poor souls who have cost you both your Blood and your life.

7. Finally, if it is reasonable for someone inspired by love to wish to give this satisfaction to Jesus Christ—although at the risk of a hundred thousand lives (if he had that many) and with the loss of everything that is sweetest and most agreeable to nature—you, my soul, will never find anyone more deeply obliged to undertake it than yourself. Courage, then, my heart! Let us blessedly lose ourselves in giving this satisfaction to the Sacred Heart of Jesus Christ. He deserves it, and you cannot refuse it to him if you do not wish to live and die ungrateful to his love.

These are the motives that animated Father Lalemant's zeal to come and to die in the midst of this barbarism. There was no one more innocent than he, for he had left the world in his tender youth, and in the nineteen years he had been a religious in our Society, he had always had a conscience so pure that the least shadow—I will not say of sin—but of thoughts that might approach it and were not at all culpable served only to aid him to unite himself more completely to God.

After his arrival here among the Hurons, he had applied himself so energetically to learning their language—a thankless task, if ever there was one—and subsequently had made so much progress in it that we did not doubt that God wished to use him in these regions only for the advancement of his glory. The charity of Father Lalemant found no difference between the study of the higher sciences that had occupied him until then and the thorny difficulties of a barbarous language with nothing attractive about it except what beauty his zeal for the salvation of his neighbor led him to find in it. Not least of the difficulties in this country is the necessity of becoming a child at the age of thirty-nine in order to learn to speak.

At all events, he finished his course quickly; but in this short time, he fulfilled all the expectations that earth and Heaven could hold for his labors. He died in the cause of God, having found in this mission country the Cross of Jesus Christ that he came here to seek, and whose bloody stains he gloriously bore in his own body.

Although in leaving the world, he had left the share of honorable offices that his birth would have given him, I can truly say that the robe he has purpled with his blood is a thousand times more precious than the purple of kings or even the loftiest expectations that the world could have promised him.

Father Lalemant was born at Paris on October 31, 1610. He entered our Society on March 24, 1630; he died in it on a bed of glory, March 17 of the present year, 1649. The Hurons named him *Atironta*.

PIERRE CHASTELAIN

INTRODUCTION

When Father Pierre Chastelain died in 1684, there was no longer any Le Jeune or Ragueneau in Canada to measure his greatness for us or to gather up his precious writings. Indeed, we would not have even a single page if the *Relation* of 1637 had not included one of his letters—a small masterpiece—and if in 1648 he himself had not published a book of meditations for the use of the Sodalities of Our Lady in France.[1]

Chastelain was born at Senlis in 1606 (some say 1603 or 1604) and entered the Society in 1624, at the same time as Charles Garnier. Together they pursued their studies in Paris, and together they embarked for Quebec, where they arrived in June 1636. Together, also, they were sent almost immediately to the Hurons, joining the other missionaries there on August 12 of that same year. In 1640, after spending several years at different posts, he was named spiritual Father of the mission and lived at Sainte-Marie des Hurons, probably holding this office until his departure for Quebec in 1650.[2] He remained in that city as preacher and confessor until his death. It was there that he became associated with

---

[1] Thw. 19:184 gives a letter of Chastelain that recounts various facts concerning the mission. Nothing remains of his correspondence with Marie de l'Incarnation. The preface of a treatise against paganism by the Canon Deslyons (Paris, 1670) cites two extracts of letters of Chastelain, and the author states that he corresponded with him for twenty-five years.

[2] Rochemonteix 2:69, n. 4, quotes from the catalog of the mission for 1648, in which Chastelain is listed with the title of *praefectus spritualis*.

the venerable Marie de l'Incarnation and became director of the mystic Catherine de Saint-Augustin, a hospital sister.

Father Felix Martin thinks that the book published in Paris in 1648 under Chastelain's name cannot be his, "because his first fourteen years in Canada were spent in the Huron mission, where such work was impossible." [3] But in addition to the facts that the preface of the volume refers to the author's stay in this region, that the title page bears the name of the place: *E nova apud Canadenses Francia*, and that it is dated 1646, a time when Chastelain was working in Canada, the work itself, as we shall see later, mentions the Canadians several times. Furthermore, we know that Chastelain remained in the principal mission residence for long months at a time while the other missionaries were traveling around the neighboring villages (cf. Thw. 21:144). During the endless winters, he did not lack the leisure necessary for composing these pages. Father Larivière (*La vie ardente de saint Charles Garnier*, p. 168) also points out that Chastelain was obliged by his office to give regular spiritual conferences to his Jesuit companions. If Chastelain could not write this book in the country of the Hurons, how can we explain that Jean de Brébeuf, and later Jérôme Lallemant and Paul Ragueneau, living under the same conditions, could compose their long *Relations*?

The *Affectus amantis Christum Jesum*[4] bears no resemblance to a powerfully conceived treatise; it is a series of

---

[3] C. Sommervogel, *Bibliothèque de la Compagnie de Jésus* (Brussels: Shepens; Paris, A. Picard, 1890–1932) 2, col. 1091.

[4] The title page reads: *Affectus amantis Christum Jesum seu exercitium amoris erga Dominum Jesum pro tota hebdomada. Auctore P. Petro Chastelain, e Soc. Jesu novae apud Canadenses Franciae, incola. Parisiis, Apud Dionysium Bechet, via Iacobei, sub Scuto Solari, MDCXLVIII Cum approbatione et privilegio*. The volume has 485 pages.

meditations on the life of our Lord, divided according to the seven days of the week. Sunday treats of the glory of Christ, Monday of the Incarnation, Tuesday of the hidden life, Wednesday of the public life, Thursday of the Holy Eucharist, Friday of the Passion, and Saturday of the Resurrection. Each of these sections is subdivided into a series of chapters of varying number and length. The text is woven from very free biblical citations, interpreted in the most diverse senses, following the manner used by the Fathers of the Church.

The doctrine of Chastelain is certainly not original, but his piety shows a remarkable theological and dogmatic soundness. His ease in utilizing Scripture presupposes a comprehensive reading in the Catholic tradition and a deep, tranquil understanding of Christian mysteries. In his lengthy expositions, there is nothing affected, facile, or narrow. What is more important and perhaps newer, however, in comparison with the spiritual works of the times, is his marked insistence on the apostolic perspectives of the Christian life and on the universal salvation that comes to us in Jesus Christ. The last text translated in this selection is significant in this respect,[5] and hardly ever do we see pages from the seventeenth century that can compare with it. The other French Jesuits, for example, made their reflections turn almost exclusively around problems of the interior life and most frequently spoke of the apostolate only as a flowering of the life of union in a chosen individual. Chastelain, who, along with his companions is confronted with the problem of the

---

[5] In the last part of his work, Chastelain will return to these themes and speak of the Church, the reconciliation of men with God, and the salvation of all nations. He will quote Saint Paul at great length. Cf. *Affectus amantis Christum Jesum*, pp. 384ff.

salvation of entire nations, is more inclined to enlarge his thought and take up Pauline themes on the Mystical Body of Christ.

The second passage we cite is much more classical. It was chosen purposely because Chastelain here develops the benefits of the hidden life, showing that the real obstacle to contemplation is the lack of self-renunciation—that if Christ commands us to live in the midst of the crowd and the tumult, he will not abandon us there. The spiritual formulae of the conference master sometimes seem to be closer to those that a Marie de l'Incarnation would write; for example: "Even when I act in public, you are established in the center and in the core of my heart, my tabernacle and yours." The spiritual formulae are pinpointed and developed, however, from those that precede and could not have been written except by a man with an apostolic vocation: "May your Spirit become twofold in me—human and divine, interior and exterior." If the stream of grace arises in the interior and if action alone produces spiritual nullity, the ultimate necessity, then, in the apostolate is to reconcile the human and the divine, the interior and the exterior. Quoting from the *Imitation of Christ*, Chastelain wrote: "If, however, you seek Jesus in all things, you will surely find him. Likewise, if you seek yourself, you will find yourself—to your own ruin."[6]

The letter that Chastelain wrote to Father Le Jeune in 1636 is much more valuable to us than his book as a source for knowing him as he really was and seeing how his apostolic

---

[6] *Imitation of Christ* 2:7, trans. Aloysius Croft and Harry F. Bolton (Milwaukee: Bruce, 1940), p. 65. We have not quoted further from the book of Chastelain since we intend to publish in this book only those pages in which the Jesuits of New France recount directly their spiritual experiences.

life summed up his whole being. Let us disregard the humor, the joking character, and the sympathetic mockery toward himself, which are but the signs of a supreme interior liberty and a refinement of culture. That is all secondary. What interests us most is that by these few sentences, Chastelain shows himself a great connoisseur in spiritual matters, putting aside the traditional modes of expression and developing new formulae to translate his experience. He has a perfect mental grasp of his own personality in the three phases that constitute it: the exterior, the interior, and that most interior of interiors where God gives him not a "sensible" but a "divine" understanding of the favors he has granted him. Under the cloak of language that is natural and not the least bit technical, we perceive the warp and woof of the two classic nights of the soul—that of the senses and that of the spirit—with their prefiguration of Heaven and their total lack of any dependence upon his exterior affectivity and even, in a certain sense, his interior movements. What Chastelain experienced in the depths of his soul is the grace of God recognized as grace, his favors perceived as favors, as merciful acts of the Lord who has redeemed us and who thereby reveals to us our inherent unworthiness. Because of this view of our radical incapacity to receive his gifts, we are literally crushed under the weight of his beneficence, which we can neither resist nor yet perfectly correspond to.

But all these elements are fundamental and basic. We must emphasize that it is the exceptional apostolic situation in which Chastelain worked that brought to climactic perfection, in a manner no less exceptional, all the dynamic forces of his personality. His most secret experience was inseparable, as he himself said, from the mission he had received and was a help in plodding along the "most difficult roads" in obedience to the commands of his superiors. It was because he had passed through the tribulations of an apostle that he had been heaped with grace by the "so great God of love and goodness" and had been inundated with consolations.

Could this missionary have possibly expounded more profound truths in so few words, very simple words, but words that carry as far as a pebble from a child's slingshot? We easily understand, in reading and rereading his letter, why his superiors named him confessor and spiritual director to the group of mystics working among the Hurons. To an obvious religious maturity he united the gifts of the analyst and a personal knowledge of the workings of God— qualities that our Lord is accustomed to unite in those whose duty it is to guide the privileged objects of his love.

LETTER TO
REVEREND FATHER LE JEUNE

August 8, 1636

May God be eternally blessed! Through a special providence, he has granted us an unusually favorable opportunity for making an extremely difficult journey. I can truly say, "I kept the letter of the law which your own lips have made; my steps clung firmly to your paths" (Ps 16:4 [17: 4–5]). There is no doubt, Reverend Father, that you who take the place of God toward me in this mission have involved me in a very rugged life. Nevertheless, it is quite true that I have never felt better than I do now. I admit frankly that up to this time, I have never sat down upon the ground for even an hour without injuring my health. Here I have spent the coldest nights with no other mattress than a little heap of branches and enjoyed a completely refreshing sleep. Nor have I suffered any ill effects from the sun or the food. As to the state of my soul—in the total lack of physical comforts and even of some spiritual ones, God has continually given me the grace to know that he is doing me a favor that I shall never fully appreciate until I reach Heaven and that a thousand earthly lives could never fully repay. He has made me realize how utterly unworthy I am and how much

---

Chastelain, having arrived in New France two months earlier, was en route to the Huron country. During a stop near Lake Nipissing, he wrote to the superior of the Canadian missions, Father Le Jeune, who was at that time in Quebec. Text taken from Thw. 12:126–28.

delight, on the other hand, he derives from heaping upon me the abundance of his benefactions, the more unfit I am for them. The consolations he has given me have been more divine than material and so delightful that I would have given up a thousand times more than I did for a God so lavish in his love and goodness toward me.

Please, Reverend Father, thank him for me and beg him never to cast me off because of my coldness and ingratitude.

THE LOVE OF CHRIST

I

Lord Jesus, we are all very small in stature and unable to see you, even in passing, because of the crowd.[1] We must climb above the crowd if we wish to see you pass. We must leave, at least for some time during the year, the crowd of men and mount the tree of contemplation, so that for a few days we may see you more clearly. The crowds of the highways prevent our smallness from catching sight of you—a sight that in our passage through this life is necessary from time to time. It is necessary for your glory, for the good of our neighbor, and even for our own welfare. Furthermore, the tumult of secular activities presses on the weakness of our human spirit so strongly that it impedes our seeking light and truth.

Choose this, then, O my soul, and mount this tree; or at least flee from the crowds temporarily, hide yourself from them, descending, so to speak, without them into a hidden cave or grotto. Here you will find Christ again; here you will be filled even to satiety with his graces for many months, not merely for several hours, for you were beginning to perish from hunger among men who are lacking in all things,

---

This is the beginning of part 3, chap. 9, of *Affectus amantis Christum Jesum*, pp. 140–42. The treatise is written in Latin; text obtained in microfilm from the Bibliothèque nationale, Paris.

[1] This is a consideration of the episode of Zacchaeus (cf. Lk. 19: 1–10). We do not attempt to indicate all the scriptural references in this work, since they are too numerous.

or if not totally lacking in them, are at least quite miserly with them. Unless the grain of wheat, O my soul, falling to the earth, dies, and unless it is in some way buried and hidden, it will bring forth no fruit. Unless you likewise, dead to secular interests, are also buried in some fashion, not only hidden in the sepulcher of your heart but also sometimes in a remote place and separated from the society of men, you will be sterile and unfruitful to God, to your neighbor, and to yourself. For man cannot build a lofty edifice if he has not first spent a long time in the bosom of the earth and, thus hidden, established his deepest foundations. Nor can the Christian soul erect and complete the edifice of his perfection unless he has placed its most solid basis through a hidden life of sufficient duration.

My soul, flee the crowd when charity and obedience permit it, since even in the number of good men evil ones are often hidden. Even in the best fields, abounding with excellent grain, there are often weeds. Judas alone would have led the whole band of apostles to unjust and impious murmuring if the good and wise Master had not restrained and curbed the forces of that wicked man. The devil himself very frequently mingles with the holy. Marvel, then, O my soul, at his boldness. On one occasion, when the sons of God were coming to present themselves to their Master, Satan also was in the midst of them. O impudence! Woe to you when you are alone, O my soul, because you are alone in the sense that you are secluded with the demon. This is not the solitude I seek for you; all I seek is that you flee the crowd even of the sons of God, not that you may remain alone, but that you may converse with the Son of God in seclusion. There, indeed, there will be present no one worse than you; there will even be no wicked person present if you are good, or at least wish to be good. Proud Satan cannot bear the companionship of the sons of the true God. Immediately after Judas had taken the morsel, Satan entered into him; as soon as he had taken it, Judas left the group. Truly, how could the Spirit of Darkness bear the presence of the Sun? Judas fled and sought a hidden place. Not those holy and blessed retreats that Christ loves and wishes us to love and that he sometimes chooses for you as for a friend, and where he is your director. Such is the Kingdom of Heaven and such is Heaven's King: like a treasure hidden in a field, like gold hidden in the depths of the earth, like the precious pearl hidden in its shell. You will not find Christ in the marketplaces, but you will find him only in the sequestered spots, unless he himself sends you forth to the crowded open places. However, he who sent you there will not leave you solitary. Absent yourself from all other places if you wish to find him and him to find you. He who shall have lost his soul shall find it again and come upon it. If the multitudes cannot find you thus lost, you will be safe, and lost to your great advantage.

Lord Jesus, if I am held by my office and my duty to live a life in public, produce in me, then, a life not only private but at the same time truly hidden. Develop in me your twofold spirit, my Jesus, my Father, human and divine, interior and exterior. Make your life twofold in me; and if I must perform my duty in public, grant that my intention may remain hidden. Light my lantern, Lord, and illuminate my shadows that I may place within you my hidden places, my retreat. While, also, I am acting in public, may you place your tabernacle and mine in the center and very depths of my heart, for you live most freely in our depths. And if it so happens that there comes a time when anyone shall say to me: "Behold, he is in the desert", I must not go out; or if they say, "Behold, he is in that secluded spot", I must not believe them. Certainly when charity or obedience requires me to be occupied in the bustle of the city squares, nevertheless, you always love and dwell in the desert of my soul and in the depths of my heart. Grant, therefore, that while, like Martha, I am busy with external service, like Mary I may devote myself to you alone and be interiorly attentive to you.

But when the time for even exterior recollection comes, the time of freedom from all external concerns, that is, the time of the Spiritual Exercises during the annual retreat, grant that I may freely cast off all my activities. When it shall be in accordance with your will that I, alone and naked, converse with you in solitude, grant that I may resemble Job, your servant, who, when all was stripped from him with your permission, rent also his clothing, which alone of all his earthly goods was left to him, and thus appeared naked before you. Truly he had nothing left that the devil could take from him or of which the devil could further despoil the servant of God, your servant, or with which to attract him to external goods. Grant, I beseech you, that I also may offer to you even the hair of my head, that I may cast out all my superfluous thoughts, lest by them, as if by my hair, I might be grasped and led by my adversary wherever he wishes; lest he succeed in leading me away from you, O my whole and only Good!

Therefore, in this state, I pray that the humanity of my Savior alone may appear to me; may all other humanities and all other creatures be hidden from me. Then shall I be satisfied, and even happy. O humanity, charm of divinity, lovable food! May I be captivated by you and nourished by you![2]

II

Rise,[3] O my soul, illuminate Jerusalem, for the light is coming and the glory of God is rising above you. Behold, it appears in the substance of our mortality, so that it may refresh you by the new light of its immortality. Divine Jesus, come, illuminate not only this Jerusalem, which must be destroyed thoroughly, but also that one against which the gates of Hell will not prevail. Enlighten your Church, the assembly of nations, by your preaching of your doctrine, your Gospel. The nations, indeed, must walk in your light, and the kings in the splendor of your birth. Thus your Father has promised us, he who has sent you into this world: "Behold I gave him as a witness to the peoples, as leader and teacher of the nations." This he also indicated to you— that this is why you have come. "It is not enough that you are my servant to raise up the tribes of Jacob and to convert the common people of Israel. Behold, I have given you as a light to nations, that you may be my salvation to the ends of the earth."

The kings shall see and the princes will arise and adore because of the Lord who is faithful and the Holy One of

---

[2] The chapter continues with a hymn to the humanity of Christ.

[3] We translate here part 3, chap. 13, pp. 157–59. The title of this section is "The Soul Once More Invites Christ the Lord to Manifest Himself Not Only to the Jews, but Also and Especially to the Pagans". Chastelain here expresses his vehement desire for the conversion of the Indians, a conversion that would be, from his point of view, nothing but the manifestation of Christ.

Israel, who has chosen you. More than that, you yourself, speaking in our favor, say with the prophet: "They have sought me, those who formerly did not ask; and they have found me, those who did not seek me. I appeared to those who did not seek me, and I have been found by those who did not ask about me, and I said: 'Here I am; here I am, for a nation which did not invoke my name.'"

Lord Jesus, your Father has promised many things in your regard, and it is necessary that first of all you take care of the business of your Father. "As the dew falls from the heavens" (these are his words), "and the snow, and as these do not return to the heavens in the same manner as they came, but water the earth, penetrate it, cause it to germinate, give seed to the sower and bread to him who eats; thus shall my word be, which will come from my mouth. It will not return to me empty, but it will do all that I wish and will succeed in those undertakings for which I have sent it", said the almighty God.

My Christ, unless you hasten to come out of your house and hurry to appear outside your native land—more important still—unless you hasten to bring with you the heritage of all nations, you will return to your Father almost without fruit. That is why, thanks to you, on the land of the pagans, the pine tree must grow in place of the valerian, and the myrtle must increase in place of the nettles, and the Lord must be named in eternal signs that will not be taken from him. The Lord Jesus, when he is called by name from Heaven, will be visible to all nations. Jonah was the sign only for the Ninevites. There is more here than Jonah. You, Lord, are to be a sign for all the nations, especially for the perverse generation of the Jews. Wicked and adulterous, and wishing to see a sign from you, yet they did not wish you as their sign. Therefore, reveal yourself to every creature, and truly thus is it written of you that we have received on that day the Root of Jesse, who stands as a sign for the people. Do not, then, remain longer hidden; it is necessary that you be a sign openly. However, I do not wish anyone to complain if, indeed, at the time of your common and public life, you sometimes took aside your friends with whom you conversed intimately and led them apart to a high mountain to become transfigured before them. I know, I know that these favors are not granted in public, but if you do not judge it good that your countenance gleam as the sun in the presence of everyone, at least, let it be evident to them how amiable and how much to be adored it is.

Joseph, the dearest of all his sons to his father, having been sent to his brothers, was merely a figure of your mission, my Jesus, in which your Father said to you: "Come, I shall send you truly, in human flesh, to men, your brothers." Immediately you responded: "I am ready." To anyone asking what you seek, do you not answer, as did Joseph: "I am looking for my brothers"? O divine Jesus, if we are all your brothers, seek, then, all of us—the barbarians and the pagans; seek also the Canadians, and not only those who are called more savage than the savages because they said: "Come, let us kill him!" Seek also those who would place you, not in an abandoned cistern, but in a new tomb. Truly, in the midst of such brothers, you can say: "I am seeking my brothers." You will desire and you will find none but wicked, wild beasts. And if sometimes men do approach you with fraternal words, in their hearts they are thinking only the speech of enemies. Indeed, the voice may sometimes be that of Jacob, the voice of a good brother, but the hands will be those of Esau, the hands of a cruel brother. And, in the end, there will be hands more cruel even than those of Esau that will be placed on you, their dearest Brother. Certainly they will be very different from the real Jacob and from the Holy One of Israel, those who will imitate by trickery the voice of Jacob but have instead the cruel hands of Esau. O divine Jesus, although you are infinitely of greater worth than Joseph, there will be those, the most despicable of your brethren, who, not moved by pity, will not repeat the words of Joseph's brothers: "What good is it to us to kill him and hide his blood? Would it not be better to sell him?" Lord, truly you will be sold and will be killed by your brothers.

I do not fear, Lord, to predict to you these things as I invite you to manifest yourself. It is for this reason, of your own free will, that you offered yourself for us and that you were constrained until this was accomplished in you for the salvation of nations.

SAINT ISAAC JOGUES

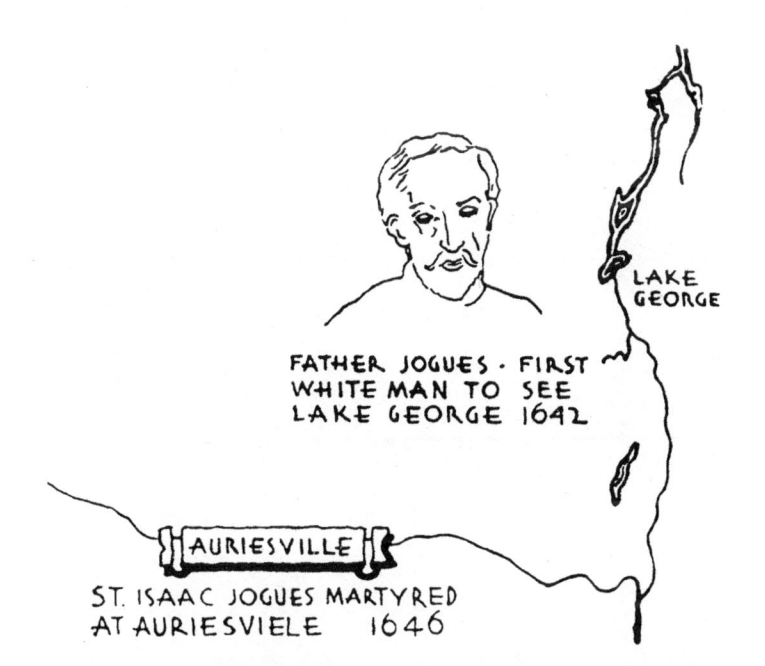

FATHER JOGUES · FIRST WHITE MAN TO SEE LAKE GEORGE 1642

LAKE GEORGE

AURIESVILLE

ST. ISAAC JOGUES MARTYRED AT AURIESVIELE 1646

INTRODUCTION

Among the martyrs in Canada, Isaac Jogues is without question the one most beloved by children, not only because his life is crisscrossed with numerous adventures, but because his soul is candid, his heart always inflamed, ready for new enterprises; and because he is a poet—a poet who dreams of Heaven and whom only little children are able to understand.

Jogues was born at Orléans on June 10, 1607. He attended Jesuit schools, then entered the novitiate in Paris on October 24, 1624. He finished his philosophical studies in 1629 and was appointed to teach at the college in Rouen. As was the custom at that time, he followed his students from the fifth form through the humanities, inclusive. In 1633 he returned to Paris, to the Collège de Clermont, where he completed three years of theological studies and was ordained priest. He was then appointed to Quebec, where he arrived on July 2, 1636.

We have three letters to his mother that he wrote during this time. In them he shows that he was always perfectly himself. The affection and tenderness toward his family revealed in these letters, and which he emphasized over and over, did not in any way hinder his zeal. His mother's solicitude, the source of so many benefits in the past, did not prevent his describing in detail the hard life he had embraced. He had not the least fear of worrying her, because to the recital of his hardships he joined the expression of an unmixed joy in working in these far-off regions for the salvation of souls. No shrinking back into his sensitiveness, no introversion appears throughout the whole account of the "inconveniences" he met with. Nor did he forget that he was still, in the eyes of his mother, a priest and a religious, and he gave her simple spiritual counsels—strong, discreet, respectful—that in no way resembled a lesson learned by rote but sprang spontaneously from his heart.

A short time after his arrival at Quebec, he was sent to the Hurons, where, it can truthfully be said, he did nothing extraordinary. Father Lucien Campeau points this out very clearly:

> He always takes the second place. In all his ministries, he accompanies another Jesuit, whom he treats as his superior. If the two of them are involved in some unusual episode, it is always the other who extricates them—the other, who frequently has had no more experience in the missions than he, and oftentimes less. It is the others who found the missions: a Daniel, a Pijart; the others who conduct the expeditions: a gentle Garnier, a Raymbaut; the others who confront and resolve difficult situations.[1]

This appraisal of his character is confirmed in the note recording the graces he received on May 11, 1638: Jogues withdrew to pray, but on the advice of Father Chastelain, he sang the psalm intoned by Father Pijart; he acquiesced to the duty of according all favors to God, using the words of Father Chastelain. Even the Church has corroborated this secondary position of Jogues by placing him after the leader, Jean de Brébeuf, in the list of Canadian martyrs, even though Jogues was martyred first.[2]

---

[1] "Portrait de saint Isaac Jogues", *Lettres du Bas-Canada* (September 1952), p. 134.

[2] The eight martyrs canonized in 1929 by Pope Pius XI are the following: Jean de Brébeuf, Isaac Jogues, Gabriel Lalemant, Charles Garnier, Noël Chabanel, Antoine Daniel, René Goupil, and Jean de la Lande.

In his apostolate, Jogues never showed himself an innovator. To be sure, he learned the Iroquois language during his captivity, but any other Jesuit in his place would have done the same. There is no doubt, either, that he quickly perceived the strategy that the enemies of the Hurons were planning to pursue during the next five years, and he informed the French governor of its details. But he did not have a mental acuteness equal to that of Brébeuf, by which the latter could distinguish what was orthodox from the superstitious, what was sound from the weaknesses in the religious practices of the Indians. Jogues was not even sufficiently interested in externals to describe the customs of the Iroquois and to show, for example, how they differed from the Hurons. When he spoke of their manner of offering food to the demon *Aireskoi*, it was merely to explain his abstinence; when he narrated the trial by fire that a Huron woman underwent, his chief purpose was to describe how he baptized her. His prudence in the midst of the Iroquois was more than tinged with apostolic impatience. He certainly never allowed himself the bold and magnificent gestures that brought death to René Goupil. He never made a frontal attack, but neither did he feel he should keep silence for months, or even years, while waiting for the hour of grace. Nor does it belittle him to say that he never perfectly understood the mentality and psychology of the savages.

On the other hand, when we read the pages wherein he recounts his dream of May 11, 1638, we are forced to acknowledge that Jogues was a very exceptional person. These are the words of a great mystic, expressed in sublime poetry. Not only does he recognize that he has had an extraordinary experience, but he knows he should reveal it. The passage in which he relates earthly liturgies to heavenly ones is executed in masterly fashion, which, without the ear at first perceiving it, changes the register of the celestial harmonies. In this, Jogues is the greatest of all the missioners of New France. The spiritual notes of Brébeuf, which are also clear, never contain a lyricism comparable to that which flows from the pen of his fellow martyr; nor do we find that veritable explosion of love that is ancillary to the perfection of his language. The Protestant writer Parkman was correct when he said that "he [Jogues] could have become a famous man of letters." [3]

In 1642, returning from a trip to Quebec via the Saint Lawrence River, Jogues was taken prisoner by the Iroquois. In the midst of the unspeakable sufferings caused by a captivity prolonged for more than a year, he described in the same lofty literary style the happenings of these long months. The entire opening passage of his letter to the provincial in France—a letter more than fifty pages long—is devoted to a discussion of his linguistic scruples, his difficulty in choosing between the use of French and Latin, his fear of committing mistakes in style. For a prisoner who was locked up and half-starved, even lacking a thumb, this is, to say the least, an unusual procedure. The humanist in him was to die only with the saint.

Another striking feature of Jogues' writing is his astonishing sense memory. Undoubtedly his isolation permitted him to review his sufferings very often, and the possibility of expressing himself freely to his superior favored this verbosity. But what details of the pains he endured, what precision in the unfolding of varied and successive scenes! In all these minutiae, he revealed himself; and if he spoke at length of the sorrows of others or of their spiritual and

---

[3] Quoted by Rochemonteix 2:20.

moral wretchedness, it was only to emphasize that he was their echo and equally tainted. If ever anyone wished to prove that stoic heroism has no relation to sanctity, it would suffice for him to read these pages of Jogues, from which arise innumerable lamentations, unnumbered cries of grief and distress. Yet how often all this is illuminated by a faith that is never denied, by a hope that accepts all and that in no single instance even suggests the least desire for vengeance against his tormentors!

Perhaps it is these qualities, united to a perfect assimilation of Holy Scripture, that never give this long exposition of himself the aspect of an intimate diary. Jogues was conscious of living a great drama—one that surpassed him—that of the Redemption. He spontaneously applied all this to himself, especially the words of the Psalms; but he also included the great biblical texts that give fullness of meaning to suffering: Job, Lamentations, Isaiah, the books of the Maccabees, the Epistles of Saint Paul. Rarely did he refer to the accounts of the Passion, as if he feared to identify himself too easily with Christ, his Master and Lord.

Not for an instant, furthermore, did Jogues allow his suffering to enclose him within himself. He wrote that he could have escaped but remained to fulfill the duty that God had given him. His care for others pervaded him completely and made him not only bear all manner of hardships but time and again risk terrible punishments. During all these months, he was conscious of not belonging to himself, and although more than once his love for prayer and solitude impelled him to withdraw into the woods, he reminded himself of his duties as apostle and Jesuit and chose the fraternization that was so painful to him. This extremely sensitive person, this dreamer, wished nothing else than the captivity that wounded him constantly, even to the depths of his soul. He experienced a very real and poignant fear that he would stray from the road that God seemed to be marking out for him and that, painful as it was, he knew to be the road of love. This conformity to the divine plan explains his hesitation, so incomprehensible to the Dutch captain who offered him a means of escape at the end of August 1643.

The heart of Jogues, always ready to be moved, to take alarm, to weep, to drink deeply with all his vitality of even the least terrestrial and celestial comforts, was not that of an indecisive or timorous person. He always chose the less important place and willingly sought shelter behind those stronger than he. He was, however, capable of forming his own opinions tranquilly, resolutely, in the manner typical of truly gentle persons. He was also in character when he took a secondary place, choosing it spontaneously as do those members of religious communities who lean upon their stronger brethren, hiding under a fragile exterior an unsuspected strength of soul and freedom of spirit. Let us read a passage from a letter to Jogues' mother, quoted by one of his early biographers. At the time of his writing, Jogues was teaching at Rouen, and his family had asked him to be present at the wedding of one of his brothers:

> It did not even enter my mind to speak of this to my superiors. The pressing duties of my classroom responsibilities do not permit me to leave the house for a single day. Besides, my presence at this ceremony was not necessary. The prayers I can say for blessing on such unions, whether near or far, are the most affectionate marks I can give you of the interest I take in this wedding.... I ask my brothers and sisters to be assured that I offer these prayers for their well-being and prosperity very often. I hope to be able to do this even more frequently during the coming year, in which I shall

have the happiness of being ordained priest, unworthy as I am of such a grace.[4]

These lines do not indicate any hardness, yet they are completely devoid of any hesitation, any anxiety, any uncertainty. The same clearness and the same force predominate in the decisions that Jogues made throughout his life. It was a free man who, knowing only too well the dangers that threatened, nevertheless agreed to travel to Quebec. Taken prisoner on the return journey, it was the same free man who accepted the position of captive, to the surprise of the Iroquois. It was again the same free man who refused to carry burdens, who left the scene of his torture to go warm himself in his cabin, and who refused to eat food consecrated to heathen idols, even when he would have had very good reasons for acting differently. Especially when there was question of the glory of God, as he himself explained in discussing the letter that he felt he must send to the French governor, there was not a trace of fear in his heart.

On the other hand, this gentle man was not obstinate. Although he had chosen to live and to die among the Iroquois without ever seeking to escape, when the Dutch offered him an opportunity, he agreed to reconsider the matter during a night of prayer. As his vigil progressed, he saw vanishing one by one all the reasons he had had for remaining. The prolonged explanation that he made of this new free choice is a model of a decision made under the eye of God, in firmness of judgment, with clearness in regard to variables, and motivated by the desire to obey God alone. It is truly difficult to determine what we admire most in Jogues.

---

[4] This text is quoted by the Abbé Forest in his biography of Jogues, *Vie de R. P. Isaac Jogues d'Orléans*, p. 15.

Is it the richness and depth of his feelings? Or is it the vigor of his spirit, infrangible in captivity, torture, and starvation? A man in full possession of his physical forces and in the recollection of his cloister could not have acted with greater clearness and control.

In the last analysis, the explanation of the whole personality of Jogues is his ardent nature, on fire with love, a man who was made for great friendships and for the excess of love. When, as a prisoner, he dreamed of his native Orléans, he saw himself in a bookstore asking for a work on piety "that he could read in the solitude of his room, in company with two or three very dear friends". The *Relation* of 1647, which contains the account of this vision, did not include this phrase, perhaps because it was considered hardly edifying for a religious. Nevertheless, it betrays to us one of the secrets of the soul of Jogues. His temptation had been, indeed, to seclude himself in his room and there to enjoy God with his beloved books and a few very dear friends. The call of God, to which he responded with ardor, led him to become the friend—or rather, the intimate—of those whom God wished to entrust to his care, far from his home, his culture, his inclinations; in the cold, under the "Sign of the Moon", in solitude, amid brutality. When Jogues was looking for the body of René Goupil, his beloved brother whom he found already dead, his picture of himself is that of a lover beside himself:

> I returned there, I clambered up the hill at whose foot the torrent raced. I descended it, I scoured the woods on the farther side, but all in vain. I probed with a stick and with my foot the bottom of this surging river, which the nocturnal rains had grossly swollen, undeterred by the depth of the water, which reached all the way up to my waist, or by its cold.... What groans I poured out! What tears I shed, tears that mingled with the raging waters of the stream. I

chanted to you, my Lord, the psalms that Holy Church ordinarily reserves for the Office of the Dead!

There we have Jogues—Saint Isaac Jogues—martyr of the Holy Catholic Church. His was a marvelous humanity, a heavy fruit of the loving tenderness of our God. For it is divine love that little by little crept into the heart of this man. When we try to retrace his spiritual evolution to the end of his captivity, his extant writings provide only a few landmarks. In his letters to his mother, he seems all afire with apostolic zeal. The very real sufferings endured on his voyage and during his stay with the Hurons are absorbed in the joy of working for the Kingdom of God in this far-off country. He suffered, but it is as if he suffered not, so deeply did he now drink of the happiness of realizing his desires, cherished from the days of his novitiate.[5] He himself said that he had health sufficiently robust to withstand every trial, that neither his long sea voyage nor the rough food of the country caused him the least discomfort. By this joy in suffering, characteristic of all the Jesuits of Canada, Jogues shows further that it was sufficient for him to breathe with all his avid soul the ordinary air of the mission. His dream of May 11, 1638, opened to him a more personal path to perfection. His soul was carried toward God by the sweetness and fullness of love, and he was henceforth to show himself "more attached to the supreme fatherland and to heavenly joys". There is in this text no allusion to the hardships, to the miserable life of the missionary, or to any interior difficulties. Simply, all the most beautiful human songs seemed to him unworthy of comparison with those we shall be privileged to hear "in the palace".

---

[5] Cf. the note of Louis Lallemant, novice master of the saint: "My brother, you will die nowhere but in Canada" (F. Martin, *Le R. P. Isaac Jogues*, p. 5).

Four years passed during which he and his companions fulfilled their apostolic tasks. Then came his terrible captivity, during which Jogues was struck both bodily and spiritually with intense sufferings, the very description of which makes us shudder. The Iroquois covered him "with innumerable blows on the head, the neck, and the rest of his body", and day after day he awaited his death. That apostolate for which he had come to this land and to which he aspired with all his being was reduced to helping at rare intervals a few Frenchmen and Hurons. He was crushed; his most generous desires were reduced to nothingness. From this time on, he suffered death, even the death of the cross. Thus, during the course of one night, that black night into which his senses and his spirit had entered, he was again transported to Heaven—not the paradise of his childhood, the secure haven of delights and sweetness, but that paradise in which one contemplates the sacrificial Lamb, who retained all his sweetness even when led to the slaughter. In this dream, which Jogues recounts at great length, the image of the Lamb is combined with that of the heavenly Jerusalem and of Christ, our Judge and Leader. Jogues understood that he was not a prisoner in the wretched Iroquois village, but that he was a guest in the heavenly city; he perceived that it was not the barbarians who had "struck him long and savagely with their sticks on the shoulders, on the neck, and on the head", but his Judge in person, "in a ravishingly beautiful palace"; and after having thus beaten him, it was the same Judge who "embraced him, banishing his cares, and filling him with consolation completely divine and utterly inexplicable".

Now all was consummated in the dialogue of love. There was nothing further Jogues could receive from God himself until "that divine judgment, in which are purified all those who are to be admitted to this holy city and by whose favor the stones of which it is built are put into their places". Suffering was now integrated with Jogues' previous vision of paradise, and whatever individuality it retained disappeared entirely, taking on the dimensions of the heavenly Jerusalem described by Saint John in the Apocalypse. It was love—redemptive, crucifying, universal—with which Jogues was clothed in this hour. Certainly that love did not prevent him from suffering, but by means of it and through the transformation it wrought within him, he achieved his desire "to procure for himself an untold number of crosses" and to feel the goodness of God despite his burdens.

It may be somewhat surprising that we impute so much importance to the discussion of these two dreams. First of all, in the eyes of Jogues himself, they were clothed with a decisive character, and we have merely echoed and emphasized his own words. Further, we have already noted in the general introduction to this book that he was not the only one to receive visits from God during his sleep. Le Jeune and Brébeuf, not to omit Chaumonot, had more than once savored these secret contacts during the night. In the history of Christian life, we can enumerate a multitude of saints to whom God has spoken—with no shadow of doubt—while they were resting from their fatigues, beginning with Saint Joseph himself. Certainly we are here touching upon the very delicate problem of the mysterious relations between the human psyche and the supernatural action of God. But is it too farfetched to think that sleep, which liberates the unconscious levels of our personality, will also allow to appear better than the state of wakefulness the depths where God works in us, where we receive him and accept him as our absolute Master, who created and who continually re-creates us? Even—and especially—if we admit that every dream is the realization of a desire, why should not the deep-seated desires of the saint or of those most faithful to God manifest themselves here? Why should not those desires we cherish most fondly and those which to the men of God are essentially more than merely thwarted instincts—why should they not rise up when our daily occupations are laid aside? In his two dreams, Jogues saw realized his vehement desire for paradise, not with the characteristics of a childish image, but with the symbolic forms of Catholic tradition. During his captivity especially, at a time when daily reality was crushing him and he was pierced from all directions by mortal anguish, his dream translated the most infrangible aspiration of his soul: to accept the blows as a well-merited chastisement in order to be embraced by his Judge; to prepare himself by his sufferings to sing the praises of the sacrificial Lamb; to enter into the holy city and there to contemplate its marvels, there to listen to the clear voices that his poetic sensitiveness sought in vain on the earth where he was now groaning. To suppose—an idea that would seem to us an injury to the divine power, which acts as easily during the night as during the day—to suppose that even if the Lord did not enter directly into the heart of the sleeper, does not Jogues, by this dream, at least reveal the best wish of his heart—that desire for paradise—that desire in which he integrates his sufferings and his apostolate? What comfort it was for him who was persuaded that he was a wretch, far from his God, to state that his foundations were rooted only in love of his Lord and the acceptance of extreme pain, for that is the gift of love!

There may be present here, however, a temptation to see in this God-who-strikes an unconscious transposition of the need of being beaten, which, psychologically, Jogues might feel. But, without taking into account the fact that the image of God as Judge and Avenger is very scriptural and that it is found even in the New Testament, when, for example, Jesus chased the merchants from the temple with blows of a lash, we must still remember that the sleeping prisoner definitely received "on the shoulders, on the neck, and on the head" very real blows, which he in no way desired and which he even sought to evade by running between the two rows of Iroquois who were striking him. Furthermore, in the letters to his mother, there is nothing to indicate any lack of interior freedom on his part. This child, who had been without doubt frail and weak, perhaps even of an extremely delicate health, through the solicitude of his mother and with the grace of God grew into a forceful and vigorous man.

The pages written in the course of Jogues' captivity, which reveal to us the outstanding graces he received in dreams or in visions, are the last in which he left us his interior secrets. There still remained for him three years of life. In the month of August, 1643, he was hidden by the Dutch, who had arranged his escape; but the fury of the Iroquois from whom he had fled was so great that his benefactors felt it advisable to wait until calm was somewhat restored before letting him leave Renselaerswich. Hence, he remained concealed there for six weeks for fear of being discovered by the Iroquois, who constantly prowled about the neighborhood. It was not until the end of September that he finally arrived at New Amsterdam (now New York), the capital of New Belgium. There he received the most devoted care from the Dutch Protestants and special attentions from the "minister", that is, the pastor. The general assembly of Holland had long since ordered the liberation of Father Jogues, at the request of the queen regent of France.

On November 5 he left the settlement of the Dutch and, after a rather rough crossing, landed in England on

December 24. The next day, Christmas Day, found him at Basse-Bretagne. His joy at being once more in the bosom of his family was complete. A companion priest wrote to the Fathers of the Society who were still in new France: "Here he is, as happy and cheerful as if he had suffered nothing. He is as eager to return to the Hurons with all the accompanying dangers as if such discomforts were his only assurance of salvation. He can hardly wait to recross the ocean once again to go to the aid of those poor people and to finish the sacrifice he has begun" (Thw. 25:72).

Actually, in the spring of 1644, he re-embarked for New France and arrived at Quebec at the end of June. A short time later, he was sent to Ville-Marie, modern Montreal, where he remained for two years. Throughout this entire period, there was talk of peace with the Iroquois. Attempts had been made with more or less success, and soon, because the French governor judged it expedient to send an ambassador to them, Father Jogues, who knew the customs and the language of that nation very well, was designated for this mission. In the letter that he wrote to his superior on May 2, 1646, in reply to the orders he had received, he described how his spirit was seized with fear and how his mortal nature trembled at the thought of undertaking such a venture. For, if he knew how to speak the language of the Iroquois, he also knew their duplicity and had no confidence in a lasting peace. When he had regained control of himself and had placed his hope in the goodness of God, he thought it well to expose discreetly all his doubts to his superior. The order to proceed, however, was not retracted. He left on May 16 and returned to Three Rivers on June 29, having accomplished his mission but not without having passed through great dangers. Whether it was because his superiors failed to realize the magnitude of the perils or because they had a very lively desire for a mission to be founded in this hostile land, Jogues was once again sent among the Iroquois—but only after many months of hesitation and delay, it is true. When at length he set out on his journey on September 27, he made his final farewells to his friends. On October 18 he was killed by a tomahawk blow. The next day the same fate befell his companions: the *donné*[6] Jean de la Lande and a Huron. In a note to a fellow Jesuit before his last departure, he had written: "*Ibo et non redibo*"—"I shall go, but I shall not return." Father Campeau wrote that this declaration is "neither a prophecy nor a presentiment; it is a conclusion that Jogues drew from his experience. He had a moral certitude that he would die in performing this act of obedience."[7] He had found the death he had longed for, and this time God spared him any new tortures.

We have assembled here all the texts of Jogues that we could locate. Father Félix Martin, either in his biography of the saint (Paris, 1873) or in the book that he entrusted to Father Bressani,[8] has already quoted most of these writings, not without taking more than a little liberty in some places. For each one of them, we will indicate in a note the source from which we have taken it and the original language in which it was written.

The letters to Jogues' mother present a special problem. One of his earliest biographers, the Abbé J. B. Pierre Forest,

---

[6] The *donnés* were exemplary Christian men who voluntarily bound themselves by contract to serve the missions for life in whatever capacity and place the Jesuit superior might assign to them. They rendered invaluable services to the Jesuit priests and brothers, and soon became coadjutor brothers.

[7] "Portrait de saint Isaac Jogues", *Lettres du Bas-Canada*, p. 139.

[8] *Relation abrégée de quelques missions des Pères de la Compagnie de Jésus* (Montreal: John Lovell, 1852).

quotes in his *Vie de R. P. Isaac Jogues d'Orléans*[9] eight letters or fragments of letters, most of which consist of only a few sentences. It seems that Abbé Forest had had access to several original letters that he obtained from the family of Jogues, but instead of scrupulously recopying them, he had, according to the custom of the times, abridged them and suited them to the tastes of his readers. Father Martin, who also retouches the passages that he obtained either from Abbé Forest or in their original form, left in the archives of the Collège Sainte-Marie a duplicate copy of a letter whose source he does not reveal to us. This is the first letter we reproduce here. The second is an exact copy of the one that Abbé Forest cited in his book, since there is no way to compare any variants that may have crept in. As for the third, quoted by the same author and by Father Martin after him, we found a more complete manuscript copy in the Municipal Library at Orléans. This copy, which probably dates from the beginning of the nineteenth century, seemed to us to be much better, for the literary style is authentic seventeenth century, which, however, does not necessarily mean that it is a perfect reproduction of the original, since copyists sometimes make mistakes.

Aside from the short passage concerning the marriage of Jogues' brother, which we quoted above, we have also omitted several of the abbreviated passages included by Abbé Forest because they were too brief to be of any great interest. Should anyone be interested in seeing them, he can find them in the work of Father Félix Martin.

---

[9] This life must have been written in 1792. The archives of the Collège Sainte-Marie in Montreal have a copy, made either from the original or from another copy, which was found before 1873 in the archives of the École Sainte-Geneviève in Paris. This document is now mislaid, if not definitely lost.

INTRODUCTION

The long recital of Jogues' captivity, written in Latin for the provincial of France, also presents a difficulty. It is accessible to us in its entirety in the work of Alegambe.[10] However, the *Manuscrit de 1652* furnishes us with the first quarter of this letter, and the copyist affirms under oath that he used the handwritten document of Jogues himself. Could the martyr have written two successive versions, one for his provincial in France and the other for his superior in Quebec? The question is very difficult to solve, because while the early pages of the text in the *Manuscrit* contain a certain number of sentences that are not included in Alegambe, in the later portions it is the latter that is clearly more complete.[11] Indeed, one can even wonder if the omissions of the *Manuscrit de 1652* were not intentional since all incidents that could shock one's modesty or recall the sufferings that a certain Huron woman inflicted on Jogues are suppressed. We list in our notes the most important variants in the two texts. The *Relation* of 1647 contains a French version of certain passages of this letter, much rearranged and edited (cf. Thw. 31:18). Father Bressani (cf. Thw. 39:174–224), at the end of his *Breve Relatione*, wrote an Italian translation, which in the beginning seems to follow the text of Alegambe, but which gradually summarizes rather than translates.

The other documents included here are taken either from the *Relations* or from the *Manuscrit de 1652*.

---

[10] Cf. *Mortes illustres et gesta eorum de Societate Jesu* (Rome, 1657), pp. 619–32.

[11] The translation contained here is made directly from the Latin of Alegambe. Father Roustang followed the opposite procedure, working first from the *Manuscrit* and using the text of Alegambe only when the former was exhausted.

LETTERS TO HIS MOTHER

1636–1637

My dear and honored mother:[1]

Certainly I would be failing in the first and most essential duty of a devoted son toward a good mother if, when ready to set sail, I should not bid you a last farewell. I wrote to you last month from Rouen, through the kindness of Monsieur Tanzeau, who offered to take charge of my letters, and told you that I was leaving for Dieppe, from which port we hoped to embark about Holy Week. But the winds were contrary and the weather was not right for us, so that we were detained up to the present time and could not leave. I trust that God is going to give us a prosperous and happy voyage, especially because so many persons who are pleasing to him are praying for us. Please try also to contribute something to the success of our trip by your prayers, and even more than these, by the generous submission of your will to the divine will. We must always seek to accommodate our desires to the desires of the divine Goodness, which can only be very sacred and highly respected by us, since they come from a heart most desirous of our good.

---

[1] A copy of the original of this letter is kept in the archives of the Collège Sainte-Marie in Montreal. The original is in the archives of the Ursulines of Quebec.

I am sure, as I have already told you many times, that if you accept this little sorrow as you should, it will be an act extremely pleasing to God, since, for his love, not only would it be right for you to give one son, but all your other sons, and even life itself, should that be necessary. For a little worldly gain, some men cross the sea and endure at least as much as we do, but for the love of God, we are unwilling to offer what these men do for their worldly affairs.

Farewell, my dearest Mother. Thank you for the great love you have always given me and especially for the tender devotion shown at our last meeting. May God reunite us in his holy paradise if we do not ever again see each other here on earth.

Please remember me to my dear brothers and sisters, to whose prayers and to yours I recommend myself with all the affection of my heart.

> Your devoted son and obedient servant in our Lord,
>
> Isaac Jogues

Dieppe, April 6, 1636

P.S. We shall leave tomorrow, please God, that is, the second Sunday after Easter, or at the latest, Monday morning. Our vessels are already at the pier. Please make my affectionate excuses for not writing to Monsieur Houdeline.

Dear and honored Mother:[2]

At last it has pleased Our Lord to allow me to land on the shores of New France, the goal of my long aspirations. We sailed from Dieppe April 8, nine vessels together, and we arrived here eight weeks after our departure. I landed at an island called *Miscou*, where two of our Fathers serve the French who have begun a settlement here. These Fathers are making valiant attempts to convert the Indians living here. After spending two weeks on the island, I embarked in another vessel, which took me to *Tadoussac*. That is the spot where the large ships must stop and smaller barks and lighter vessels go up the Saint Lawrence as far as Quebec, a French settlement that is growing larger day by day. I arrived there July 2, the Feast of the Visitation of Our Lady.

My health has been so good, thank God, both on sea and on land that I have surprised everyone, since it is very unusual for one to make such a long trip without suffering at least a little from nausea or seasickness.[3] The vestments and sacred vessels for Holy Mass have been most useful to me. I have offered the Holy Sacrifice of the Mass every day the weather was favorable—a happiness I should have been deprived of had not our family generously provided the holy vessels for me. It was a great consolation to me personally, and one that our Fathers did not enjoy on their trips in preceding years. Officers and crew also profited by the Holy Sacrifice, since the eighty persons on board could not

---

[2] We quote this letter according to a manuscript copy in Abbé Forest, *Vie du R. P. Isaac Jogues d'Orléans*, p. 20.

[3] Father Charles Garnier, who had crossed with Jogues, had been quite ill. He wrote to his father: "I pass over in silence the other inconveniences and the seasickness, which destroys our courage." Quoted in *Lettres du Bas-Canada* (June 1949), p. 28.

otherwise have assisted at Holy Mass for two whole months. Because I had received faculties for hearing confessions, they all received the sacraments of penance and Holy Eucharist on Whitsunday, Ascension Day, and Corpus Christi. God will reward you and Madame Houdeline for the good you have thus enabled me to do.

For the rest, Mother dear, you shall have letters from me once a year, God willing, and I shall expect yours. Please send them to Paris at the beginning of March so they can arrive at Dieppe before our ships set sail. It will always be a consolation for me to hear from you and from our family, as I have no hope of seeing you again in our lifetime. May God in his goodness unite us all in his holy abode to praise him for all eternity! For this we must work most zealously as long as we live, managing the time granted us so well that we may do in life what at our death we shall wish to have done. And what a consolation there will be on that day for a soul that departs satisfied in conscience that he has served God with as little imperfection as possible and has endeavored everywhere and always to do what was most agreeable to the divine Majesty! Such were the thoughts and the motives that have urged us to beg with so much importunity to be sent to these countries, where, since there is so much to suffer, we can also give to God such sincere proofs of how much we love him.

If I could give you some good advice, or if you were in need of it, I would recommend that you place yourself in the hands of some holy director to whom you would entrust the guidance of your soul and who would require you to receive the sacraments more devoutly. Devotion, which has always brought you pleasure, should now more than ever absorb your entire attention. Your advanced age and the rest you are now able to enjoy make this practice more convenient for you.

I write this to you from a distance of more than a thousand leagues. Perhaps I shall be sent this year to a nation called the Hurons. They live more than three hundred leagues from here. They seem to be willingly disposed to embrace the Faith. However, it makes no difference where we are, provided we rest in the arms of Providence and in God's holy grace. This is the prayer I offer at the altar every day for you and all our family.

> Your most devoted and affectionate servant and son, according to God,
>
> Isaac Jogues, of the Society of Jesus

Three Rivers, August 20, 1636

P.S. I have just received orders to get ready to go to the mission of the Hurons in two or three days.

❧

Dear Mother:[4]

Peace and grace of Our Lord!

As only one opportunity of writing to you is offered every year, and even that one is uncertain and subject to change, I cannot let it pass without performing my duty toward so good a mother. I feel sure that you will be happy to know of the special providence that divine Goodness has exercised

---

[4] A manuscript copy of this letter is kept in the municipal library at Orléans (MS 975:52°).

over me since granting me the grace of coming to this Huron country. I wrote to you last year in the month of August, if I remember rightly, just when I was starting out on my journey to this country where I desired so ardently to be. I left Three Rivers, a French settlement on the Saint Lawrence River, on August 24, Saint Bartholomew's Day. I embarked in a canoe with some of the savages of that region who come every year to buy from the French whatever they need. This canoe is like a tiny boat, made of very thin birch bark, and it accommodates five or six persons at the most, along with the merchandise purchased from the French. I left, then, in one of these canoes, the only Frenchman with five savages.[5]

It is true that the inconveniences one must endure on these journeys are great, but the love of God, who calls us to these missions, and our desire to do something for the conversion of these poor barbarians render it all so delightful that we would not exchange our hardships for all the pleasures of earth. The traveler's food is a little Indian wheat or Turkish wheat (these are the names they give to corn), crushed between two stones and boiled in water without any seasoning—no salt, no vinegar, nothing but plain water. While on the trip, which generally takes about twenty-five or thirty days, we sleep on high, frightening cliffs that border on this great river, or sometimes on level ground, but always under the "Sign of the Moon". The position one must take in the canoe is very strained and uncomfortable. You cannot stretch out your

---

[5] Jogues uses the words "barbarians" and "savages" with no connotation of scorn. He loved with his whole heart these Hurons to whom he was ministering. We must remember this when he uses the same terms with the same meaning for the Iroquois. Everyone, even the Indians' greatest admirers, employed this terminology for the natives of North America in the seventeenth and even in the eighteenth centuries.

legs, for the place is narrow and crowded. You hardly dare move for fear of upsetting the boat. You keep perpetual silence because you cannot speak a single word in the Huron language. Novelty adds an increase of pain to these inconveniences, which, joined to the barbarism of these savages in whose company you are, tries a man's patience exceedingly.

On this journey, we met some sixty to eighty rapids or waterfalls that descend from such great heights and with such great force that often canoes that go too close are crushed by them. Since we were paddling against the stream, we were not exposed to this danger. However, we often had to land and walk over rocks and through tangled woods to make a detour, carrying on our backs all our packs and luggage, even the canoes at times. These portages would frequently extend for one, two, or even three leagues. For my own part, I carried not only my own small baggage, but I also aided and relieved our Indians as much as I could. Toward the end of our journey, when we came to the portages I mentioned above, it became necessary for me to carry on my shoulders a child ten or eleven years old who belonged to one of the canoes of our group and who, because of the great fatigues of the journey, had fallen ill and was unable to walk. By dint of great exertion, instead of the twenty-five or thirty days ordinarily required for this trip—sometimes extending even to forty—it took but nineteen days to reach the spot where five of our Fathers were residing, some of whom have been in this country five or six years. The two who came last had arrived here only one month before me.[6]

---

[6] The manuscript has a lacuna here. The two priests were Fathers Chastelain and Garnier, who had left France at the same time as Jogues and who arrived in the Huron country on August 12 and 13, 1636. Cf. Thw. 13:20.

Thus has Providence vouchsafed to keep me full of strength and health to this day.[7] God grants me grace to be far more contented amid the privations inseparable from our position than if I were enjoying all the comforts of the world. He makes himself felt with far greater sweetness. He guards us among the savages with so much love; he gives such abundant consolations in the little trials we have to endure that we do not even think of regretting what we have renounced for his sake. Nothing can equal the satisfaction we enjoy in our hearts while we impart the knowledge of the true God to these heathen. About 240 have received baptism this year: among them I have baptized some who now surely are in Heaven, since they were children one or two years old.

Can we think the life of man better employed in any other labor than this good work? What can I say? Would not all the labors of a thousand men be well rewarded in the conversion of one single soul to Jesus Christ? I have always felt a great love for this kind of life, for such an excellent profession, for one so closely akin to that of the apostles. Had I to work for this happiness alone, I would

---

[7] Jogues did not tell his mother that he had been seriously ill some time after his arrival. This is the account Father Le Mercier gives of the way that he was cared for: "His fever was not diminishing at all, which caused us quite a bit of anxiety in regard to his illness; we concluded therefore that he should be bled; all we needed was to find a surgeon. We were all so skilled in this profession that the sick man could not decide who should open his veins for him, and we, as many as we were, were waiting only for the Father superior to put his blessing on the operation before taking the lancet in hand and striking the blow. However, he resolved the problem himself. In view of the fact that he had once bled a savage with quite favorable results, he hoped, God willing, that his second experiment would be equally successful and that what he was lacking in skill would be supplied by charity. We saw the good results of the operation that very day; his blood stopped flowing, and his fever abated a great deal" (Thw. 13:94).

exert myself to the utmost to obtain this favor, and I would be more than willing to give a thousand lives for it.

I beg you, dear Mother, if you receive this letter, by the tender love of Jesus Christ, to thank God for me for this extraordinary favor—a favor so earnestly wished for and craved by so many servants of God endowed with qualities far above those I possess. Always keep in mind, also, that everything we do must be done for God, for his glory; that all earthly things are capable of absorbing our souls completely but can never satisfy them.

Only God is important; therefore, all our love, our confidence, our affections, our thoughts, our desires, our ambitions—all, I repeat—must be completely consecrated to him. You are now at an age and in a position of life that demands greater detachment from worldly concerns and closer union with God through prayer, more devout exercises of piety, more frequent reception of the sacraments—all of them so many channels by which God communicates to us the abundance of his grace. I have no doubt that you will make good use of these means in the near future to obtain for yourself the sovereign good of man, which is God. These are the wishes and desires you should have, now more than ever. These same wishes and desires are made daily for you, dear Mother, at the altar, at Holy Mass, by your devoted servant and son in Our Lord,

Isaac Jogues, of the Society of Jesus

Ontario, country of the Hurons, June 11 [1637]

P.S. Please tell my brothers and sisters that I love them dearly in our Lord and that I pray to him daily for them at Holy Mass.

IN THE LAND OF THE HURONS

A Dream

1638

On Tuesday, May 11, on the day before the vigil of the Feast of the Ascension of our Lord Jesus Christ, while I was studying the Huron language with Father Chastelain[1] in the early afternoon, I felt very sleepy and asked him to permit me a few moments of rest. He suggested that I go to the chapel and rest a little while before the Blessed Sacrament, remarking that he was in the habit of doing this and always felt refreshed not only physically but also spiritually. He said that in such sleep, he had even occasionally enjoyed much celestial happiness.

I arose, but I felt that I could not without irreverence sleep in the presence of the majesty of my God, whom I should rather fear and adore; I went out, then, to a nearby grove, much confused to realize that others even in their sleep were more closely united to God than I was in the very act of prayer. I lay down, then, in a mossy spot.

This text, written by Jogues in Latin, is found in the *Manuscrit de 1652*, pp. 221–23. Ragueneau is in error when he dates it 1637; the day before the eve of the Ascension fell on May 11 in the year 1638.

[1] Father Pierre Chastelain was then thirty-two years old, one year older than Jogues. They had arrived in Canada at the same time.

While I was sleeping, it seemed that I was singing Vespers[2] as usual with the other Fathers and members of our household. On one side of the chapel, Father Pijart[3] stood near the door; I was a little farther inside. I do not know who else was present or where they were placed in the chapel. Father Pijart began the first verse of the psalm: "My words with open ear receive, O Lord, and to my groan attend" (Ps 5:1). I do not know exactly the number of it. As he could not continue it alone, we two finished it together. When the chant was ended, I seemed to be no longer in our cabin, but lying in a place I did not recognize. Suddenly, I heard other verses from psalms being sung (I forget which ones they were), having reference to the happiness of the saints and the delights they enjoy in the Kingdom of Heaven. The chanting was so beautiful and the melody of the voices and instruments so harmonious that I have no recollection of ever having heard anything like them. It even seems to me that any human melodies, no matter how sweet, would be cacophonous in comparison. Indeed, it would be an insult to compare such harmony with any on earth.

On fire with a love so great, so ardent, so burning, I was borne aloft to God by this most admirable concert of the angels, and my poor heart could scarcely bear such an overflowing of sweetness. My heart seemed to melt and flow away under this inexplicable wealth of divine love. I experienced this feeling especially while they sang the verse I remember so well: "O let us enter, then, his dwelling place, fall down before the footstool of his feet" (Ps 131 [132]:7).

When I heard this, though I was still half-asleep, I began at once to think that it was all in accordance with the

---
[2] Vespers were sung on Sundays and feasts of the Church. Cf. Thw. 6:40.
[3] Father Pierre Pijart, born in 1608, returned to France in 1650.

words Father Chastelain had spoken to me. When I woke completely, all had disappeared. Yet so great a consolation remained in my soul that even now the mere recollection of its sweetness fills me with inexpressible delights. The result of all this is that I seem to have a greater love for our heavenly homeland and the eternal joys of Our Lord. O happy moment, all too brief![4] I do not think it lasted longer than the space of a Hail Mary. "If, O Lord, you deal with us thus in our exile, what will you give to us in our home?"[5]

---

[4] *Felix hora, brevis hora* is probably a quotation from the later pseudo-Bernard. The nearest expression that we can find in Saint Bernard is *Rara hora et parva mora* in his *Super Cantica*, 23, 15 (J. Leclercq, ed., *S. Bernardi opera* [Rome, 1957], 1:148, l. 20).

[5] After this final sentence, the manuscript has the word *August*, which has been interpreted as indicating a quotation from Saint Augustine. We were unable to locate such a quotation and therefore wondered if perhaps Jogues meant that he had written this text in the month of August of that year.

PRISONER OF THE IROQUOIS

A Dream

1642

After the death of my dearest companion of happy memory, René Goupil, when I was being sought every day to be put to death also, my soul was filled with anguish. What I am now going to relate happened during my sleep.

I had gone out of our village as I usually did in order to groan more freely to you, O my God, to "pour out in [your] presence all my care; and in [your] presence bare all my anxiety" (Ps 141:3 [142:2]). When I returned, everything seemed changed. The tall palings that surrounded our village on all sides were transformed into very beautiful towers, battlements, and walls. These did not have the appearance of being newly erected but seemed to belong to a city built long ago and now honored because of its antiquity. While I stood in doubt whether or not this really was our village, some savages whom I knew by sight came out and assured me that it truly was our little hamlet. Filled with wonder, I approached this strange city. I passed through the first gate, then I saw incised into the pillar of the second gate, which was at my right as I entered, two capital letters: L N, with the image of a small lamb, slaughtered. At first I wondered who could have done this; how could the

---

This text is given in Latin in the *Manuscrit de 1652*, pp. 97–104.

barbarians, who had no knowledge of our letters, have cut these characters? Then, while I was trying to find an explanation of this, I saw above me, placed as if on a rolled-up scroll, the three words LAUDENT NOMEN EJUS,[1] and below each word was the corresponding letter: L..... N..... and a figure of a lamb. At this, my soul was illumined as if by a great light; it seemed to me beyond any doubt that those souls especially praise the Lamb who in their distresses and tribulations try to imitate his gentleness; those who, like the sheep before the shearer and the lamb brought to slaughter, are silent (cf. Is 53:7).

This sight gave me courage, and I passed through the second gate of this strange city. The portal was built square, of polished marble, and it provided the base for a long arcade that was arched and vaulted—most beautiful to see! About the middle of this arcade, on the side opposite the one by which I entered, I saw that a military guardhouse had been erected; it contained arrows, cannonballs, all sorts of weapons. There was no one to be seen either in or near it. Then the thought came to me that even if I did not see anyone, I ought to salute the military insignia as was customary. So, turning in that direction, I uncovered my head. Immediately, a soldier on sentinel duty, standing on the same side of the street by which I was advancing, called out: "Halt, there!" Now, either because I was facing the opposite direction or because the novelty of the sights before me was engrossing my attention, I neither saw nor heard the sentinel. Therefore, a second time and in a sharper tone, he shouted: "Halt, there, I say!" Then, recovering myself, I stopped short. The soldier continued: "Is this the way you

---

[1] Ps 149:3. The *Manuscrit* has an illustration here of a scroll with a lamb sketched below it.

obey the sentinel guarding the royal palace? Why should I have to order you twice to halt? I must take you immediately to our judge and leader (for those two words I knew—the first one dealing with laws, the other a military term). He will sentence you according to your boldness." "O my friend," I tried to explain, "I stopped as soon as I heard your voice; I did not continue to advance!" But he paid no attention to my excuses and hurried me off to where the judge was sitting. He was on the same side of the road along which I had been walking.

A short distance beyond the garrison, on the other side of the road, there was a door that led into the palace. This place resembled those large halls in the Palais de Justice in France that are called "Golden Galleries", or those beautiful places that can still be seen in some famous old monasteries, called "chapter rooms" (for I remember well the appearance of both sorts of places). The palace was outstandingly beautiful. Within the hall, there was a venerable old man, full of majesty, resembling the "Ancient of Days" (Dan 7:9). He was dressed in a rich purple cope, not wearing a biretta on his head but a skullcap. Nor was he seated on a throne; he was quietly walking about the room, rendering justice to his people, from whom he was separated by a sort of balustrade.

I saw at the gate of this palace a large crowd of people of all stations of life, as we are accustomed to see in Europe. A few of them were well known to me, and they asked me for news of the Huron country. I was saying to myself: "This is good; they know who I am and that, innocent of any wrongdoing, I have been brought before this judge. Therefore, I will be dealt with leniently." How wrong I was! The judge listened to the soldier who had brought me here and, without interrogating me at all, drew from beside him a switch or rod out of a bundle like those that were formerly borne before the Roman Consuls. He beat me long and severely with that switch, on the shoulders, then on the neck, and finally on the head. Although only a single hand had struck me, I felt as much pain as I had experienced at my entrance into the first village of the Iroquois when all the young men, armed with sticks, had inhumanly beaten me. Under those blows, however, I did not utter any complaint, nor did I permit a single groan to escape my lips. I suffered all the pain inflicted on me, enduring it patiently as punishment for my baseness. Finally, my judge, as if admiring my patience, sweetly embraced me, thus banishing my sufferings. He filled me with a consolation that was wholly divine and entirely inexplicable. Brimming over with celestial joy, I kissed the hand that had struck me. As if in ecstasy, I cried out: "O my Lord and my King, 'Your crook and staff—they comfort me!' (Ps 22 [23]:4)." When I had finished speaking, he led me to the door of the palace and left me on the threshold.

After I awoke, I began to think deeply about what I had seen. There was no possibility of doubt that God had wrought wonders in my soul, not only because of the admirable and apt relationship of all the marvels I had seen—marvels whose likeness I could never have imagined—but especially because of the burning love that my judge had kindled in the depths of my heart when he had embraced me and I had burst out my paean of praise. Even after many months, the sweet remembrance of these sights can draw from me tears of the tenderest consolation.

As I stood there on the doorstep, the thought came to me that this city, placed as it was so extraordinarily in the place usually occupied by our village, was the abode of the blessed into which I was not worthy to enter but where I would be able to gain admittance someday if I persevered with patience and fidelity to the end. I hoped that this village in which I had already suffered so much and continued to suffer would be transformed for me into this holy city.

It was strange, I thought also, that in this city, which I considered as our village, because it was placed exactly in the same spot, or at least very close to it, as our little settlement—it was strange that I saw no savages. When I was entering the gate, I had seen a few coming out but not a single one inside. Could it be that "nothing defiled will enter it" (Rev 21:27); "outside are dogs, the sorcerers, the immoral persons, the murderers, the idolaters, and everyone who loves and practices falsehood" (Rev 22:15)?

I thought that the garrison (in which I had seen no one) was that of the angels, who watched over this city, which was celestial rather than terrestrial. Finally, the tribunal and the judge, to whom I had been led and where I had received the blows, I considered to be the divine judgment, in which are purified all those who are to be admitted to this holy city, or at least are allowed to become the stones that construct it when

> By many a salutary stroke,
> By many a weary blow that broke
> Or polished with a workman's skill
> The stones that form that glorious pile;
> They all are fitly framed to lie
> In their appointed place on high.[2]

Finally, when I had been brought back to the threshold, I was left standing there, not allowed to enter the holy city.

---

[2] Vespers hymn from the Office for the Dedication of a Church. The translation here is that of J. W. Irons, in Matthew Britt, *The Hymns of the Breviary and the Missal* (Benziger: New York, 1922), p. 344.

Nevertheless, I turned around at least to see the place I could not enter, and I beheld many streets like those Saint John describes in Revelation—pure, clear, breathing forth sanctity itself. The blows that had been rained upon my back I interpreted as the exterior torments I had undergone when among the barbarians; those on the neck as the scorn, mockery, and insults as well as the yoke of slavery to their service; those on the head as the hatchets or flames, even death itself. However, I was surprised that I had been subjected to the blows of the judge and yet not admitted into the holy city, and I asked myself, "Can it be that, living as I do in such barbaric cruelty that seeks daily to put me to death, I shall not die, but shall continue to live?" I had not been admitted, but sent away, so I thought that I would not die soon.

The blows that I had received on the head also could be interpreted as representing the profound torments of my soul. That confirmed still more strongly the idea that I should believe what I frequently saw in my sleep, namely, that I was following someone, but with smaller steps; now I believed that it was my dearest companion,[3] whom the eternal happiness of the saints had received, while I continued to follow him with my eyes from a distance and through narrow, winding paths. I sighed sometimes, even while following him snatched from me, when I was attracted by the beauty of the temples that I came across on my way and into which I entered to pray. And when I delayed there for a long time, attracted either by the beauty of the place or by the sweetness of the singing, then more than ever did I grieve that I had lost him.

---

[3] He is here referring to René Goupil.

PRISONER OF THE IROQUOIS

Several Visions

1642–1643

Following the example of Saint Bernard, disciple of the beech trees,[1] in that secluded place where for many reasons I frequently went to say my prayers, but especially because I had carved a cross there on a huge tree, I was overcome with sorrow because the Indians hated me so much. Here the following incidents took place:

I seemed to be present at a council of many Fathers of our Society whom I had known when they were alive and whose virtue and merits I held in great esteem. I do not have a distinct recollection of who was there, however, except Father Jacques Bertrix.[2] I have some slight remembrance of seeing the face of Father Étienne Binet[3] in the group, and an even more vague one of Father Pierre Coton.[4] I begged all of them, with an ardent love, to commend me to the holy Cross so that it might receive me as a disciple of him

---

The original text is found in the *Manuscrit de 1652*, in Latin, on pages 104–7.

[1] Cf. Guillaume de Saint-Thierry, *Vita prima S. Bernardi*, 1, 4, 23; *PL* 185:240.

[2] Father Jacques Bertrix, rector of the colleges at Rouen and at Bourges, died in 1639.

[3] Father Étienne Binet (1569–1639) was a prolific spiritual writer, several times provincial superior of the Paris Jesuits. He had been a fellow pupil at the Collège de Clermont in Paris with Saint Francis de Sales and remained his close friend throughout his life.

[4] Father Pierre Coton (1564–1626) was also the author of several spiritual books. He served as *prédicateur* at the court of Henri IV and later became provincial superior in Paris.

who had been suspended upon it and that it might not repudiate me, its fellow citizen—an idea that had never before come to me, even in meditation. I claimed the title of fellow citizen because I had been born in a city whose metropolitan church was dedicated to the holy Cross.

At another time, when I was in the grove where I usually prayed, I seemed to be in Orléans, the city of my birth, in the cloister of the Cathedral of the Holy Cross. From there I went to the shop of a bookseller whom I knew very well. I asked him if he had some new book on piety, as they call them. He answered that he had one that he valued very highly, entitled *Famous Men*. When I heard this, I felt an overwhelming desire to examine the book, so I asked him if he would lend it to me for a few days. I assured him that I would return it promptly, just as soon as I and a few of my most intimate friends had read it in the quiet of my room. The bookseller was a little unwilling to let me have it because he considered it so valuable. Meanwhile, some other persons in the shop were talking about their tribulations and misfortunes; each one was relating what he had suffered. I made myself bold enough to say that I, too, had suffered something for God. After some time, since I did not see the book I wanted on the counter any longer, I asked one of the clerks to look for it and bring it to me. Without asking the owner, he brought it to me, and when he placed it in my hands, I heard a voice saying: "This book contains the lives of men illustrious for their sanctity and for their hearts courageous in war." [5]

---

[5] The title of the book that Jogues dreams about, *Illustres pietate viros et fortia bello pectora*, may perhaps be a faulty quotation for 1:10 of the *Aeneid*: *Insignem pietate virum*. The last words are an exact quotation of 8:150–51:
   Accipe, daque fidem. Sunt nobis fortia bello
   Pectora, sunt animi, et rebus spectata juventus.

These are the very words I heard; they stamped this truth upon my soul, namely, that it is only through many tribulations that we enter the Kingdom of Heaven. Now, as I was leaving the shop, full of happiness at possessing the book, it seemed as if the whole store was covered with crosses. I told the shopkeeper that I would return because I wished to buy some of the crosses that he had in such great quantities and in so many types.

On another occasion, hidden in my retreat in the woods, with the snow piled high about me and my body tormented by hunger, cold, and nakedness, considered the scum of the earth, the vilest of men, by these degraded barbarians, I endured intense agonies also in my soul because of all my sins and culpable negligences. All the bitter pangs of death and the terrors of Hell invaded my heart at the thought that the savages were about to kill me, as they had so often threatened. The following then transpired, bringing me peace:

Very distinctly, I heard a voice that proved to me how false this distress of my heart really was and advised me to think of God only in his goodness (cf. Wis 1:1) and to cast all my anxiety on him (cf. 1 Pet 5:7). I heard also those words that I had noted long ago in the letters of Saint Bernard to his monks: "Serve God in that charity and love that casts out fear; such love does not seek any reward."[6] These two counsels were given to me very opportunely, for my soul was burdened with an excessive fear—not a filial, but a servile, fear. I did not have sufficient confidence in God. Besides, I was lamenting because I was being hurried to judgment, in the middle of my life, as it were, without having paved the way with any good works. I should rather

---

[6] Cf. Saint Bernard, *Epist. 143*, 3; *PL* 182:300A.

have been grieving because of my multitudinous offenses and negligences toward God.

This advice indeed reanimated my sorrowing soul and stirred up within me a burning love of God. That fire of love was so vehement that in the fervor of my soul, even before I had returned to myself, I added to what had been told me, using once more the words of Saint Bernard: "It is not unjust that he claims our life for himself since he gave up his own for us."[7] After this, God so greatly enlarged the soul of his servant that I could even joyfully return to the village where I firmly believed I would be beaten to death as soon as I entered.

---

[7] Ibid., 182:299D.

PRISONER OF THE IROQUOIS

*Letter to the Governor
of New France*

June 30, 1643

Dear Sir:

This is the fourth letter[1] that I have written to you since I was captured by the Iroquois. Time and paper fail me to repeat here what I have been telling you all along. Couture and I are still living. Henri (one of the two young men taken prisoner at Montreal) was brought here on the eve of Saint John's Day.[2] He was not beaten with clubs at the entrance to the village as we were, nor, like us, has he had his fingers cut off. He and all the Hurons brought with him into this territory are still living. Be on your guard everywhere; new bands are always setting out, and we are convinced that until fall, the river[3] will not be free of our enemies. In this place, there are nearly three hundred guns

---

The *Relation* of 1643 states that this letter was written by Jogues partly in Latin, partly in French, and partly in Huron, so as to confuse the Iroquois. The archives of the Society of Jesus in Rome hold a copy of this letter in Latin, in the handwriting of Saint Charles Garnier (cf. ARSJ, 98, 379). Thw. 24: 294–96 has the text in French.

[1] The three preceding letters are lost. Jogues must have written this one very rapidly; his style is almost breathless.

[2] On the eve of the Feast of Saint John the Baptist, June 23.

[3] The Saint Lawrence.

and seven hundred Iroquois. The Indians are quite skilled in handling firearms. They have various streams and waterways by which they can reach Three Rivers. Fort Richelieu is a little more difficult to approach, but they are not completely hindered from arriving there.

The Iroquois say that if those who took and killed the French at Montreal had known that you had ransomed the Sokokiois from the Algonquins and then released them, they would never have put them to death. It seems that they had left in the middle of the winter, before that news came. Nevertheless, quite recently a band set out with that fellow De Mathurin (Father Brébeuf knows him well) in charge—a situation just like that during which we were captured last year. This troop intends to capture some Frenchmen as well as some Algonquins. Do not let any consideration for us prevent you from doing what serves the glory of God.

The plan of the Iroquois, as far as I can see,[4] is to make prisoners, if they can, of all the Hurons; and, after killing the most influential ones and a large portion of the others, to unite the two tribes into one, having a single country. I have great compassion for these poor people, several of whom are already baptized Christians and others catechumens, ready for baptism. When will relief from these misfortunes be brought? Only when all are captured? I have received several letters from the Hurons, along with the *Relation*, which was captured near Montreal.[5]

---

[4] Jogues had a perfect understanding of the strategy of the Iroquois, which they systematically pursued during the next few years.

[5] The *Relation* for the mission for the year 1642 was captured by the Iroquois from a convoy of Hurons who were taking it to Quebec with the annual letters.

The Dutch have tried to ransom us, but in vain; they are continuing their efforts even now, but I am convinced they will not succeed. I become more and more determined to stay here as long as our Lord wishes me to. I will not go away, even if an opportunity should present itself. My presence consoles the French, the Hurons, and the Algonquins. I have baptized more than sixty persons, several of whom have already arrived in Heaven. That, and the will of God, to which I unite my own, are my consolations. I beg you to recommend that prayers be said and that Holy Masses be offered for us, and above all for him who desires to be forever, Your Excellency,

Your very humble servant, in the Society of Jesus,

Isaac Jogues

Village of the Iroquois, June 30, 1643

PRISONER OF THE IROQUOIS

*Letter to His Provincial
in France*

August 5, 1643

Reverend and dear Father:

Pax Christi!

When I decided to write to you, Reverend Father, I was at first uncertain as to which language I should use—Latin or French—for after so long a lapse of time in using either, I have almost forgotten both. I find it equally difficult to express myself in each. However, I chose Latin for two reasons. The first was that I could thus express certain thoughts in the language of Sacred Scripture, a source of great consolation to me in my adversities.[1] The second was that I want this letter to be a little out of the ordinary, so I used the more formal language. Your great charity, Reverend Father, which has so often in the past generously excused my shortcomings, will do so once more, I am sure, if I, who became a savage in custom and costume eight years ago and now even more than ever live like one and dress

---

This letter is translated from the Latin; Alegambe edition, pp. 619–32.

[1] Jogues always quotes from the Vulgate, in which the order of the sentences sometimes differs from the Greek text. The Kleist-Lilly and Kleist-Lynam translations that we quote are made from the Greek. The citations here are numbered according to these latter texts.

like one, commit errors in grammar and style. I also fear that in my ignorance of the language, I may also show a lack of learning; that I will not "recognize the time of my visitation" (Lk 19:44) and that I will forget the duties God assigned to me here—those of preacher of the Gospel, Jesuit, and priest. I am impelled to write to you, Reverend Father, so that if by chance this letter should ever reach your hands,[2] you and all the Fathers of our province will come to my aid with your prayers and by offering the Holy Sacrifice of the Mass. Here in this cruel country, in the midst of the Iroquois and the Maquas,[3] I am certainly in need of your help. You will understand how serious my condition is and how much I owe to God when you read this, and I am sure that you will gladly offer your good works—I know how much protection they can provide for me in my distress.

We set out from the country of the Hurons on June 13, 1642, with four small boats—they call them canoes—and twenty-five persons, five of whom were Frenchmen. The journey was extremely difficult for many reasons, but especially because there were at least forty portages where we had to carry both the canoes and our baggage on our shoulders. Our ordeal was further increased by fear of our enemies, who every year skulk along the roads leading to the French settlements and capture many prisoners. Last year Father Jean de Brébeuf barely managed to escape them. In addition to all this, they had recently sent back unharmed to their countrymen two

---

[2] Jogues wrote his letter from the settlement of the Dutch, where the Iroquois had come to transact business. He does not doubt that his captivity will soon be ended.

[3] The Maquas were the nation of Iroquois closest to the Dutch; the French called them Agniers.

French captives in an effort to make peace. Unfortunately, the conditions they proposed were extremely unfair. Later they renewed hostilities and were put to flight by our cannons. They threatened then that if ever again they took a Frenchman captive, they would apply more cruel tortures to him than to any other prisoner, and after excruciating torments, they would burn him alive over a slow fire.

The superiors were aware of the dangers of this journey but considered it necessary for the glory of God. They appointed me to undertake it, but in such a way that I could have refused if I had wanted to. But "I did not resist: I have not gone back" (Is 50:5). I willingly, even joyfully, undertook the mission imposed upon me by obedience and charity. If I had asked to be excused, the task would have fallen to someone much better than I.

We left Sainte-Marie des Hurons and, after suffering all kinds of adversities—fear of our enemies, hardships of travel, losses, shipwrecks—arrived safe and sound at the residence named La Conception de la Bienheureuse Vierge thirty-five days later. This is the residence, or settlement, of the French at Three Rivers. The name "Three Rivers" is due to three inlets of a most beautiful stream nearby, which flows into the great Saint Lawrence River. We gave heartfelt thanks to God and stayed there, and at Quebec for about two weeks.

While we were there, we transacted our business and remained to celebrate the feast of our holy Father Ignatius. On August 1 we began our return trip to the land of the Hurons. On the second day of our journey,[4] very early in the morning, some of our men discovered fresh footprints

---

[4] The ambush of the Iroquois was laid at the entrance to the islands that enclose Lake Saint-Pierre, southwest of Three Rivers. The missioners are thus traveling southward on the Iroquois River.

on the shore. Some of our companions said they were made by enemies, but others maintained that they were those of friends. Eustache Ahatsistari, who was acknowledged as leader because of his exploits in war, declared: "These men are enemies. Judging from the number of tracks, I would say there are not more than three canoes. So, even if they are very brave, we are more numerous than they and need not fear such a handful of enemies." Indeed, there were about forty in our group now because a few men had joined us.

We continued our journey but had hardly gone a mile when we fell among the enemy. There were about seventy men, twelve canoes, and they had separated into two groups, one on each side of the river. When we came to the place where they had prepared their ambush, hiding themselves in the tall grass and the reeds, they fired on us with their cannons, of which they had a great number, but they did not kill any of us. At the first sound of the cannons, almost all the Hurons abandoned our canoes (for we were traveling near the shore because the middle of the river is very rapid). Fleeing in panic, they hid themselves deep in the woods. We were left alone, we four Frenchmen, with a few Christians and catechumens. Having commended ourselves to God, we resisted the enemy, but since we were so few—about twelve or fourteen—against thirty, we were quickly overcome by their superior number. We fought bravely, nonetheless, until our companions, having caught sight of other canoes coming from the opposite bank, lost heart and fled. One of the Frenchmen, named René Goupil, who was fighting among the first, was captured, along with a few Hurons.

When I saw this, I neither would, nor could, flee. Besides, how far could I go without shoes?[5] Of course, I could

---

[5] The Indians always removed their shoes when entering their canoes.

have concealed myself among the grasses and reeds and thus could have withdrawn from the danger. But how could I leave even one Frenchman and some Hurons who were already captured—or those about to be taken—without having baptized them? That is why, although the enemy had left me standing in the place where the skirmish had occurred in order to pursue the fugitives, I called one of those who had remained behind to guard the prisoners and begged him to take me prisoner with the other Frenchman. As I had been his companion on the journey, I now wanted to be his companion in danger and in death. The guard could scarcely believe me and, not without fear, came over to me and took me to the other captives.

Then I said to René Goupil: "My dearest brother, God has led us in a marvelous way, but he is the Lord: let him do what is good in his sight (cf. 1 Sam 3:18); as it has pleased the Lord, so it is done: blessed be the name of the Lord" (Job 1:21). After this, I heard his confession and absolved him. Then I went to the Huron captives and, after instructing them, baptized them one by one; and since new captives were always being brought back from flight, I always had new work to do. Finally, that valiant Christian leader, Eustache Ahatsistari, was brought back. When he saw me, he said, "I had taken an oath, Father, that I would either live or die with you." My heart was so filled with grief at this that I did not know what to answer. The last one to be dragged in from flight was Guillaume Couture, who had set out from the Hurons with me. This man, in the midst of the general confusion, had fled with the others into the forest; and, as he was a young man not only of courageous disposition but strong in body and fleet of foot, he had put a great distance between him and his enemies. Then, all of a sudden, he looked around him, and seeing that I was not with him, he said to himself: "Shall I desert my dearest

Father, a prisoner of these savages, and escape without him? Never!" Then, returning along the path by which he had fled, he was taken prisoner of his own accord. Would to God that he had escaped and not increased the number of sufferers. In such circumstances it is no consolation to have companions in misfortune, especially when they are those whom we love as much as we love ourselves. Such is the quality of those men who, although laymen, put aside all worldly interest and devote themselves completely to the Hurons for God and the Society.

One could never imagine the horrible types and the severity of the torments to which this man was subjected. The hatred of the Iroquois had been aroused against all the French, but it was especially violent against him because they knew that he had killed one of their chiefs in battle. They began, then, by stripping him naked; they tore off his fingernails with their teeth; they gnawed off his fingers little by little; they pierced his right hand all the way through with a broad sword. Despite the intense agony he suffered from all these tortures, he told me later that the remembrance of the Passion of Our Lord Jesus Christ had fortified him and even brought him great joy.

When I saw him there, stripped of his garments and bound with ropes, I could not contain myself. I tore myself from my guards and ran to him through the midst of the enemies who had brought him there. I embraced him with great affection and exhorted him to offer to God those pains, for himself and for all those who were tormenting him. The savages were at first surprised at what I had done, but then, as if they had recovered their senses and concentrated their hatred, they assailed me with their fists, with sticks and cudgels; then they left me half-dead on the ground. Two of them then took me, scarcely breathing, to the place where

I had been standing. Others then fell upon me, tore off almost all my nails, and gnawed off my two index fingers with their teeth—all of which caused me incredible pain. They did the same to René Goupil but left the Hurons unharmed.

When all had returned from their pursuit, during which two Hurons had been killed, they took us to the other side of the river, where they divided among themselves the booty from our twelve canoes (eight had joined us in Quebec). Their prize was very rich, for in addition to the personal belongings of the Frenchmen, we had twenty packages containing sacred vessels, vestments, books, and other articles of that nature—great wealth, surely, in view of our extreme poverty among the Hurons. While they were engaged in dividing the spoils, I baptized some of my fellow captives who had not yet received the sacrament but were sufficiently instructed. Among them was a venerable old man— eighty years of age—who, when the Iroquois ordered him to climb into a canoe with the others, objected: "How can I, old and decrepit as I am, go into a distant and foreign country? No, I shall die here." Since he refused to leave, he was slain in the same spot where he had been baptized.

Filling the air with jubilant shouts, "as conquerors rejoice after taking a prey" (Is 9:3), they led us captive into their country. In all, there were twenty-two of us, since three of our men had been killed. We suffered many hardships— thanks be to God—on the journey (which took thirty-eight days) from hunger, excessive heat, threats, blows, and the cruel hatred of the savages, in addition to the excruciating pain of our wounds, which had not healed but were festered so horribly that maggots were developing in them. But what seemed to me the cruelest of all their torments was that, when we were exhausted after five or six days of traveling, they came up to us with no semblance of anger and in cold blood tore out our hair and our beards and scratched us deeply with their fingernails, which they keep sharply pointed, in the most tender and sensitive parts of our bodies. All these sufferings were external, however. My interior sufferings were much more intense when I saw that sad procession of Hurons, now slaves of the Iroquois. Among them were many Christians, five of them converts of long standing and pillars of the infant Huron Church. I will admit naïvely that from time to time I could not restrain my tears, deploring their lot and that of all my companions, but even more filled with anxiety for the future. For I saw that the Iroquois would forbid the practice of the Christian Faith to these Hurons and to innumerable other nations unless God by a special providence should intervene.

On the eighth day of our journey, we met a band of two hundred savages setting out on the warpath. These were the ones who had formerly been put to rout, although superior in numbers, by the honorable governor of New France, Charles de Montmagny, Knight of Malta. Two of them had been killed and several others wounded.

Because it is customary for these barbarians when setting out for war to employ their cruelty as a prelude, thinking that the outcome would be favorable in proportion to their severity, they fell upon us in this frame of mind. First they gave thanks to the sun god, to whom they ascribe success in wars. Then they fired their muskets as a sign of good fortune. Each one then went into the nearby woods to cut clubs with which to beat us. They ordered us to get out of our canoes, and having arranged themselves in two parallel rows, they forced us to "run the gauntlet" between them, beating us ferociously with their cudgels. I was the last of all and consequently more exposed to their blows. Halfway up the hill, which we were then forced to climb in order to reach a platform they had erected on the summit, I was overcome by pain and weakness. I fell, thinking I would die right there, because I neither could nor cared to rise.

How long and how violently they struck me, only he knows—he for whose love and glory it is sweet and blessed to suffer. Finally, moved by a cruel mercy because they wished to take me alive to their country, they stopped beating me. That is why they carried me, half-dead and all covered with blood, to the stage. Some of the blows they had rained upon me had so battered my face that the blood flowing down from it had completely soaked my shirt, the only one I had left.

Then they ordered me, scarcely breathing, to come down from the platform; and again heaping upon me insults and opprobrium, they covered me once more with innumerable blows on the head, the neck, and the rest of my body. This letter would become much too long if I were to try to enumerate in detail what we French had to bear. They burned one of my fingers and crushed another with their teeth. They twisted my other fingers—the ones they had already chewed on—and so strained the ligaments that even now, though healed, they are still frightfully deformed. But the lot of my companions was not any better.

What follows shows that God was taking care of us, that he was pleased with us and had not abandoned us in our miseries. One of the barbarians, breathing out blood and savagery, came up to me, although I was hardly able to stay on my feet. He took hold of my nose with one hand, getting ready to cut it off with a huge knife that he held in the other. What could I do? I who had thought I was destined to be burned alive over a slow fire, groaned inwardly to my God and waited motionless for the blow. But my aggressor, as if restrained by a divine force, stayed his hand at the very moment of striking.

About a quarter of an hour later, he came toward me once more, as if ashamed of his timidity and softness, and prepared to do the same thing. Once again, an invisible force held him back and he went away. Twice his weakened hands had fallen to his sides. If he had fulfilled his purpose, that would have been the end of me because the Iroquois are not accustomed to let those so mutilated continue to live. At length, late at night and the last of all, I was led away by those who had brought me there. They gave me no food—indeed, I had hardly touched any for several days. I spent the rest of the night in great pain. But even more agonizing than my physical sufferings was the sight of my poor Hurons suffering like torments, especially Eustache, whom they tormented most cruelly. They had torn off both his thumbs and through the wound in his left hand had thrust a pointed stick all the way up to his elbow. He bore all this like a true Christian, with an extraordinary courage.

The following day we met still more canoes filled with warriors. They cut off some of the fingers of our companions and instilled great fear in all of us. Finally, on the tenth day of our trip, toward noon, we abandoned the canoes and finished the journey—a matter of four more days—on foot.[6] The fatigues of carrying on our poor wounded shoulders all the baggage from the canoes was added to all our other hardships. Surprisingly, they showed themselves quite lenient to me at this time and gave me only a very light burden to carry, either because they realized that I was too

---

[6] Here they left the waters of Lake George, which Jogues renamed the Lake of the Blessed Sacrament, in 1646.

weak to bear any more or because I refused, in my status as captive, to do their work for them. Indeed, throughout my whole period of captivity and even in the face of death, I maintained a very haughty spirit before them.

Our hunger increased daily because our stores were rapidly diminishing. We had spent three days almost entirely without food, and when we came to a village on the fourth day, we had eaten nothing but a few wild fruits we had been able to gather on the way. To tell the truth, even in the beginning of the trip, when our food supply was quite ample, I had eaten almost nothing for fear of delivering over to the fire and other tortures a body that was much too robust and too full of life: "If I must boast, I will boast of the things that show my weakness" (2 Cor 11:30). But when my poor body, exhausted by these fasts, sought nourishment, it could find nothing but water. As early as the second day, when we were worn out by our journeyings, they put a kettle on the fire as if to cook something, but there was nothing in it but warm water. We could, however, have as much of that as we wished.

Finally, on the eighteenth day,[7] which was the vigil of the Feast of the Assumption of the Blessed Virgin Mary, we arrived at the first Iroquois village.[8] I gave thanks to our Lord Jesus Christ because on that day when the whole Christian world was rejoicing at the glory of his Mother assumed into Heaven, he had called upon us to share with him his

---

[7] "The eighteenth day" is from the Alegambe edition. Father Roustang adds that in fact it was the thirteenth day, since they left on October 2 and we are now on the fourteenth.

[8] The Iroquois villages were about twenty-five miles from Fort Orange [modern Albany].

sorrows and his Cross. In truth, throughout the whole trip, we had never lost sight of the fact that the day of our arrival at the village would be a very sad one. As for René Goupil and me, we could easily have avoided this arrival, as well as the fire. Often, free of all bonds, far from our guards, late at night, we could have escaped. Even if we would not have been able to return to our own people, at least we could have died in the forest with less suffering. But he refused to flee, and I was more than willing to suffer all these extremes rather than to desert in their need, and even abandon to their death, my fellow Frenchmen and my poor Huron Christians and so deprive them of the consolations that a priest could give them.

Thus, on the eve of the Assumption, about three o'clock, we arrived at the river near their village. Some former Huron captives and the Iroquois were waiting for us on both banks of the river. The first ones told us, by way of greeting, that we were to be burned over a slow fire. The next group welcomed us with sticks, blows, and stones. And because they have an extreme aversion for a man whose hair is sparse and short, a veritable tempest exploded, particularly on me and my bald head. I still had two fingernails. These they now tore off with their teeth, and with their own sharp fingernails laid bare the bones of my poor fingers. When there on the river bank they had sufficiently glutted their cruelty and mockery, they led us to their village, which was located at the top of a hill. At the entrance, all the young men of the region, armed with clubs and cudgels, were lined up in two parallel rows on either side of the road.

We knew that if we withdrew from the number of those who were chastised, we also withdrew from the number of the sons of God; therefore, we offered ourselves with generous heart to God, who corrected us as a Father so that he might be pleased with us as he is with his sons (cf. Prov 3:11–12; Heb 12:5–8).

They set up this order of proceeding through their lines: first was a Frenchman, stripped completely, without even a loincloth; René Goupil was in the center, and I was the last of all. René and I had been permitted to keep our shirts and trousers. Some of the Iroquois had placed themselves between us and the Hurons to slow our passage through their lines and to give those who were striking us more time and opportunity to strike each of us separately.

Long and cruelly "upon my back the plowmen plowed; they drew their furrows long" (Ps 128 [129]:3). They beat us not only with sticks but with whips having metal pieces at the end. They have a great number of these, having obtained them from the Europeans. In addition to the whip lashes, one of the chiefs had a lump of iron the size of his fist tied to the end of a rope. He gave me and my companions a blow with it that almost felled me to the ground. The only thing that kept me from fainting and that sustained my strength and courage was fear that he would strike me with it a second time.

When we had run this long course through a hailstorm of blows, we came at length to the platform, or stage, erected in the center of the village. Truly, the face of each one of us was a miserable sight, but the worst of all was poor René, who, because he was not very nimble and could not run fast, had received a multitude of blows not only all over his body but also on his face, which was so raw that all we could see was the white of his eyes. However, even thus he was more beautiful than he "who had become for our sakes, as it were a leper, and as one struck by God and afflicted; in whom there is no beauty nor comeliness" (Is 53:4, 2).

We mounted the platform and scarcely had time to catch our breath when one of the savages struck all the Frenchmen three blows upon their bare backs. Then other savages began to take out their knives and climb up on the stage to cut off the fingers of a number of captives. And since a captive is more exposed to their cruelty in proportion to his dignity, they began with me because they saw that both the French and the Hurons esteemed me. It was not difficult to determine this either from the manner in which the others treated me or from my own proud conduct.

One old man led a woman toward me and commanded her to cut off my thumb. In the beginning she refused, then being constrained four or five times by the old man, she cut off my thumb at the place where it was joined to my hand. This woman was an Algonquin, that is, one of the barbarians who live near the French in New France. She had been captured about a month before. She was a Christian named Jeanne. It gives me happiness to receive such sufferings from those for whom we have come here to die, and it is to shield them from the cruelties of their enemies—both visible and invisible—that we prefer to accept the worst possible torments. Then, taking up in my other hand the severed thumb, I offered it to you, my living and true God, in remembrance of the Sacrifices that I had offered in your Church during the past seven years. Warned by one of my companions, I left off doing that for fear that they would force me to put the bloody thumb into my mouth and eat it. Then I threw it down somewhere on the platform, relinquishing it completely. They cut off René Goupil's right thumb at the first joint.

I thank God for preserving my right thumb so that by writing this letter I may invite my Fathers and Brothers to pray for us at the Holy Sacrifice, to make fervent petitions and heartfelt prayers for us in the Holy Church of God. We know that Holy Church takes special care of us under a new and twofold title, since she prays so often for the afflicted and for captives.[9]

The next day, the Feast of the Assumption of Our Lady, we spent the morning on the stage; then, toward noon, they took us to another village about two miles away. Just as we were leaving, the savage who had brought me there, regretting the loss of my shirt, was going to send me away completely naked except for a miserable, soiled loincloth. I said to him, "What, my brother, would you send me away like this, completely stripped, you who have already become so rich by taking our belongings?" Moved by pity, he gave me an old hempen cloth that had been used to wrap our baggage so that I could cover my shoulders and at least a part of my body. However, my poor shoulders, sore from all the wounds and blows they had received, refused to bear this harsh, rough material, and since it covered me so poorly, and in places not at all, while we were making our way in the heat of the sun, my "skin was burnt as in an oven" (Lam 5:10) and soon began to peel from my neck, my shoulders, and my arms.

At the entrance to the second village, contrary to their custom of beating their captives only once, they did not moderate the blows they rained upon us in the least. The Lord wished in this way to give us some resemblance to his apostle, who gloried in having thrice been beaten with lashes. Although the number of blows may have been less, they beat us more cruelly than the first ones had, because these, unhampered by others around them, directed their blows

---

[9] The text of the *Manuscrit* ends here.

more accurately. They struck us particularly on our shinbones, causing us intense pain. Stripped and bound, we spent the rest of the day on the stage and the night in a cabin on the bare ground. Persons of both sexes and all ages tormented us. As a matter of fact, we were handed over as playthings for the children and the adolescents. They threw coals and live embers on our bare flesh. We could not throw them off because our hands were bound. This is the way the Iroquois apprentice their youth to cruelty and accustom them gradually to greater tortures. We spent two days and two nights there, with almost no food or sleep. My soul was in great interior anguish because from time to time, the savages would climb up on the stage and cut off the fingers of my Huron companions, or they would bind their wrists so tightly with hard ropes that they would lose consciousness. Whereas each one of them bore his own pains, I endured those of all of them. I felt the same intense grief a loving father must experience at the sight of his sons' sufferings. Indeed, except for a few who had been Christians for a long time, I had only recently by baptism brought forth in Christ all of these.

In this, however, the Lord gave me sufficient strength to be able to console the French and the Hurons who, like me, were suffering affliction. That is why on the road as well as on the platform where that crowd spread itself out to "greet" (that is the term they give to the beatings of captives at their arrival) us, I exhorted them, sometimes individually, sometimes in general, to preserve their patience, to cling to the hope of a great reward, to remember that "we must pass through many tribulations to come to the Kingdom of Heaven" (Acts 14:21). I assured them that the time had come that had been foretold by the Lord when he said: "You will weep and lament, while the world rejoices.

You will be plunged in sorrow, but your sorrow will be turned into joy. When a woman is about to give birth, she is in sorrow because her hour has come; but when she has brought forth her child, she no longer remembers her pangs for sheer joy that a human being has been born into the world" (Jn 16:20–21). They must also convince themselves that our temporary and "present light affliction is producing for us an eternal weight of glory that is beyond all measure" (2 Cor 4:17). And certainly there was sufficient cause for me to rejoice at seeing them so well prepared, especially our early Christians—Joseph, Eustache, and two others. Théodore had been freed from his bonds when we arrived at the first village, but he died on his way back to the French settlement as a result of a bullet wound in his shoulder.

The barbarian torture platforms had not yet seen any French or Christian captives. That is why, in order to satisfy the curiosity of all, we were led, contrary to their custom, to all the towns. We had entered the third one peaceably enough, but I saw on the stage there a most atrocious sight. Four Hurons whom other Iroquois had captured elsewhere were led out to increase the number of poor wretches. Among other mutilations, the savages had removed several fingers from all of them, and the thumbs of an old man. I joined them, and after taking them aside and instructing them in the truths of our Faith, I baptized two of them on the stage itself, with rain water that had collected on the leaves of the Indian corn, several stalks of which they had given us to chew on. I baptized the other two on the way to another village while we were crossing a river.

While we were in this village, the weather turned from rainy to cold, and since we had no clothing, we suffered very much. That is why, when I was trembling with cold on their platform, I would often get down without any permission and go into any cabin at all to warm myself. Many times, though, I had hardly begun to get warm when they would order me again to climb up on their stage. Up to this time, they had not yet cut off any of Guillaume Couture's fingers. One of the inhabitants of this village could not bear this omission. He cut off half of Couture's index finger, causing him intense pain because instead of using a knife, he used a shell that was not very sharp; therefore, he had to saw back and forth on the poor sufferer's finger in his efforts to remove it. The sinews were too tough and slippery even for this, so the Indian tore off the finger with such violence that the arm swelled all the way up to the elbow—a most horrible sight. Someone, moved by pity, sheltered Couture for the two days that we spent in this village. I was quite worried about him, though, because I did not know where he was.

When night came, they took us to a cabin, where some young people were expecting us. They ordered us to sing, as they always did with captives; so we sang. What else could we do? But it was "the Lord's own song on alien soil" (Ps 136 [137]:4). After the singing came the tortures. One portion of this storm centered especially on René and me because Guillaume was no longer with us. A savage had kept him in his cabin. Therefore, they threw on me, but even more on René, their burning embers and even live coals. René was quite seriously burned on the chest.

As for me, they hung me in the middle of the cabin by the upper part of my arms, which they fastened to two stakes, one on each side, using as ropes some bark that they had taken from the trees. I thought they were going to burn me, because that is the way they proceed when they intend to burn anyone. And to teach me that if up to now

I had borne any torment with courage or patience, that it was not I who was strong but he "that gives strength to the weary" (Is 40:29), on this occasion I groaned as if I were giving up my spirit: "gladly, therefore, will I boast of my infirmities, that the power of Christ may spread a sheltering cover over me" (2 Cor 12:9). Because of the violent pain, I begged my tormentors to loosen the bonds just a little. But, justly, God provided that the more I begged them, the tighter they bound me. After about a quarter of an hour spent in this position, I would shortly have rendered up my soul if they had not released my bonds.

I thank you, Lord Jesus, that I have learned from this slight test how much you deigned to suffer for me on the Cross when the weight of your whole body was suspended not by ropes but by your hands and your feet cruelly pierced with nails.

Other bonds followed the first. They tied all of us together and fastened us to the ground to spend the rest of the night. What did they not do to us then, bound as we were to our Huron companions! What did they not try to do to me! But again, Lord, I thank you for having preserved me, your priest vowed to chastity, from the impure hands of those savages.

After staying in this village for two days, they took us back to the second one in order to decide what to do with us. Seven days had already passed, during which from village to village and from stage to stage, we had been made "a spectacle to the world, both angelic and human" (2 Cor 4:9). This, of course, was done through the dispensations of the divine Goodness, as we truly believe. But by the vilest and most savage of men, we were "laughed at and reproached" (1 Macc 10:70). Finally the savages informed us that this day we would end our lives by fire. Although, naturally, this last act held its horrors for us, the good pleasure of God and the expectation of a better life, free from all sin, made us very happy. That is why, having given both my French and Huron companions a final encouragement to persevere, to remember in their pains of body and mind to "meditate on him who in his own person endured such great opposition at the hands of sinners; then your souls will not be overwhelmed with discouragement" (Heb 12:3), I further reminded them that we would all meet the next day in our Lord, and there we would reign for all eternity. And because we were fearful of being separated, I had especially warned Eustache that if we could not be near each other, he should make a sign to me that he was sorry for his sins by placing his hand on his breast and raising his eyes to Heaven and that I would then give him absolution as I had been doing often after hearing his confession on the road and also since our arrival. Several times he received this grace by making the sign.

However, after more mature deliberation, the elders decided not to precipitate matters in regard to the French, and they agreed in an assembly, to which they had summoned us, to grant us life. They did the same for most of the Hurons, all except three—Paul, Eustache, and Étienne— whom they put to death, one in each of the three villages that constituted this nation: Étienne in the village where we were, named *Andogaron*; Paul at *Ossernenon*; and Eustache at *Teonontogen*. They burned Eustache on almost every inch of his body and cleaved open his head with a knife. He bore all this like a true Christian. Whereas all the other prisoners were accustomed to say at the moment of death, "May an avenger rise from my bones!" he, on the contrary, in accordance with the Christian spirit that had impregnated him at his baptism, begged his Huron compatriots present at the scene not to let any consideration of his fate become an obstacle to the peace that should be made with the Iroquois. Paul Ononhoraton, who died from a hatchet blow after the usual torment by fire in the village of *Ossernenon* mentioned above, was a young man about twenty-five years old possessing very great courage. It is men such as this that they prefer to put to death in order to diminish the vital forces of their enemies. The hope of a better life gave this young man a strong contempt for death, which he did not hesitate to express during the journey. When the Iroquois approached me to tear off my fingernails or to do any other harm to me, he would offer himself in my place, asking them to leave me and to vent their fury on him instead. May our Lord grant him the hundredfold with interest for that outstanding charity, through which he gave his life for his friends and for those who, while in chains, had brought him forth in Jesus Christ.

Toward evening they took Guillaume Couture, in whom they saw a young man full of strength, to the most distant village, named *Teonontogen*, and turned him over to a family of savages. It is the custom among these barbarians when they grant life to a prisoner to give him to some family as replacement for someone who died. He inherits after a fashion that man's rights and has no other master than the head of the family, who offers presents to obtain him. As for René and me, who did not seem to be too strong, they took us to the first village, where those who had originally captured us lived, and left us there to await some new command.

Then followed many long days spent without food and just as many nights spent without sleep. Wounded and bruised, suffering unspeakable torments of soul, dragging out our sickly lives, hardly able to walk, hardly able even to stand up, lacking a single peaceful moment day or night—our lives became an unbearable torment. Our wounds were not healing properly because they had not been cared for; our bodies were harassed by fleas, lice, and ticks, which our mutilated fingers made it difficult to avoid. We also suffered great debilitation from lack of food. In these regions, it can more truly be said than in any other that "the sick man does not need food." [10] That is why we were almost reduced to our last extremity—our only food was some "American wheat", as the Europeans call our Indian corn, crushed more or less between two stones and having no seasoning, except once in a while some green pumpkins. René especially suffered from hunger, first of all because he was not accustomed to such food and also because, owing to the horrible wounds he had received on his face, he found it difficult to eat. His face was still swollen, and he could hardly see. The savages noticed that we were becoming weaker and weaker and began to add to our soup a few fish that they caught near the village, and sometimes a few pieces of meat they had dried in the sun and ground to a powder. At the end of three weeks, we were a little stronger; then they came to put us to death.

The two hundred savages who had mistreated us on the journey had gone to that place in New France where the Iroquois River, as it is called, flows into the great Saint Lawrence River.[11] As they had seen a few Frenchmen placing the foundations of Fort Richelieu, they thought they would easily be able to kill some of them and make the

---

[10] Ovid: *Tristium*, Liber 3; *Elegia*, 3, 9.

[11] Jogues had been captured not far from here. For the exact place of the capture, see Lucien Campeau, *Lettres du Bas-Canada* 6 (1952), pp. 24–36.

others captive. All two hundred of them were armed with muskets. They made a surprise attack, in a single sortie, on the Frenchmen who were engaged in various labors of building the fort. At the arrival of the enemy, the small number of the French, with full realization of the superiority of the Indians, ran for their arms and repelled the flood of savages with so much courage and success that they killed two of them, wounded several others, and forced the rest to take to flight. These returned to the village, then, full of fury, acting as if they who had gone out to commit a grave injustice had instead received one. They insisted that those of us who were still living should immediately be put to death. It was a disgrace, they said, that three Frenchmen should be living here quite tranquilly while two Iroquois had just been killed. To be sure, these complaints put René and me in a most critical position. Only he who not only gives life but protects it could restrain the blow.

On the eve of the Nativity of Our Lady, one of the leading men of the Dutch settlement, which is about twenty leagues from the Iroquois, came with two other men to try to arrange for our ransom. He stayed there several days, offering a multitude of terms, promising several concessions, but obtained absolutely nothing for his pains. The Iroquois are very clever and full of tricks; to simulate acquiescence and thus not offend their petitioner, they pretended that they had intended all along to restore us to our own French settlement in a few days. Perhaps a few of them were sincere. At any rate, at the end of September—the abundant rainfall had caused much uncertainty about setting out—when the provisions were all ready and those who were to take us back had been appointed, they held a final council concerning us. Those who favored our return were in the minority; disorder prevailed in the council, and some die-hards insisted that they would never agree to our being sent back. Indeed, these troublemakers became so violent that the whole council dispersed in fear, each member returning to his own cabin or village as if in flight. So there we were—abandoned to the fury of these formidable savages who were looking everywhere for us in order to kill us. Armed with hatchets, they searched all the houses in order to find us and put us to death. By some good fortune, God had inspired me with a most unusual idea. I had conducted my companions to a field near the house where I had been living. There, completely unaware of what was going on, we were sheltered and protected. While we were out there in the field, the fury, which would surely have been vented on every one of us, abated a little.

Guillaume's protectors took him back to their village. As for René and me, when we realized that everyone was shouting for our return, we withdrew to a nearby hill that overlooked almost the entire village, and there we prayed. Far from all witnesses and disagreeable distractions, we put ourselves completely into God's hands and at the disposal of his holy will. We were walking along the road to the village, reciting Our Lady's rosary, and had already reached the fourth decade when we met two young men who ordered us to return to the village. "My dear brother," I said, "we do not know what these men may intend to do to us in the midst of all that disorder." Therefore, we recommended ourselves very insistently to God and his holy Mother, Our Most Blessed Lady.

We were still praying when we entered the village. Hardly had we entered when one of those who had come to get us took out a hatchet he had concealed under his clothing and struck René so violently on the head that he fell half-dead to the ground, calling on the holy name of Jesus. (We had frequently exhorted each other, that, being mindful of the rich indulgences attached thereto, this holy name would seal our voices and our lives.) As for me, when I saw the bloody hatchet, I knelt down where I was, took off the cap I was wearing and, recommending my soul to God, awaited a similar blow. When I had knelt there a few moments, the man ordered me to get up because, he said, he was not permitted to kill me since I was in the custody of a different family. Rising quickly, then, I ran over to my dearest companion, who was still breathing, and immediately gave him the absolution he had been receiving every other day after his confessions. Then, before my eyes, the savage struck him two more blows, which put him among the number of the blessed.

He was a man thirty-five years old,[12] most admirable for his simplicity, the innocence of his life, and his patience in adversity. He was always perfectly resigned to the will of God, whose presence he perceived in everything, and was filled with a holy love for him. Truly, Reverend Father, he is most worthy of being considered as one of ours, not only because he had spent several months very satisfactorily in the novitiate of our Society and because at the command of our superiors—to whose will he was always perfectly conformed—he had come to the Hurons in order to help the Christians with his medical skills and knowledge. Another reason—the strongest of all—was that a few days before his

---

[12] In regard to René Goupil, see the account written by Jogues (pp. 311ff.). If according to the strict letter of the law, Goupil could not be considered a member of the Society, there has, nevertheless, been a continuous tradition in the Society to consider the *"donnés"* as their children. As noted on p. 272 and on pp. 313–14, he pronounced vows to the Society before his death.

death, filled with a desire to unite himself still more closely to God, he pronounced the vows of the Society, dedicating himself to it as much as was possible for him. Without a shadow of doubt, in life as in death, pronouncing the holy name of Jesus as his final word, he always showed himself a true son of the Society. Furthermore, I love and venerate him not only as a brother but as a martyr of obedience and even of the Faith and the cross. He was very pious, and since he had been living among Indians who were either Christians themselves or were accustomed to Christian practices, he prayed to God for a long time every day. This amazed the Iroquois, who had never seen anything like it. It was his piety, really, which ultimately caused his death. One day, when he was in the cabin where he lived, he took off one of the children's caps and made a large Sign of the Cross on his forehead and on his breast. The child's grandfather, a very superstitious old man, thought this was a hex of some sort and told his nephew to kill René. The child's mother told me all this later, explaining that it was the reason for Rene's murder.

But let us continue our story. I had stayed quite peacefully for quite a long time in the cabin to which I had been assigned originally, when suddenly I was sent to another. It was, indeed, the cabin of the man who had cut off my thumb and who was the declared enemy of the Algonquins and, consequently, of the French. I expected at every moment to be struck on the head with a hatchet, and the other Iroquois also were waiting for the same thing. Those who had loaned me a few pieces of clothing immediately claimed them because they did not want to lose them at my death.

The next day, I was very uneasy about the disposal of the body of my dearest companion. I decided to go out and look for it, regardless of the danger, and to bury it if I could. I found that he had been most shamefully dragged, completely naked, by means of a rope tied about his neck, through the village and then thrown into the river.

As I was going out of the village, I met the old man in whose cabin I had been living. He advised me not to go. "Where are you going? You are only half-alive; everywhere, they are trying to put you to death, and here you are, looking for a corpse that is already half-decayed. Don't you see those young men, filled with anger, who are going to kill you?" (A few Iroquois, fully armed, had preceded me as I was leaving the village.) But I feared nothing, disturbed as I was by that great anguish of soul, since "to die means gain" (Phil 1:21) when one is performing an act of mercy. So I continued on my way. When he saw that I was set in my resolution, he asked another savage to accompany me.

Then, with his help, I found the dear body, which the dogs had already half-eaten. I covered it with a pile of stones in a place where the river was not too deep, intending to come back the next day with a pickax so I could bury him secretly. I was greatly afraid that they would exhume him.

Two young men were waiting for me when I returned to take me to their village and there put me to death. Not knowing what they wanted, I said that I was in the power of those in whose house I was living and that only with their permission would I accompany the young men. And I surely would have done it.

Seeing that they could obtain nothing in this way, the next day one of them, who had been wounded with his brother at the time of our capture, hatchet in hand, ready to kill me, hurried out to the field where I was working.

Fortunately, the head of the house met him on the road and forbade him to do it.

Thus, the Lord has taught me to "cast all my anxiety on him, because he takes care of me" (1 Pet 5:7), to fear nothing from men because "the Lord protects my life" (Ps 126:1), and "not a hair on my head will perish" (Lk 21:18) without his permission. Since I had been unable to accomplish my purpose that first day, I left the next morning very early with a hoe and a pickax to go out to bury the body. But they had taken away my brother. I returned there; I scrambled up the hill at the foot of which that torrent flowed. I ran down the other side; I scoured the woods on the opposite side, but all in vain. I probed with a stick and with my foot the bed of the river, which the nocturnal rains had swollen considerably, not being deterred by either the depth of the water, which came up to my waist, or by the cold (for it was already the first of October). I thought it possible that the violence of the torrent could have dislodged it. I asked those whom I met if they knew anything about it. But because these are lying people and talk to please rather than to tell the truth, they falsely asserted that he had been dragged far down the river; this statement was in reality not at all true. What groans did I not send forth! What tears I shed, tears that mingled with the rushing waters of the stream! And to you, O Lord, I chanted the psalms that ordinarily the Church reserves for the Office of the Dead!

However, when the snows had melted, I learned from a few young men that they had seen the scattered bones of a Frenchman who had been killed. I hurried to the place and gathered up the half-gnawed bones—remnants of the dogs, the wolves, and the crows—and particularly the skull, broken into several pieces. I respectfully kissed these relics and then placed them in the ground, so that, if it should be

God's will, someday I could transport them to a holy and Christian country like the great treasures they were.

In truth, God delivered me from many other dangers that I knew of and many that I was ignorant of, despite the bad will and the threats of the Iroquois. But I cannot refrain from recounting the following incident. In our cabin there was an idiot who asked me to cut off for him two handbreadths of a piece of material that in all measured only seven and that covered me very scantily, if at all. "But", I answered him, "you see, my brother, how I tremble from the cold at night under this small, light cloth! However, do as you wish." He was offended at this excuse, and later, when I entered the cabin of the baptized Hurons (I instructed them every day and "suffered the pangs of childbirth for them until Christ is formed in them" [Gal 4:19]), he came after me and ordered me severely to return to the house. When I returned, he sent for the murderer of René so that I could be killed by the same hand as he. They looked for him but could not find him. The next day, I was sent out with two women to the field of the man with whom René used to live. Ostensibly, it was to take something to him, but in reality, they wanted to give him a chance to kill me. (As a matter of fact, two days before that, the son of the wife of one of the chiefs had died in our house, and they had offered me as a sacrifice to his Manes.) These women were carrying some pumpkins, some ears of corn, and other victuals of this type to pay for putting me to death. "But I—like to one deaf, I do not hear; like to one dumb that opens not his mouth. I am become a man that does not hear, as one that has no answer on his lips. In you, indeed, O Lord, I trust" (Ps 37 [38]:14–15). Calling to mind, also, the sweetness of him who was "led as a sheep to the slaughter" (Is 53:7), I was going to my death, praying to the Lord with David: "See that their evil deeds recoil upon my foes; and may your plighted word destroy them all" (Ps 53:7 [54:5]). In the middle of the road, we met the murderer they were seeking. Having caught sight of him in the distance, I recommended myself to God one last time, begging him to receive my soul, crushed as it was by such torments and anguish. However, I was still not yet worthy of death because of my sins.

Then, while he passed us by peacefully, we met his mother, who said something to the two women that I could not hear. They began to tremble and, fleeing from me, left me standing in the middle of the road. (They realized, of course, that I had understood their intentions.)

Two months of constant fears and dangers had now passed since our arrival, so that "day after day I face death" (1 Cor 15:31) in a life more torturous than any death. No study of the language was possible for me. What good would it do to learn it, since at every moment I expected to die? The village was my prison; I fled the crowded places; I loved the solitudes in which I prayed to the Lord to deign to speak to me, his servant, and to give me strength in the midst of such great anguish of soul and body. Truly, if in these torments "as a prodigy I appeared to many", it was God who was my "mighty helper" (Ps 70 [71]:7). By his generous goodness, he aroused the courage of his afflicted one. I had recourse very frequently to Sacred Scripture to sustain me; it was my only "refuge and strength, a mighty helper in distress" (Ps 45:2 [46:1]). I reverenced Holy Writ very highly, and I wanted to die with its holy words on my lips.

It so happened that of all the books we had brought along for the use of the French who were living with the Hurons, the only one that fell into my hands was the Epistle of Saint

Paul to the Hebrews, paraphrased by Monsignor Antoine Godeau, bishop of Grasse. I always carried this book with me. I also had a picture of Saint Bruno, founder of the famous Order of Chartreux, to which there had been attached numerous indulgences. Besides these, I had fashioned for myself, more or less crudely, a wooden cross. The result was that if ever death should surprise me—death that was always before my eyes—fortified by Holy Scripture, by the gifts and indulgences of Holy Mother Church, whom I had always loved but now with a very special tenderness, fortified also with the Cross of my Lord, I should be able to embrace death willingly.

We were now in the middle of October, a time when the barbarians left their villages and went out to hunt deer,[13] trapping them or killing them with their muskets, which they had learned to handle very skillfully. The time, therefore, that the savages put aside for feasting and amusing themselves was for me only a period of increased sufferings. A few of them were assigned to me as companions. In the beginning they were amazed at me but ended with mockery and finally with hatred.

Mindful of the duties God had imposed on me by sending me here, I began to teach them, as prudently as I could, the worship of the true God, the observance of the Ten Commandments, the teachings of the Church concerning Heaven and Hell, and other mysteries. To be sure, they listened to me in the beginning, but when they saw that I frequently repeated the same teachings, and most especially when the hunt did not bring the hoped-for success, they

---

[13] It is not really deer that they hunted, but a type of moose, with webbed antlers. The Canadians still hunt them today.

declared that I was a demon and the cause of their poor hunting.

The outstanding reason, however, for which their bad will turned into rage and fury was this. All of these people have the custom when hunting, fishing, in war, or in illness to invoke a spirit whom they call *Aireskoi*. Whoever desires success in hunting, fishing, or other similar pursuits takes viands and the best portions of their victuals and asks the oldest member of the household or of the whole village to bless it (if I can use such a term here—they consider the blessings of some people more efficacious than others). This old man, standing opposite him who holds the viands, pronounces these words in a loud, distinct voice: "O demon *Aireskoi*, behold, we offer you these viands, with which we prepare a feast for you to eat so that you will show us in what place there are deer and that you will lead them into our nets." If this ceremony takes place outside the hunting season, they say, "... so that you will grant us to see the spring once more, to taste the fruits, and to return to the hunt in the fall." If they are praying for a sick person, they say, "... so that you will grant us to regain our health."

As soon as I heard this formula, I was seized with a fierce hatred for the superstition of the barbarians, and I made a firm resolution never to eat food that had thus been offered. They interpreted my abstinence as contempt for their demon and the cause of the lack of success on the hunt: "They hated me without just cause" (Jn 15:25).

Their hatred was so violent that they would no longer listen to my teaching or answer my questions when I used their language, because I employed it to refute their foolishness. I decided then to devote that time to spiritual exercises. Each morning, I went "out of the midst of Babylon" (Jer 50:8), that is, out of our cabin, where they maintained an almost continuous cult to their demon or to their dreams. I would "flee to the hills" (Gen 19:17), that is, to a neighboring summit. In that spot, I had removed the bark of a huge tree to form a large cross, and there I would spend entire days, sometimes meditating and praying, sometimes reading the *Imitation of Christ*, which I had come upon a little while before. I was alone with my God in these vast regions, honoring him and loving him.

This practice was hidden from them for a while, but when they found me there one day, praying as usual before my cross, they were more furious than ever, saying that they held this cross in horror since it was unknown to them and to their European neighbors (the Dutch heretics). While I had always purposely avoided praying openly in their cabins or kneeling down in order not to give them cause for even a slight complaint (one must indeed always be prudent, especially with these savages, who were not at all accustomed to these acts of worship), nevertheless I did not feel that I should deprive myself of the practices of piety related to my spiritual life and therefore much more important in my eyes than my temporal life. I surely thought that these pious exercises would be useful in their time, that is, when the time for their conversion would come, that hour "which the Father has fixed by his own authority" (Acts 1:7).

Truly this intense hatred by the savages caused me many sufferings—hunger, cold, the scorn of the vilest men, and cruel resentments of certain women. Since almost all the meat taken during the hunt was used to pay these women, they held me responsible for their small profit and their poverty. Hunger caused me the most distress, since almost all the food that they took at this time had been offered to their demon in oblations of the sort I mentioned before, and consequently, I spent many successive days with nothing to eat. I would return to the cabin in the evening and see our Egyptians seated around their fleshpots, and I would be strongly tempted to yield to the many reasons that presented themselves to my mind as excuses for acting differently; however, not once, by the grace of God, did I permit myself to break my resolution.

On the contrary, when I was hungry, I would say to my Lord: "We will be sated with the blessings of your house" (Ps 64 [65]:5); "when I wake to life, your sight will be my bliss" (Ps 16 [17]:15); in paradise you will fill all the desires of your starving servants; you will "settle peace within their borders, and fill them with the choicest wheat" (Ps 147:14).

The cold also caused me much suffering when the snow was high and I had no covering but a short coat, already well worn. It was worse at night, when I was forced to lie down naked on the bare earth or on harsh pieces of bark from the trees. Although there were numerous deerskins in the cabin, the Indians would not give me even those no one was using. What was even worse, if during a very severe night, the intense cold would drive me to take a skin secretly, my tormentors would get up immediately and take it away from me, so great was their hatred toward me. My poor skin was always, to use the words of David, "clothed with rottenness and the filth of dust, it is withered and drawn together"[14] by the cold. My whole body was one huge pain because of this. But when my exterior sufferings were joined to interior ones, then, indeed, my pain became unbearable. I would recall how I had been covered with the blood of my dear companion; and those who came from the village where Guillaume lived[15] told me he had been killed with the most cruel torments and that I would be

---

[14] Jogues believed he was quoting a psalm, but the citation is from Job 7:5.
[15] Guillaume Couture was really still alive; he was released a few years later.

put to death in the same way when I returned to the village. In addition to this, I would recall my past life, so blameworthy because of my numerous sins and my infidelity to God. I groaned at being stopped in the middle of my course, having no good works to send before me, rejected by my God, and without the sacraments. Truly, in this situation, where I wanted to live and dreaded to die, I would moan with distress and say to my God: "When shall there be an end to my miseries and griefs? When will you 'bring calm after the storm and fill us with joy and exultation after our tears' (cf. Tob 3:22)? 'If those days had not been shortened, my flesh would have perished'" (Mk 13:20).

I had recourse to the support of Holy Scripture, my usual refuge, certain passages of which I kept in my memory. It was these that taught me to "think of the Lord in goodness" (Wis 1:1), even if I felt no sensible devotion, and to recall that "the holy one shall live by faith" (Heb 10:38). I would explore these passages; I would probe the smallest streams in my efforts to quench my constant thirst. I would "con his law by day and night" (Ps 1:2). "Were not your law my great delight, I should by now have perished in my grief" (Ps 118 [119]:92). "Then would a swollen stream have swept us off. Blest be the Lord who did not give us up—a victim to their crunching teeth" (Ps 123:5–6 [124:4–5]). "We were crushed beyond measure, beyond our strength, so that we were not sure of even continuing to live" (2 Cor 1:8). And I would say, misquoting Job: "Even if he did not cause us to die, I shall hope in him."[16]

Having thus spent two months in that retreat where I had become, like Saint Bernard, the disciple of the beech trees, I thought of nothing but God. Because all the natives hated

---

[16] What Job really said: "He can kill me, still I will hope in him" (13:15).

me and could stand me no longer, they sent me back to the village before the usual time. During the trip, which took eight days, loaded under the enormous weight of food that I was carrying, I had become, as it were, a beast of burden before God; still, I tried to remain always with him, not knowing what awaited me in the village. A few of those who had preceded us into the village had spread all sorts of rumors about me. On the road, since I was almost naked and spent the largest part of the night outdoors, I suffered very much from the cold, because the wounds of my fingers, which had closed up only toward the middle of January, were still not completely healed. In the village, they gave me a thin skin to use in addition to the old coat I was wearing. In this clothing, still rather insufficient, I went through the streets begging Our Lord to let me join his saints, those souls who had served him "dressed in sheepskins and goatskins, destitute, distressed, mistreated. The world was not worthy of them" (Heb 11:37–38). And every day, I saw the savages well covered with the woolens and the vestments that had been in great supply in our baggage, while day and night I was stiff with cold. But that was not too important. What bothered me most was to see those men use for secular purposes the vestments that had been destined for use at the altar. One of them had even taken two humeral veils, from which he fashioned stockings of a sort—a use for which the sacred vestments manifestly had not been destined.

Throughout this whole period, which lasted until about the middle of January, I could say before God: "To this very hour we are victims of hunger and thirst; we are poorly clad and knocked around; we are vagabonds and wear ourselves out with manual labor. When men call us ugly names, we speak well of them. When they persecute us, we bear it patiently. When they insult us, we speak gently. We have practically become at present the world's scum, the scapegoat of society" (1 Cor 4:11–13).

Toward mid-January, when our masters returned from hunting, they gave me some skins so that I could clothe myself a little better. Besides, a man from Lorraine who was living with the Dutch, our neighbors, sent me as a gift an outfit of clothing like they sold to the Indians, because he had heard that I was suffering from the cold. This was a relief to my hardship. More comforting still was the care taken of me by an old woman who had lost her only son a short while before. This noble woman (for even the savages have their nobles) took care of me, and the Lord let me find favor in her eyes. But these were only slight comforts in the midst of an immense distress.

When finally I realized that I was still living—more or less—I began to study the Iroquois language, and since not only the local assemblies but those of the whole region were held in our cabin, I began to teach a few of the older ones the truths of our Faith. These men asked me many questions concerning the sun, the moon, the face that the moon showed us, the limits of the earth, the magnitude of the ocean, the rise and fall of the tides, the place where, as they had heard, the sky met the earth, and many other facts dealing with natural science. Adapting my teaching to their mentality, sometimes I would satisfy their curiosity, and sometimes I would amaze them. They would then say: "We would really have done a very stupid thing to kill this man"—but nothing threatened me more frequently than death.

I forced myself to lead these creatures to the knowledge of their Creator; I refuted their old wives' tales about the ways in which the world came into being, one of the most fantastic of which ascribed the creation to a turtle. I showed them that the sun had neither intelligence nor life, least of all was it a god, and that if they, being filled with delight at its beauty, considered it a god, how much more beautiful is the Lord who made it. I added that *Aireskoi* was not a god but a devil and that he was not telling the truth when he said that he was the author and preserver of life, the distributor of all the good things they enjoyed. If these poor savages had not had more difficulty in believing than in being convinced, their conversion would have been accomplished. But the Prince of this world, who because of the Cross is rejected by a great portion of the universe, seemed to have fled from this region to a strong place, with the result that this kingdom held for thousands of years in the power of Satan could not be taken except by the passage of time and the invincible constancy of the soldiers of Christ. From time to time, however, Christ, the true Lord of these regions, as of all others, chose for himself a few souls not only among the infants who went immediately to Heaven but also among the adults whom I baptized in illness or in captivity. I instructed several other sick natives, but they did not respond to my teaching, and several of them rejected me. Still others agreed with what I said, prompted by a sort of politeness that made them think it rude to contradict a person who spoke to them—a politeness that can deceive a man who is not on his guard.

Sometimes I would go to the neighboring villages to console and strengthen the Christian Hurons, "whose knees have not been bowed before Baal" (3 Kings 19:18 [1 Kings 19:18]), and to give them absolution after hearing their confessions. Everywhere I spread the truths of God as well as I could; I comforted the dying, but especially did I encourage the children who were in danger. That was my only consolation in all the trials of my soul. One time when I was in a neighboring village, I baptized five children; shortly afterward, on another visit to that place, I learned that all five of them had gone to Heaven.

In activities of this nature and in a piecemeal study of the language (how can one really learn a language without writing it?), two months passed. About the middle of March, when the snow had thawed, the savages took me with them on a fishing expedition. In our party there were an old man, an old woman, a young boy, and myself. We walked for four days before we came to a lake, where we caught nothing but a few little fish. The Indians use the whole fish—the meat is dried or sometimes eaten fresh, while the intestines are used to season their soup. All their eating habits, even that of swallowing the bloody intestines of deer, half-rotten shellfish, frogs that they ate whole, without roasting or cleaning them—head, feet, everything—all of these became, if not agreeable, at least tolerable, through hunger and habit, or at best, a lack of something better. How many times during the course of these trips or in some peaceful solitude "by Babylon's great waters, there we sat and wept as we remembered Sion's hill" (Ps 136 [137]:1). Not only did we weep over Sion exulting in Heaven but also praising God on earth! How many times did we not ask: "How can we sing the Lord's own song on alien soil?" (Ps 136 [137]:4.) The woods and the mountains echoed and reechoed with the praises of their Creator, such as they had not heard since the time of their creation. How many times did I not carve on the huge trees of the forest the holy name of Jesus so that the demons would flee at the sight of it and tremble at hearing it! How many times did I not cut out the bark of the trees in the form of the most holy Cross of the Lord so that his adversaries would flee when they came upon it and so that you, my Lord and my King, might reign in the midst of your enemies, the enemies of your Cross, the heretics and pagans living in these regions, and all the demons who triumph in these lands.

That is one of the reasons why I was so happy that the Lord led me into solitude at the season when Holy Church recalls the Passion, so that I could recall so much more easily his celebration of the Passover and the bitterness and gall that followed, and that, being mindful and remembering, my soul languished within me (cf. Lam 3:20). That is also why, when I had finished the work that was assigned me in my condition of slave to these barbarians (it was my duty to go to the forest and cut down and carry to the cabin the wood for our fires), I spent almost all my time before the cross that I had carved in a huge pine tree far from the cabin. They did not permit me to enjoy this holy leisure very long, however. Too many days had passed without my customary terrors. On Monday of Holy Week, one of the men of our village came to us. This is the reason for his coming:

Ten Iroquois, among them the son of the one who had cut off my thumb and in whose cabin I was living, had gone out on the warpath in the middle of summer. We had had no news of them during the rest of the summer; no news in the fall or in the winter. We concluded that they had perished, since we had heard from our neighbors that they had all succumbed to the cruelty of their enemies. Thus, at the beginning of the summer, when a prisoner who was brought in and questioned while we were away testified that the report was correct and that all of them had been killed, the Iroquois sacrificed this prisoner to the Manes of the youth with whose father I was living. But the prisoner was too lowly to make satisfaction for the noble youth. Therefore, a messenger came to the lake where we were fishing to bring me back, so that, added to the other prisoner, my death should recompense that of the young noble. This was the decision arrived at by a few wicked old women and a decrepit old man. The next day we set out, like fugitives, under the pretext that there were enemies in the region. We arrived in the village on Holy Thursday. On Good Friday, then, on the day that Our Lord had consummated his life for me, I would also end mine; and he who in dying had given me the life of my soul would also grant me the eternal life of my body.

Then, on the day that I was to be put to death, the rumor was circulated—no one knew how it started—that those who had been thought dead were really still living and were bringing in a group of twenty-two prisoners. God thus put an end to the hostile plans of these barbarians and showed me that "I should cast all my anxiety on him because he takes care of me" (cf. 1 Pet 5:6). No one knew better than I that if he did not watch over me, I would surely fall.

Thus, snatched from these perils and from others, although I felt a little natural joy, nevertheless I regretted always being dragged back to new griefs and very cruel torments, back to a life more painful than any death. Both the successes and the reverses of these savages caused me to suffer, for if any one of them was killed in combat, I was proposed as a victim to his Manes, but if—as almost always happened—they brought back prisoners after having killed several others, these were always French or friends of us French, and so my poor heart would be torn with new pangs.

Naturally, I liked my place of retreat and solitude, where I was not hurt by the customary cruelty of the savages; I took my repose in God more freely and with greater satisfaction. But I knew, too, that Leah, despite her afflicted eyes, was more fruitful than Rachel and had more children (cf. Gen 29:17–31); I also called to mind the Constitutions of the Society, which require us to prefer the salvation of our neighbor to our own retirement and solitude; therefore, I willingly remained in the house. Indeed, by staying in the village, I could study more extensively the Iroquois language, and better still, I could see to the baptism of the children and the instruction of the adults. I was sorry that several times while I was away, someone died, either an adult who had not been instructed or an unbaptized infant.

Our barbarians, returning from their wars, had brought back, then, twenty-two prisoners, six of whom belonged to a nation against which they had never before waged war. These poor victims, contrary to all justice and right, were beaten, clubbed, and mutilated, according to the Iroquois custom, and had their fingers cut off. Five others were to be put to death (for all the rest were children, young girls, or women, and so would become slaves), and I was concerned for their salvation because I did not know their language. Nevertheless, with the help of God and one of them who knew both languages, I instructed them, using also the few words of their tongue that I knew, and thus succeeded in baptizing them. This took place on Easter Sunday.

On the Feast of Pentecost, the Iroquois brought in some more prisoners, namely, three women with little children. They had killed the men because of us French. After grossly mistreating these poor captives, they led them into the village, completely nude, without even a loincloth, and there cut off their thumbs. They burned one of them all over her body, a brutality they had never before committed, and then threw her onto a large pile of wood. This new atrocity was noteworthy, for each time they approached this woman with burning firebrands, an old man pronounced these words in a loud voice: "Spirit *Aireskoi*, we offer you this victim, whom we are burning for you, so that you may be sated with her flesh and always make us victorious over our enemies." The poor woman's body was cut into pieces, carried into various villages, and eaten with avidity. On one occasion during the winter, regretting, so to speak, their abstinence in regard to several victims whose flesh they had not eaten, they had solemnly sacrificed two bears to their demon and addressed him thus: "It is our just chastisement, O Spirit *Aireskoi*, that for so long a time we have taken none of our enemies captive. [It was true that during the summer and the fall, they had not captured a single Algonquin, their special enemies.] We have sinned against you by not eating and by throwing aside our last prisoners, but if in the future we succeed in taking any, we promise you that we will eat them in the same fashion that we are now going to eat these two bears." And so they did. Under the pretext of taking this poor woman a drink of water, I baptized her on her funeral pyre, because I had not been able to approach her earlier.

On the eve of the Feast of the Nativity of Saint John the Baptist (about whom it was said that "multitudes of people will rejoice in his birth" [Lk 1:14]), my usual sufferings were greatly intensified when more prisoners were brought in—eleven Hurons and one Frenchman—not to mention three others, whom they had killed and then scalped (the Iroquois prided themselves on bringing home the hair still attached to the skin of those they had killed), nor ten other Hurons, whom they treacherously deceived by simulating friendship and then put to death. Among these were several well-known Christians. Truly my soul was shaken by the realization that my sins were the cause of this punishment—a chastisement God had announced to his people, saying: "And I will turn your feasts into mourning and all your songs into lamentations" (Amos 8:10)—since on Easter, Pentecost, and now on the birthday of Saint John the Baptist, new pains had poured out upon me. Nor was this the end. My pangs were multiplied a hundredfold when, as a result of a disaster suffered by a hundred Hurons, some of them were delivered to the flames after being most cruelly tortured by the neighboring nations. "Woe is me, wherefore was I born to see the ruin of my people" (1 Macc 2:7).

Indeed, in these terrible agonies of spirit, and in others like them, "my life is wearing out with grief; my years are one long sigh" (Ps 30:11 [31:10]). "He scourges me for my sins" (Tob 13:5) and has gnawed at my soul like a moth. "He has filled me with bitterness; he has inebriated me with wormwood" (Lam 3:15), "because the comforter, the relief of my soul, is far from me" (Lam 1:16). "But in all those things we are more than victorious through him who has loved us" (Rom 8:37), until the day when "he who is to come will come, and will not delay" (Heb 10:37).

Although it is true that I could probably have escaped had I so wished by appealing either to the Europeans or to neighboring savages, I had decided that with the help of God's grace, I would live and die on the Cross, to which our Lord had affixed me with himself. Indeed, if I should leave, who would console the French prisoners or absolve anyone who wished the sacrament of penance? Who would remind the baptized Huron captives of their duties, instruct the new prisoners who were continuously being brought in, baptize the dying, and support those agonizing in their torments? Who would regenerate the children with the holy waters of baptism and see to the salvation of the dying adults and see to the instruction of those who were still in good health? And, in truth, I felt that it was not without a special providence of the goodness of God that, at a time when on the one hand men who were not acquainted with the true Catholic religion, and on the other, a fierce war with the savages (and consequently with the French) prevented our holy Faith from being brought to these regions—is it not, I say, without a special providence—that I fell into the hands of the savages, against my will, certainly, and that even until now has preserved me, despite their barbarous desires to put me to death. God had willed this, it seemed to me, so that through me, his unworthy instrument, all these might receive instruction, faith, baptism, and eternal life, according to his divine plan. Since the time I was taken prisoner, I have washed in the waters of baptism seventy souls, young and old, of five different nations and languages, that thus they might stand before the Lamb, "men of every tribe and tongue and people and nation" (Rev 5:9).

That is the reason why every day "on bended knees, I beseech the Father from whom every family in heaven and on earth derives its origin" (Eph 3:14–15), begging him, if this be his will, to put to naught the plans of those—Europeans or savages—who sought to deliver me or to restore me to my own people. The savages have talked at great length about my return to Quebec. And the Dutch, my protectors, even while I write this, have offered and continue to offer countless rewards for my ransom and that of my companions. I have gone to them twice; they have treated me with the utmost courtesy. They have done everything possible to obtain release for me and mine. And even more than that, they have heaped presents on the savages who were holding me captive so that they would treat me with consideration.

But I am weary of this long, rambling letter. I beg you, Reverend Father, to claim me, despite my unworthiness, as one of your sons. If I have become a barbarian in custom and costume; if, worse still, I have become almost godless in such a disrupted life, nevertheless, I still wish to die as I have always lived, that is, as a devoted son of Holy Church and of the Society.

Obtain for me from God, Reverend Father, through your Holy Masses, that I may on this latest occasion employ to advantage the graces he gives me, although in the past I have abused so many of them. Surely your goodness owes that to your son who trusts in you, for I lead a most miserable life in which any virtues I may ever have acquired are constantly in danger. Faith, certainly, in such dense shadows of infidelity; hope, in such long and harsh trials; charity, amid so much corruption and the deprivation of all the sacraments. Chastity, surely, which, although not seriously threatened by lures of pleasure, is nevertheless endangered by the sight of the free intimacies between the sexes, by the liberties they take to dare and to do anything at all, and especially by their indecent exposure. Indeed, we must here witness willy-nilly what under other circumstances would repel not only the curious spectator but even the depraved.

For this reason I complain daily to my God, begging him not to leave me without help among the dead; imploring him, I repeat, so that in the midst of so many defilements of the flesh and of superstitious cults of demons, to which he has exposed me stripped and defenseless, as it were, he may keep my heart perfect in observing his decrees (cf. Ps 118 [119]:80), so that, when the Good Shepherd shall come to gather "the scattered sons of Israel" (Ps 146 [147]:2), "he may gather us from 'mongst the heathen tribes, that we may celebrate his holy name" (Ps 105 [106]:47). Fiat! Fiat!

> I remain, Reverend Father, your humble servant and son in Jesus Christ,
>
> Isaac Jogues

Please, Reverend Father, be kind enough to greet my dear Fathers and Brothers, all of whom I love and revere in Christ, and ask them to remember me in a very special way in their Holy Masses and in their prayers.

Colony of Renselaerswich, New Belgium, August 5, 1643

ACCOUNT OF HIS ESCAPE

*Letter to
Father Jérôme Lalemant*

August 30, 1643

On the Feast of Saint Ignatius, our holy Father, I set out from the village where I was a captive in order to follow and accompany some Iroquois who were leaving, first for trade and then for fishing. When they had finished their little business, they stopped at a place seven or eight leagues below a Dutch settlement located on the banks of a river. Here we carried on our fishing. While we were setting out our snares for the fish, we heard that a squad of Iroquois, having returned from a pursuit of some Hurons, had killed five or six of them on the spot and taken four prisoners, two of whom had already been burned in our village with extraordinary cruelties. At this news my heart contracted with a bitter and sharp pain because I had not seen, consoled, or baptized those poor victims. Consequently, fearing that a similar tragedy would take place in my absence, I said to a good old woman who, because of her age and the care and compassion she felt toward me, called me her nephew, and I called her my aunt—I, then, said to her: "My aunt, I would very much like to return to our cabin;

Father Jérôme Lalemant was at that time superior of the Huron mission. Jogues traveled southward with the Iroquois, passing Renselaerswich; later they will stop there. French text in Thw. 25:42–60.

I am getting very weary here." It was not that I expected greater ease or less pain in our village, where I suffered a continual martyrdom at seeing with my own eyes the horrible cruelties that were practiced there, but my heart could not endure the death of any man without my procuring for him holy baptism. The good woman said to me: "Go, then, my nephew, since you are weary here; take something along to eat on the way." So I embarked in the first canoe that was going up to the village, always taken and always accompanied by the Iroquois. While we were in the Dutch settlement, through which we had to pass, I learned that our whole village was aroused against the French and that they were only waiting for me to return in order to burn all of us. This is what had happened:

Among several bands of Iroquois who were warring against the French, the Algonquins, and the Hurons, there was one that decided to go near Fort Richelieu[1] to spy on the French and the savages who were their allies. A certain Huron of this band, captured by the Iroquois and settled among them, came to ask me if I wanted to send some letters to the French, hoping, perhaps, to surprise someone by this bait. I did not doubt that our French would be on their guard, and I saw, moreover, that it was important for me to give them some warning of the plans, the arms, and the treachery of our enemies. I found a bit of paper on which to write to them—the Dutch granted me this charity.[2]

I knew very well the dangers to which I was exposing myself; I was fully aware that if any misfortune befell these warriors, they would hold me responsible and blame my letters

---

[1] Fort Richelieu was on the right bank of the Saint Lawrence, at the mouth of the Iroquois River.

[2] He is talking about the letter of June 30, 1643, translated on pp. 244ff.

for it. I could foresee my death, but it seemed pleasant and agreeable to me, devoted to the public good, and the consolation of our French and of the poor savages who listen to the words of our Lord. My heart did not quake at the thought of all that might result from sending this letter, since it concerned the glory of God. Accordingly, I gave my letter to the warrior that had offered to take it. He did not return. The story that his comrades brought back was that he carried it to Fort Richelieu and that as soon as the French had read it, they fired their cannons on the whole band. This frightened them so much that the greater portion of them fled, completely naked, abandoning one of their canoes, in which they had three muskets, some powder, and some lead, along with some other baggage. When these reports were brought into the village, a loud clamor arose that my letters had caused them to be treated like that. The rumor spread everywhere and finally came to my ears. They reproached me for having done this evil deed; they talked of nothing but burning me, and if I had been in the village when these warriors returned, fire, rage, and cruelty would have taken my life. My danger was doubled when another troop, returning from Montreal, where they had set ambushes for the French, said that one of their men had been killed and two others wounded. Everyone considered me guilty of these adverse encounters; they were out of their minds with rage and could hardly wait for me to arrive.

I listened to all these rumors, offering myself without reserve to Our Lord and committing myself in all and through all to his most holy will. The captain of the Dutch settlement where we were, well aware of the evil intentions of those barbarians, and knowing, too, that Monsieur le Chevalier de Montmagny had prevented the savages of New France from coming to kill the Dutch, revealed to me a means of escape. "There is a vessel at anchor", he said to me, "ready to sail in a few days. Board it secretly. First it will go to Virginia, and from there it will take you either to Bordeaux or to La Rochelle, where it will dock."

I thanked him very respectfully for his courtesy. I warned him that the Iroquois would probably suspect that someone had aided my escape and might cause some trouble to his people. "No, no," he answered, "do not be afraid; this is a wonderful opportunity for you. Embark. You will never find a more certain way to escape." My heart was perplexed at these words, wondering if it would contribute more to the greater glory of our Lord to expose myself to the danger of the fire and the fury of the barbarians in the hope of bringing salvation to some poor soul. I said to him then, "Sir, the matter seems to me to be so important that I cannot answer you right away; give me, if you will, a night to think it over. I will commend the problem to our Lord; I will examine the arguments for both sides; tomorrow morning I will tell you of my decision."

Though greatly surprised, he granted my request. I spent the night in prayer, earnestly beseeching our Lord not to let me reach a conclusion by myself, to give me light to know his holy will, that in all and through all, I wished to follow it, even to being burned over a slow fire. The reasons that could keep me in the country were consideration for the French and for the savages. I felt much love for them and a great desire to help them, so much so that I had resolved to spend the remainder of my days in captivity for their salvation. But now I saw that the face of the matter was quite changed.

In the first place, in regard to our three Frenchmen, led captive into the country with me, one of them, René

Goupil, had already been murdered at my feet. That young man had the purity of an angel. Henri, who had been taken at Montreal, had escaped into the woods. While he was watching the cruelties practiced upon two poor Hurons, roasted over a slow fire, a few Iroquois had told him that he would receive the same treatment, as would I, too, when I returned. These threats made him resolve to plunge himself into the danger of dying of hunger in the woods or of being devoured by some wild beast, rather than to endure the torments inflicted by these half demons. Seven days had passed since he disappeared. As for Guillaume Couture, I saw scarcely any further way of aiding him, for they had placed him in a village far from the one where I was, and the savages kept him so busy here and there that I was no longer able to meet him. Besides, he himself had said to me, "Father, try to escape. As soon as I notice that you are gone, I shall find the means to get away. You know well that I remain in this captivity only for the love of you. Try, then, to escape, because I cannot think of my own liberty and my life unless I see that you are safe." Furthermore, this good youth had been given to an old man who assured me that he would let him go in peace if I could obtain my deliverance. Therefore, I saw no further reason that would oblige me to remain for the sake of the French.

As for the savages, I was without power and beyond hope of being able to instruct them. The whole country was so stirred up against me that I could no longer find an opening to speak to them or to win them over. The Algonquins and the Hurons were forced to withdraw from me as from a victim destined for the fire, for fear of sharing in the hatred and rage that the Iroquois felt against me. I realized, moreover, that I had some acquaintance with their language, that

I knew their country and their strength, and that I could, perhaps, better obtain their salvation by other ways than staying with them. I realized also that this knowledge would die with me if I did not escape.

These wretches had so little inclination to free us that they transgressed the law and custom of all these nations. A savage from the country of the Sokokiois, allies of the Iroquois, had been seized by the Upper Algonquins and taken prisoner to Three Rivers or to Quebec. There he was released and given his liberty by the intervention of the governor of New France at the request of our Fathers. This good savage, seeing that the French had saved his life, sent to the Iroquois during the month of April some valuable presents so that they should release at least one of their French prisoners. The Iroquois retained the presents but did not release anyone. Treachery is perhaps unknown among these peoples—for they inviolably observe this law, that whoever touches or accepts a present offered to him is bound to fulfill what is asked of him through that present. That is why when they do not wish to grant what is asked, they return the presents or make others instead.

But to return to my subject. When, before God and with all possible impartiality, I had weighed the reasons that influenced me either to remain among these barbarians or to leave them, I believed that our Lord would be better pleased if I took the opportunity to escape.

The next morning I went to greet the honorable Dutch governor and told him the resolutions I had formed before God. He summoned the men in charge of the ship, told them his intentions, and exhorted them to receive me and to keep me hidden—in a word, to take me back to Europe. They answered that once I had set foot on their vessel, I could be sure that I would not leave it until I reached Bordeaux or La Rochelle. "Well, then," the governor said to me, "return with the savages, and toward evening, or during the night, steal away softly and move toward the river. There you will find a small boat, which I will keep ready to take you secretly to the ship." I very humbly thanked all these gentlemen and then withdrew from the Dutch, so that I could better conceal my intentions.

Toward evening I retired with ten or twelve Iroquois into a barn, where we spent the night. Before lying down, I went out to see in what direction I might most easily escape. The dogs of the Dutch, untied at that time, ran up to me. One of them, large and powerful, threw himself on my bare leg and seriously injured me. Immediately I went back into the barn; the Iroquois closed it securely and, the better to guard me, came to lie down beside me, especially the one who had been charged to watch me. Seeing myself surrounded by those wretched men and the barn wall closed and dogs all around that would surely betray me if I tried to go out, I felt that I could not escape. I complained gently to my God, because, although he had given me the idea of escaping, he had also "shut up my ways with square stones" (Lam 3:9). He had "placed my feet on spacious ground" (Ps 30:9 [31:8]), but now he seemed to be stopping up my exit and impeding my paths. And so I spent a second night without sleeping. When day was dawning, I heard the cocks crow. Soon afterward, a servant of the Dutch farmer who had lodged us in his barn entered it by some door or other. I went up to him softly and made signs to him (for I did not understand his Flemish) that he should keep the dogs from yelping. He went out at once, and I after him, having previously gathered up all my belongings. They were few enough—a Little Office of the Blessed Virgin, a little

Gerson,[3] and a wooden cross I had made for myself to preserve the memory of the sufferings of my Savior. When I was outside the barn, without having made any noise or awakened my guards, I crossed a fence that enclosed the yard around the house, and ran straight to the river where the ship was. This was all the service that my poor leg, severely wounded, could render me. (I had had to run a good quarter of a league to reach the river.) I found the boat as they had said, but because the water had subsided, it was aground. I pushed it to try to get it into the water. I could not do this, because it was too heavy. Then I called to the ship for someone to bring a skiff to ferry me—but nothing happened. I did not know whether or not they had heard me; at all events, no one appeared. Daylight, meanwhile, would soon reveal to the Iroquois that I had stolen their prisoner from them. I feared that they might surprise me in my innocent crime. Worn out with shouting, I returned to the boat and prayed to God to increase my strength. Then I did so well that, by turning it end over end and pushing with all my might, I finally got it into the water. Once it was afloat, I jumped into it and went all alone to the ship, where I climbed aboard without being noticed by any of the Iroquois. The Dutch immediately stowed me down in the hold; and, the better to conceal me, they put a huge chest over the hatchway.

Two days and two nights I was in the belly of the vessel, with such discomfort that I thought I would suffocate and die from the stench. I remembered then poor Jonah, and I prayed that I might not flee "from the face of the Lord"

---

[3] An edition of the *Imitation of Christ*. [Thomas à Kempis is the book's most probable author, but at time when this letter was written, the Imitation of Christ was often attributed to John Gerson.—ED.]

(Jon 1:3), and that I might not separate myself from his will. On the contrary, should my escape not tend to his glory, I prayed that he would overthrow all my plans and detain me in the country of these infidels. The second night of my voluntary imprisonment, the minister[4] of the Dutch came to tell me that the Iroquois had indeed made quite a disturbance and that the Dutch inhabitants of the country were afraid that they would set fire to their houses or kill their cattle. They are justified in fearing these savages, since it is they themselves who provided the excellent muskets handled so expertly by these same savages. I replied, "If the storm has arisen on my account, I am ready to appease it by losing my life."[5] I had not the slightest desire to escape at the expense of even the least man of their settlement.

The furor finally waxed so great that I had to leave my cavern. All the mariners were offended at this, saying that the promise of security had been given me in case I could set foot in the ship and that I was being taken away at the very moment when they would have had to bring me there if I had not already come; that I had put myself in danger of my life by depending on their word for my escape; that their promise must be kept, whatever the cost. I begged them to allow me to leave, since the captain who had planned my escape was asking for me. I found him at his house, where he then kept me concealed. Since all these comings and goings had occurred at night, I was not yet discovered. I could easily have advanced some arguments to defend myself in all this turmoil, but it was not for me to speak in my

---

[4] This Protestant pastor was named Jean Megapolensis. He had come from Holland with his wife and four children. The Dutch Protestants were very kind to Jogues.

[5] Jon 1:12. Jogues continues his meditation on the situation of Jonah.

own cause, but rather to follow the orders of another, to whom I willingly submitted. Finally, the captain told me that it was necessary to yield quietly to the storm, to wait until the minds of the savages should be more calm, and that this was the universal opinion. So there I was, a voluntary prisoner in his house, where I am now writing you this letter. And if you should ask my thoughts about all these adventures, I would tell you:

First, that the ship that had been prepared to save my life sailed without me.

Second, that if Our Lord did not protect me in a manner that was almost miraculous, the savages, who come and go here at every moment, would certainly discover me; and if ever they are convinced that I have not gone away, I will of necessity be turned over to them. If they were so angry at me before my flight, who can imagine what treatment they would now inflict on me, finding me once more in their power? One thing is certain: I would not die an ordinary death. The fire, their rage, the cruelties that they would invent, would snatch my life from me. May God be forever blessed! We are constantly in the bosom of his divine and always adorable providence. "As for yourselves, the very hairs on your head have all been numbered. Away, then, with all fear; you are more precious than whole flocks of sparrows. And yet, not one of them can drop dead to the ground without the consent of your Father" (Mt 10:30–31, 29). He who cares for the birds of the air does not cast us into oblivion. I have been hidden now for twelve days; it is quite improbable that misfortune will reach me.

In the third place, you see the great need that we have of your prayers and of the Holy Sacrifices of all our Fathers; obtain this help for us from all, so that God may make us worthy and well disposed to love him. May he make me strong and courageous to suffer and endure for him; may he give me a generous constancy to persevere in his love and in his service. This is what I should like to have more than anything. Pray for these poor nations who burn and devour one another, that at last they may come to the knowledge of their Creator and render to him the tribute of their love. "I have all of you in my heart ... during my imprisonment" (Phil 1:7). I am, with all my heart and affection, etc.

Renselaerswich, August 30, 1643

AFTER HIS RETURN TO FRANCE

Letter to a Priest

January 5, 1644

After all, my sins have rendered me unworthy to die among the Iroquois. I am still living, and God grant that it may be to mend my ways. I realize it was a great favor for God to permit me to endure something for love of him. I often say with gratitude: "How good it was for me to come to grief, that I may learn what you ordain" (Ps 118 [119]:71).

On November 5 I left the Dutch settlement in a fifty-ton ship that took me to Falmouth in England the day before Christmas. I arrived in Basse-Bretagne, between Brest and Saint-Pol de Léon, on Christmas Day in time to have the blessing of hearing Mass and offering my devotions. A good merchant whom I met took me at his own expense to Rennes, where I arrived today, the eve of Epiphany. What happiness, after having lived so long among savages and having associated so long with Calvinists, Lutherans, Anabaptists, and Puritans, to be at last among the servants of God, in the Holy Catholic Church, and still more, to be among my brothers in the Society of Jesus! This joy is but a slight foretaste of the happiness that will someday be ours in paradise, God willing, when the Lord will gather "the scattered sons of Israel" (Ps 146:2 [147:2]). When will God

---

French text in Thw. 25:64–66.

withdraw his hand from us poor French and our poor savages? "Woe is me, wherefore was I born to see the ruin of my people?" (1 Macc 2:7.) My sins and the infidelities of my past life have made the hand of the divine Majesty very heavy on me and justly angered him against me. I beg you, Reverend Father, to obtain for me, from our Lord, a perfect conversion. May this little chastisement, which he has given me according to his purpose, help me to improve. Is it true that Fathers Raimbault, Dolbeau, and Davost are all dead? They were ready for paradise, and New France has lost in a single year three men who had labored very zealously there. I do not know whether or not a copy of the *Relation* from the Huron country has been received this year. The first copy was captured, along with the Hurons on their way to the French, in the month of June and was returned to me in the country of the Iroquois, with a large package of letters that our Fathers at the Huron missions were sending to France.[1] If I had known that God intended to deliver me, I would have brought it back with me when I went to visit the Dutch. As it was, I left everything in the cabin where I had been staying. I will write at greater length another time; this is all I can manage for the first day of my arrival.

Rennes, January 5, 1644

---

[1] Cf. the letter of Jogues to the governor, June 30, 1643, pp. 244ff.

AFTER HIS RETURN TO FRANCE

Letter to
Father Charles Lalemant

January 6, 1644

"Now I know that the Lord has sent his angel and rescued me from the power of Herod and from all that the Jewish people were expecting" (Acts 12:11). At last I am delivered! Our Lord sent me one of his angels to release me from captivity. The Iroquois had come to the Dutch settlement toward the middle of September and, after making much disturbance, finally accepted some presents from the captain who was sheltering me, to the amount of about three hundred pounds, which I will strive to repay. When all was calm once more, I was sent to Manhattes,[1] to the governor in charge of their whole territory. He received me kindly, gave me a new habit, and then arranged for me to board a ship that crossed the ocean in the middle of winter. We landed in England and there took another boat, a collier, to Basse-Bretagne. I was reminded of you and your arrival at Saint-Sebastien—I was wearing my nightcap on my head and had no other luggage. The only difference was that I was not dripping wet from a second shipwreck.[2]

Text taken from Thw. 25:62. Father Charles Lalemant was in Paris at that time, procurator for the mission in Canada.

[1] New Amsterdam—modern New York.

[2] Reference to the two shipwrecks that Father Charles Lalemant experienced in 1629, when he was trying to bring help to his brothers in Canada.

MISSION TO THE IROQUOIS

*Letter to
Father Jérôme Lalement*

May 2, 1646

Most Reverend and dear Father:

The letter you were kind enough to write to me, Reverend Father, found me engaged in the exercises of my annual retreat, which I began after the departure of the canoe that carried my letter to you. It was a good time for retreat, because the savages were all gone hunting and we have a little silence. Would you believe that when I opened your letter, Reverend Father, at first my heart was seized with fear that what my soul had longed for and prized exceedingly was really going to happen. My poor nature, which remembered all that had gone before, trembled. But our Lord, in his goodness, calmed me, and will calm me still more. Yes, Father, I desire all that our Lord desires, and I desire it at the risk of a thousand lives. Ah, how sorry I would be to lose such a wonderful opportunity, an opportunity in which my ministry might perhaps provide the

---

Taken from the *Manuscrit de 1652*, pp. 108–10. Jogues had just received orders to leave for the Iroquois territory, and he knew these savages well enough to be acquainted with the risk he was taking. He returned, however, a few months later, after his task as ambassador of peace was completed. Father Jérôme Lalement was superior of the Canadian mission at that time; Father Ragueneau had replaced Lalement as head of the Huron mission.

only means of salvation to certain souls. I hope that God's goodness, which has never failed me on former occasions, will still continue to assist me and that he and I, we together, will be able to trample underfoot all the difficulties that beset us. It frightens me to be "in the midst of fallen peoples" alone, without Holy Mass, without Holy Communion, without confession—without sacraments and sacramentals. Nevertheless, God's holy will and his sweet command are well worth that deprivation. He who by his holy grace has preserved us without these aids for eighteen or twenty months[1] will not refuse to continue his favor. We have not thrust ourselves into this position but undertook this work solely and only to please him, undertook it in opposition to all our natural instincts and inclinations. One thing I have noticed about all these comings and goings of the Iroquois is that I see very few from the first two villages, and yet it is with these that we must deal principally, and it was to these two villages that those who were recently slain belonged. Almost the only ones to come were from the third village, the one where Couture was held. They say that ordinarily they do not make war in these territories. It is not among these latter that we shall have to live, but among the first, those whom we do not see here at all. I thank you, Reverend Father, very sincerely for sending me the Ten Commandments in Huron. Please send the other teaching materials when you can. It is principally prayers, formulae for confession, and other instructional items of that sort that I need. I who am now your debtor on many grounds will be still more indebted to you for your kindness. I have not forgotten about the

---

[1] It was really a matter of sixteen months, since Jogues, taken in August 1642, was in France for Christmas 1643.

account of the capture and death of our good René Goupil, which I should have sent you long ago, Reverend Father. If those who are to take these letters can wait until I write it, I shall send it with this one.[2] If God wills me to go to the Iroquois, my companion should be virtuous, docile, courageous, one who is willing to suffer anything for God. I would like someone who can make and handle canoes, so that we can go and come without depending on the savages. Will you again be so kind, Reverend Father, as to remember me to all our Fathers.

Your very humble and obedient servant,

Isaac Jogues

Montreal, May 2, 1646

---

[2] This sentence makes it possible to date the account of the death of René Goupil.

MARTYRDOM OF RENÉ GOUPIL
BY THE IROQUOIS

René Goupil was a native of Anjou who, in the bright promise of his youth, had urgently requested to be received into our novitiate at Paris. He remained there some months and gave much edification. Ill health deprived him of the happiness of consecrating himself to God in holy religion—despite a strong desire to do so. When his health improved, he went to New France to serve the Society there, since he had not had the blessing of giving himself to it in Old France. And, so as to do nothing in his own right—although he was fully his own master—he submitted totally to the guidance of the superior of the mission. He was employed for two years in the menial duties of the house, which he performed with great humility and charity. He was also assigned to caring for the sick and the wounded at the hospital and tended them very skillfully. His natural aptitude for the art of healing was joined to a supernatural affection and love; he saw Our Lord in the person of his patients. He left so sweet a remembrance of his goodness and his other virtues in this region that his memory is still held in benediction.

When we came down from the Hurons in July 1642, we asked Reverend Father Vimont to let us take him with us, because the Hurons had great need of a doctor. He granted our request.

Title and text, *Le Martyre de René Goupil par les Iroquois*, taken from the *Manuscrit*, pp. 289–301. For the date of writing of this account, see p. 310 note 2. Many of the facts contained here had already been given in the letter of August 5, 1643 (pp. 247–93).

I cannot express the joy this good young man felt when the superior told him that he might make the journey. He knew well the dangers that threatened those who traveled on the river; he knew equally well how intensely the Iroquois were enraged against the French. Yet no fear of these perils prevented him from submitting to the least indication of the will of him to whom he had voluntarily committed all his concerns. With ready obedience, he set forth with us for Three Rivers.

We left Three Rivers on the first of August, the day after the feast of our holy Father Saint Ignatius. On the second, we met the enemy, who, separated into two bands, were awaiting us with the advantages of superior numbers and attacking from the land. We were not only separated in our scattered, flimsy birch-bark canoes, but we were also in danger of overturning into the water.

Almost all the Hurons had fled panic-stricken into the woods, leaving us alone and unprotected. Immediately we were seized. It was then that Goupil manifested his unusual virtue. As soon as he realized that we were prisoners, he said to me: "Oh, my dear Father, God be blessed! He has permitted this; he has willed it—may his holy will be done! I love it, I desire it, I cherish it, I embrace it with all my heart!" In the meantime, while the enemy were still pursuing the fugitives, I heard his confession and gave him absolution, not knowing what might happen to us as a result of our capture. When our attackers returned from the chase, they fell upon us like mad dogs, with sharp teeth, tearing out our nails and crushing our fingers. He endured all this pain with patience and courage.

His presence of mind in so grievous a situation was particularly apparent in this, that he aided me wherever he could, despite his own intense pain, in the instruction of the Huron captives who were not Christians. I was engaged in preparing them individually, just as they came. René, however, called my attention to a poor old man named Ondouterraon, who would probably be among those whom the savages would kill on the spot, since it was their custom always to sacrifice someone to the heat of their fury. While the enemy was engaged in dividing the plunder from our twelve canoes, I took advantage of their preoccupation to instruct the old man unhurriedly. The spoils were great, because our canoes had been laden with supplies for our Fathers who were working among the Hurons. I had just finished washing the soul of the poor old man in the waters of holy baptism when the savages killed him—depriving him of the life of the body almost at the same instant that he gained the life of his soul. There was one consolation that we both appreciated, namely, that we would be together in this fearsome journey into the enemies' country. For me, it was an opportunity to witness many virtues.

While we were on our way, he was continually occupied with God. His words and his conversations were all expressive of submission to the dispensations of divine Providence and the willing acceptance of the death that God was sending him. He offered himself to him as a holocaust, to be reduced to ashes by the fires of the Iroquois that his heavenly Father would kindle. He sought to please him in everything everywhere. One day he said to me—it was soon after our capture, while we were still on our way to the Iroquois village—"Father, God has always given me a great desire to consecrate myself to his holy service by the vows of religion in his holy Society. My sins have made me unworthy of this grace up until now. Nevertheless, I hope that our Lord will be pleased with the offering I now wish to make him, by taking as best I can the vows of the Society of

Jesus in the presence of my God and before you." I happily granted this request, and he pronounced his vows with great devotion.

Covered with wounds as he was, he carefully dressed those of the other prisoners, nor did he neglect any of the enemy who had received some wound in the fight. He opened a vein for a sick Iroquois with as much charity as if he were serving his best friend.

His humility and the obedience he showed to those who had captured us amazed me. The Iroquois who were taking us both in their canoe told me that I must help paddle. I would do nothing of the kind, being proud even in death. A little later they gave the same command to René, and immediately he began to paddle. These barbarians tried once more, by the force of his example, to drive me to take up the paddle. When he saw how they were using him as a model for me, he asked my pardon. The liberty the savages granted us on the way offered sufficient opportunity for him to escape, and from time to time, I urged him to profit by it. As for myself, I felt I could not leave the French and the twenty-four or twenty-five Hurons who had been captured. He rejected my proposals, however, because our Lord had not thus inspired him, and he committed himself in all things to the divine will.

While we were on the lake, we met two hundred Iroquois who had come to Richelieu when the French were beginning to build the fort. These savages heaped blows on us, covered us with blood, and exhibited the furious rage of those who are possessed by the devil. All these outrages and cruelties René endured with remarkable patience and a Christlike charity toward those who ill-treated him.

When we entered the first village, where we were treated so cruelly, he showed an extraordinary patience and gentleness. He had fallen under the shower of blows from clubs and iron rods with which they attacked us, and unable to rise again by his own strength, he was carried half-dead to the center of the village and placed on the platform to which we others had already been taken. He was in so pitiful a condition that he would have inspired compassion in cruelty itself. He was all bruised from the blows, and in his face nothing but the whites of his eyes could be distinguished. But the more disfigured he was, that much more beautiful was he in the sight of angels and men and that much more like to him of whom it is said: "We saw him, as it were a leper, in whom there was no beauty nor comeliness."

We had all hardly recovered our breath when our tormentors gave him three blows on his shoulders with a heavy club, as they had done to us once before. They cut off my thumb, since I seemed to be some sort of leader, then they turned to him and cut off his right thumb at the first joint. During this torment, he murmured incessantly, "Jesus! Mary! Joseph!" During the six days that we were exposed to all those who wished to do us some harm, he showed an admirable gentleness; he had his whole chest burned by the coals and hot cinders that the young boys threw upon our bodies at night when we were bound flat on the ground. Nature furnished me with more ability to avoid some of these pains than she gave to him.

After the savages had decided to let us live, even though shortly before, they had warned us to prepare to be burned, he fell sick, suffering great inconvenience in every respect and especially from the food, to which he had never become accustomed. In that, one might truly say, "The sick man needs no food." I could not care for him, for I, too, was very sick, and none of my fingers was sound or entire.

I must hasten now to describe his death, which lacked no detail of that of a martyr.

We had been in the enemy country for six weeks. There was much confusion in the councils of the Iroquois, because some of the chiefs were quite willing that we should be taken back to our people, but others were very much opposed to it. This disagreement caused us to lose hope—I had never really had much—of seeing Three Rivers again that year. We consoled each other in regard to the divine arrangement of our affairs and prepared ourselves for whatever God might ordain for us. René did not quite realize how great our danger really was. I saw it better than he, and I often exhorted him to be ready for anything.

One day, then, we went out of the village to obtain a little solace for our stricken souls and to pray more suitably and with less disturbance. Two young men came after us to tell us that we must return to the house. I had some premonition of what was going to happen and said to him, "My dearest brother, let us commend ourselves to Our Lord and to our good Mother, Mary. I think these people have some evil plan." We had offered ourselves to our Lord shortly before with much love, beseeching him to receive our lives and our blood and to unite them with his life and his Blood for the salvation of these poor natives. Accordingly, we returned to the village, reciting our rosary, of which we had already said four decades. We stopped near the gate of the village to see what they might say to us. One of the two young Iroquois then drew out a hatchet that he had concealed under his blanket and struck René, who was in front of him. He fell motionless, his face to the ground, pronouncing the holy name of Jesus. (We had often admonished each other to let his holy name end our voices and our lives.) At the blow, I turned around and saw the bloody hatchet. I knelt down to receive the blow that would unite me to my dear companion, but, as they hesitated, I rose again and ran to the dying man, who was not far from me. They then struck him two other blows on the head with the hatchet, which killed him, but not before I had given him absolution, as I had been accustomed to do every other day after his confession.

It was September 29, the Feast of Saint Michael, when this angel in innocence and this martyr of Jesus Christ gave his life for him who had given him his. They ordered me to return to my cabin, where I expected for the rest of that day and all of the next the same treatment. Indeed, all the savages had the same thought, now that the affair was started. Several times they came to kill me, but our Lord did not permit this, preventing it in ways it would take too long to explain here. The third day, however, I went out to find where they had thrown that blessed body, for I wished to bury it at any cost whatever. A few of the Iroquois who had some desire to help me said: "You have no sense! Don't you see that they are trying to kill you, too, and still you go out. You are looking for a body that is already half-decayed, a body they have dragged far from here. Don't you see those young men who will kill you once you are outside the stockade?" But their words did not stop me, and Our Lord gave me courage enough to wish to die in this act of charity. I went out; I sought; and, with the help of an Algonquin—formerly a captive but now a true Iroquois—I found him. The children had stripped him and had dragged him, with a rope around his neck, to a torrent that flows at the foot of their village. The dogs had already eaten a part of his loins. I could not restrain my tears at this sight. I took the body, and with the Algonquin helping me, I put it beneath the surface of the water, weighted it down with large stones, and tried to conceal it so that no one would find it. I intended to come back the next day with a pickax when no one was about, in order to dig a grave for the body. I thought that the corpse was well concealed, but perhaps someone saw us—particularly some of the youths—and withdrew it.

The next day, as they were still seeking to kill me, my aunt sent me out to her field, to escape them, I think. This caused me to delay until the following day. It had rained all night, so the torrent was unusually swollen. I borrowed a pickax from another cabin so as to conceal my purpose, but when I came near the place where I had arranged my stones, I could not find my blessed deposit. I went into the water, already very cold; I went up and down the stream, sounding it with my foot, to see if perhaps the water had dislodged and carried the body downstream. I found nothing. How many tears I shed! How many hot tears of mine mingled with the torrent rushing at my feet! I chanted, as well as I could, the psalms that Holy Church is accustomed to recite for the dead.

After all my trouble, I found nothing. A woman I knew passed there and saw me in pain. She told me when I asked her if she knew what they had done with him that they had dragged him to another river nearby, one about a quarter of a league from there, with which I was not familiar. That report was false. The young men had taken away the body and dragged it into a little woods near there, where during the fall and winter the dogs, the crows, and the foxes had fed upon it. In the spring, when they told me that was the place to which they had dragged him, I went out several times without finding anything. At last, the fourth time, I found the head and some half-gnawed bones, which I buried with the intention of taking them with me if ever I should be taken back to Three Rivers, as the savages sometimes spoke of doing. I kissed the relics very devoutly several times, as the bones of a martyr for Jesus Christ.

I gave him this title not only because he was killed by the enemies of God and his Church and had placed himself, in the exercise of an ardent charity toward his neighbor, in evident peril for the love of God, but especially because he was killed on account of prayer and for having made the sign of the cross.

He had been in a cabin where he nearly always said some prayers. This did not please a superstitious old man who lived there. One day there was also a little child about three or four years old in the cabin. With an excess of devotion and love of the cross, and with a simplicity that we who are more prudent than he, according to the flesh, would not have shown, he took off his cap, placed it on the child's head, and made a large Sign of the Cross on the small body. When the old Indian saw that, he commanded a young man of his cabin, who was about to set out for war, to kill René. The young man did so, as we have said.

Even the child's mother, when I happened to be near her on a journey one time, told me that it was because of this Sign of the Cross that my dear companion had been killed. On another occasion, the old man invited me to his cabin for a meal. I said my grace before meals, making the usual Sign of the Cross. When the old man saw this, he said to me, "That is what we hate; that is why your companion was killed and why you, too, will be put to death. Our neighbors, the Europeans, do not do this." Sometimes, also, when I would be praying on my knees while out on the hunt, the Indians would tell me that they hated this custom; that because of it they had killed the other Frenchman; that for this same reason they would also kill me when we came back to the village.

I ask your pardon, Reverend Father, for the haste with which I have written this account and for the want of respect that such speed connotes. Please forgive me; I was afraid, though, that I should miss this opportunity of discharging a duty that I should have performed long ago.[1]

---

[1] Thw. 28:116–34 also has a copy of this letter. The last paragraph is not contained in the *Manuscrit*, possibly in an effort to remove the effect of a letter.

NEW HOLLAND

New Holland, which the Dutch call in Latin *Novum Belgium* and in their own language *Nieuw Nederland*, that is, New Netherlands, is situated between Virginia and New England. The entrance to the river, which some call the Nassau and others the Great North River, to distinguish it from the South River (and on some maps I have seen recently, it is called the Maurice River), is in the latitude of forty degrees, thirty minutes. Its channel is deep and navigable by the largest ships, which go up as far as Manhattes Island. There is a fort on this island—which has a circumference of only seven leagues—that was built as the nucleus of a town that is to be called New Amsterdam.

This fort, located at the point of the island about five or six leagues from the mouth of the river, is called Fort Amsterdam. It has four regular bastions, each having several pieces of artillery. In 1643 all these bastions and their pavilions were merely earthworks, most of which had collapsed, making it possible to enter the fort from all sides. There were no trenches around it. It was manned only by about sixty soldiers who were to defend this fort and another, built farther inland, against the raids of the savages. When I was there, they were beginning to reinforce the gates and the bastions with stone. Inside the fort there was a church, built of stone and quite spacious; the house of the governor, whom they call the director general, a very neatly built residence

---

The original of the account of New Holland is found at the Collège Sainte-Marie in Montreal. Father Jogues spent a few weeks at New Amsterdam in November 1643, before he returned to France. The text is included here merely to make the writings of Jogues complete.

made from brick that was fashioned locally; and the storehouses and soldiers' quarters.

On the Island of Manhattes and in its environs, there are about four or five hundred men of various sects and nations. The director general told me that eighteen different languages were spoken there. The inhabitants of the island are scattered here and there, up and down the stream, according as the beauty or convenience of the sites invited each one to settle. Some of the artisans, however, who work at their trades live inside the fort; all the others, though, are exposed to the sorties of the savages, who, in 1643, during my visit, had actually killed about forty Hollanders and burned many houses and barns filled with grain.

The river, very straight and flowing from north to south, is at least a league wide in front of the fort. Ships anchor in a bay on the other side of the island and can be defended by the fort.

Shortly before my arrival, three large ships, each able to hold a cargo of three hundred tons, had come to load wheat. Two received their full lading, but the third could not be filled because the savages had burned a portion of the grain. These ships had come from the West Indies, where the West India Company usually maintains seventeen war vessels.

No exercise of religion except Calvinism is permitted there according to their laws. However, these laws are not enforced, for besides the Calvinists, there are Catholics, English Puritans, Lutherans, Anabaptists (whom they call Mnistes),[1] and many others living in the settlement.

Whenever a newcomer arrives to settle here, the islanders furnish him horses, cows, and other livestock. They also

---

[1] Abbreviation for Mennonite.

provide him with food. He repays this aid when he is well settled. To pay for his land, he gives to the West India Company at the end of ten years one tenth of the products he has harvested.

This region is bounded on the New England side by the Fresh River, which separates the Dutch from the English. The English live very closely to the Dutch, however, preferring to have their lands among these latter, who require nothing from them, rather than depending on the English "milords", who exact rents and like to put on airs as esquires. On the other side, toward Virginia, the island is bounded by the South River, on which there is also a Dutch settlement. At the entrance of this river, the Swedes also have a settlement, extremely well equipped with cannons and people. It is thought that these Swedes are maintained by merchants in Amsterdam, annoyed because the West India Company monopolizes all the trade in these regions. It is said that a gold mine has been discovered near this river.

You can find out more about all of this in the book of the Sieur de Laet, of Antwerp, which contains a table and an account of New Belgium, as he sometimes calls it; or also by looking at the great map of Nova Anglia, Novum Belgium, and Virginia.

The Dutch have lived in these regions for a full fifty years. The fort was begun in 1615. About twenty years ago, they began to develop the settlement, and at the present time they have quite a bit of trade with Virginia and New England.

The pioneers found the lands already prepared for use. The savages had cleared the fields in former times and had begun to raise crops there. Later settlers made clearings in the woods, which abound in oak trees; the soil is rich and fertile. Deer are abundant toward autumn. Some of the dwellings here are of stone, with mortar made from crushed oyster shells, great heaps of which are found near here. They were piled up by the savages, who supply part of their diet with these fish.

The climate is very mild because the region is situated at forty and two-thirds degrees. There are plenty of European fruits—apples, pears, cherries. When I arrived here in October, I still found peaches in great abundance.

Up the river, at about the forty-third degree, the second Dutch settlement is located. Ships of 100 and 120 tons can anchor there, but no farther.

There are two items of interest in this settlement, which is called Renselaerswich—that is, the "settlement of Renselaers"—named from a wealthy merchant of Amsterdam. First, there is a wretched little fort, called Fort Orange, built of logs and having four or five pieces of Breteuil cannon and as many swivel guns. This fort is reserved for and maintained by the West India Company. Formerly it was located on an island formed by the river; now it is on the mainland, on the side of the Iroquois, a little above the aforementioned island. Second, there is the colony sent by the merchant Renselaers, who also acts as its patron. This colony is composed of about a hundred persons living in about twenty-five or thirty houses built along the river, according to their preferences. In the principal house, the patron's representative lives; the minister has his own house, where he conducts his religious services. There is also a sort of bailiff, called a seneschal, who is in charge of administering justice. These are all frame houses with thatched roofs. There is no masonry here as yet, except for the chimneys.

The forests supply many stout pine trees, from which the people make boards at their sawmill.

There are also some suitable fields, which the savages formerly tilled, where the settlers now plant corn and oats for their beer and for their horses, which they raise in great numbers. The fields fit to be tilled, however, are very few because they are restricted by the coasts and the soil is poor. For this reason, the families are widely separated, each one holding about two or three leagues of land.

Trade is open to everyone. The Dutch compete with each other, everyone being satisfied to gain some little profit. For this reason, the savages obtain their supplies very cheaply.

This settlement is not more than twenty leagues from the Agniehronons. They can be approached either by land or by water because the river on which the Iroquois dwell empties into the one that flows past the Dutch. There are, however, many shallow rapids and a waterfall of a short half-league that necessitates a portage.

There are several Indian nations between the two Dutch settlements, which are about thirty German leagues apart—that is, fifty or sixty French leagues. The Wolves, whom the Iroquois call Agotsaganens, are the closest to the settlement of Renselaerswich, or to Fort Orange. Several years ago, when there was war between the Iroquois and the Wolves, the Dutch allied themselves with the latter against the former; but after four of them had been captured and burned, peace was made. Later, because some tribes near the sea killed several of the Dutch in the more remote settlement, these retaliated by killing about 150 savages—not only men, but also women and little children. The savages, in various reprisals, then killed forty of the Dutch, burned many houses, and wrought damage reckoned at the time I was there at about two hundred thousand pounds. Troops were levied in New England. At the beginning of winter, when the grass was short and there was a little snow on the ground, six hundred men pursued the savages, two hundred of them being always on the march and one set continually relieving the other. The result was that since the savages were besieged on a great island and unable to flee easily because of the women and children, there were as many as sixteen hundred of them killed. This forced the remainder of the Indians to make peace—a peace that still continues. That occurred in 1643 and 1644.

Three Rivers, in New France, August 3, 1646

FINAL DEPARTURE

Letter to Father Castillon

September 12, 1646

Reverend and dear Father:

Pax Christi!

I received your letter, Reverend Father, asking us to give you some information about New France and especially something about me in particular.

In the middle of May, I left Three Rivers accompanied by Monsieur Bourdon, an engineer here in New France, to take a trip to the Iroquois country. We returned in good health early in July. Our honorable governor was very glad for him to accompany me so that he might become acquainted with the region. We made a fairly accurate map of the territory and were well received both by the Dutch, through whose lands we had to pass, and by the savages. The leading Europeans were not there; they had gone to the other settlement, near the sea, which is the chief trading center. We did not lack exercise on this trip, either on water or on land. We made at least one hundred leagues on foot and were usually well laden. In the village where we stayed a few days, I

French text forwarded by Father Lucien Campeau; made from the original copy in the archives of the Lyons province of the Society of Jesus, Paray-le-Monial, coll. Prat, ancienne Compagnie, tome 44, pp. 569–72, f. 233–34. Father Castillon was provincial in France.

baptized some sick children, who, I believe, are now with God. I heard the confessions of some of the Huron Christians who were there, and we exchanged presents with the Iroquois chiefs. I am making preparations to return there to spend the winter, and, unless I die there, shall return next June. The question is now under discussion at Three Rivers; the leaders think that if I do not go now, I shall certainly do so in early spring, with the help of God. But I see that considerable preparations are being made for an early departure, to which our Reverend Father superior is quite favorably disposed. It is only my own cowardice and wretchedness that present powerful obstacles to the plans God has for me and this country. Beg him, Reverend Father, to make of me what he desires, that I may be a man after his own heart. May the Lord give me "largeness of heart as the sand that is on the seashore" (see 3 Kings 4:29 [1 Kings 4:29]). May he widen my poor heart, which is so narrow; and may I, through my past experiences and the abundance of his goodness and mercy toward me, learn to rely wholly on him. I am certain that he will not withdraw or let me fall when I cast myself lovingly into the arms of his divine, paternal providence. Our Lord has granted us the beautiful gift of peace; pray that he who in his divine goodness bestowed this favor may prolong it, because that is the only condition in which we can hope for success. This peace and the trade in which the country now engages cause a noticeable change in its appearance, an increase in the number of inhabitants, and greater comfort in all respects. The country no longer seems as rough as before; we know, too, that it can produce good wheat and other necessities of life—especially this locality of Montreal, where we are, a climate much milder and more temperate than Quebec because it is in a middle latitude, namely, that of forty-five degrees.

More than eighty Huron canoes have just come down the river, bringing a large number of pelts. This promises to be a year better than last, although it, too, was very good. I do not know whether or not the gentlemen of the colony will take note of this. They could scarcely furnish the shipping when they had the trade. It is fortunate for us that God has given peace along with this change, which is of great advantage to the country. God grant that it may grow in spiritual blessings even more than in temporal, and if "he has magnified the land, may he also magnify its joy" (cf. Is 9:2). May he especially bestow the unction of his Holy Spirit upon those who labor for the spiritual interests of these nations. It is for this that I beg you, Reverend Father, to entreat Our Lord, and at the altar to be particularly mindful of a poor priest who is about to be deprived of Holy Mass for eight or nine months. This will increase more than ever my obligations to you, Reverend Father.

Your very humble and obedient servant in God,

Isaac Jogues

Montreal, September 12, 1646

I shall leave in two or three days for the trip to the Iroquois and will spend the winter there. Still, for life, all in Our Lord!

Three Rivers, September 25

FINAL DEPARTURE

Letter to a Fellow Jesuit

September 1646

Alas! Dear Father, when shall I begin to serve and to love him whose love for us had no beginning? When shall I begin to give myself completely to him who has given himself to me without reserve? Although I am extremely wretched and have made bad use of the graces that Our Lord has given me in this country, still I do not lose courage. He takes the trouble to help me do better; he still furnishes me with new opportunities for dying to myself and uniting myself inseparably to him.

The Iroquois have come to offer presents to our governor, to ransom some prisoners he was holding, and to sue for peace on behalf of the whole country. The treaty has been concluded, to the great satisfaction of the French; the peace will last as long as Our Lord shall please. It is thought necessary to send a priest among the Iroquois in order to preserve the new concord and to learn quietly what can be done for the instruction of the savages. I have reason to believe that I shall be sent, because I have some slight knowledge of the country.

French text in Thw. 31:110–12. Jogues is really making his last farewells; he was massacred on October 18.

Do you see how much I need the powerful aid of your prayers in the midst of those barbarians? I shall have to live among them almost without any liberty to pray—without Mass, without the sacraments. I shall be held responsible for any and all incidents between the Iroquois and the French, the Algonquins, and the Hurons.

But what of it? My hope is in God, who really has no need of us for the accomplishment of his designs. All we need do is try to be faithful to him and not spoil his work by our own weaknesses.

I hope that you will obtain for me this favor from Our Lord and also, that after having led so slothful a life until now, I may begin to serve him better.

My heart tells me that if I have the blessing of being sent on this mission, *Ibo et non redibo*: I shall go and shall not return. I shall be happy if Our Lord wills to finish the sacrifice where he began it. May the little blood that I shed in that land be a pledge of what I am willing to give him from all the veins of my body and from my heart. Indeed, that nation is as "a spouse of blood to me" (Ex 4:25). May our good Master, who has acquired that nation by his Blood, open to it, if he will, the door of his Gospel, as well as to the other four nations, its allies and neighbors. Farewell, dear Father; beg God to unite me inseparably to him.

SAINT CHARLES GARNIER

FATHER GARNIER MAKES A SENECA DICTIONARY

INTRODUCTION

According to the testimony of Father Ragueneau, Charles Garnier "entered so deeply into the hearts of his companions, and with so great eloquence, that all who knew him were delighted with him".[1] However, we are hardly enraptured when we read the letters he wrote to his superiors and to his family;[2] if he found his way easily into the hearts of all who met him, we, in turn, have much more difficulty in penetrating his. The last of the Jesuit martyrs of New France is indeed the least colorful. He does not have the burning tenderness of Jogues or the Olympian majesty of Brébeuf. And if we compare him with the others, we do not find, either, the decisive traits that bestow any human qualities upon him: the deep humor of Le Jeune, the whirlwind nature of Massé, the childlike intensity of Chaumonot, the sprightliness and joviality of his friend Chastelain. He is a saint, they say. Yes, but what sort of a saint?

Garnier was born in Paris on May 25, 1606. When he was still quite young, his mother died, and he and his two brothers were reared by his father, undersecretary to the king, and later chief collector of revenues in Normandy.

---

[1] *Manuscrit de 1652*, p. 254.

[2] The letters Garnier wrote to Marie de l'Incarnation are all lost. Father Le Jeune had established communications between the two in 1637. Chastelain and Garnier seem to have been especially concerned with the history of the mission. Cf. Marie de l'Incarnation, *Écrits*, pp. 100–101, 108. The letters reproduced here are taken from the *Rapport de l'archiviste de la Province de Quebec*, 1929–30. Father Florian Larivière published two letters in the *Lettres du Bas-Canada*, June 1949, pp. 28–33.

After Garnier finished his studies at the Collège de Clermont, he entered the novitiate in 1624. Here he was a fellow student of Pierre Chastelain and later of Vincent Juby and Blessed Julien Maunoir, the two future apostles of Brittany. After he finished his philosophical studies, he taught grammar for three years at Eu, a small town near the coasts of the English Channel. In 1632 he returned to Paris to study theology. Here he was reunited with Chastelain, and the following year, Jogues joined the group. In 1636 all three of them left for Quebec, and they began their apostolic work among the Hurons toward the end of the summer.

Charles Garnier often went to the Petuns in his missionary work, a tribe located south of the Huron country. Here he was killed on December 7, 1649, by a musket shot of the Iroquois, who had come to pillage the region.

Of the writings of Saint Charles Garnier, we have only some letters[3] to his superiors, and a few others to his father or his brothers. He has not left us any spiritual notes in which he revealed himself before the eyes of God alone. However, the language of his letters is very explicit, and he speaks in them almost constantly of himself and of his apostolic and spiritual experiences. Therefore, we can attempt to extract from these texts a few traits of spiritual appearance.

One thing is immediately striking: the importance of his family, and especially of his father, throughout the whole history of his religious life. Jean Garnier had at first refused to see his son enter the novitiate, for he had cherished completely different ambitions for this gifted son

---

[3] Father Florian Larivière gives the complete list of Garnier's correspondence in *La vie ardente de saint Charles Garnier*, pp. 30–31. The book also includes all historical and bibliographical information one could wish.

of his.[4] "He had had great difficulties in obtaining permission from his father to enter our Society" (*MS de 1652*, p. 252), wrote Father Ragueneau. He continued:

> But they were much greater when, ten years after his first separation, he had to accept an even more painful one, which was his departure from France to come to these missions at the end of the world. Our superiors had desired that his father should give his consent because of the obligations our Society owed to him, and for this reason, his trip was delayed for a whole year. This postponement served only to inflame his desires. (*MS de 1652*, p. 252)

We must not underestimate these facts in our attempt to understand the psychology of Saint Charles Garnier. Because of the early death of his mother, all the affection and all the authority of his father was directed toward these sons, who sought to free themselves of this domination. It is quite possible that the missionary vocation of Charles had deep roots in these circumstances, and when Ragueneau affirms that he obtained the paternal permission "with so much joy in his heart that he considered that the happiest day of his life" (*MS de 1652*, p. 253), it is not at all difficult to think that his spiritual happiness bore immeasurable psychological echoes. The "obligations" of the Society in regard to this domineering parent could have served only to complicate the problems of the son.

In the letters of Garnier, we find more than one indication of a still very lively aggressiveness that conceals from his own eyes a sincere affection and a great respect for his father. He has, for example, an unseasonable wish to see his

---

[4] There are many proofs that he learned languages with an extraordinary facility.

father become a monk. "I would like", he wrote to his Carmelite brother, "for him to stop and consider the vanity of the world but to do it in a way different from what he usually does. Although he often says that he holds the world in disdain, nevertheless, in practice, he does not show that he scorns the opinions of the world and the discourses of men, being more concerned, perhaps, in the practice of pleasing the worms of the earth than God."[5]

These are, certainly, very excellent sentiments, but they hardly take into consideration the concrete facts of life, especially the life of a man of the court. In view of the fact that all three of Jean Garnier's sons became religious—the eldest only after a rather stormy life—it is possible to suspect a certain lack of understanding of this father for the psychology of his children. It is obvious also that he was a very good Christian. The words Charles Garnier wrote to his brother do not conceal, in spite of himself, a desire to assume an ascendancy on the religious plane over the man he could not dominate on the secular level.

Even later, when Charles Garnier was actually working in Canada, this opposition to his father and the need of throwing off the paternal yoke were not absent. He wrote to his father, probably in 1638:

> I see that you are afraid I am suffering much inconvenience and discomfort here. Let me assure you that I have never enjoyed such good health as I do here. When I was in France, there was hardly a year when I did not suffer from a cold, catarrh, or some such ailment; I assure you that, since I assured you of my good health in my last letter, I have not

---

[5] *Rapport de l'archiviste*, p. 8. This whole letter describes an austere program that the Carmelite tried to impose on his father.

had any illness, neither a cold nor catarrh. So do you not think it foolish for those poor sons of this earth to treat their bodies so delicately and to go to so much trouble for their physical comfort? Alas! How miserably wretched they are, those who offend God by their inordinate care of the body, to the extent of killing those poor men who could live from their superfluities! These worldlings put on masses of flesh that do nothing but bring them to a sickbed, full of pain and suffering. And the worst is that, after all this suffering, they find themselves in Hell after death. Will some of my good friends, and even my close relatives, find themselves in this group? Please God, no!

We detect in these pages an irritation at seeing his father exercise a too-maternal solicitude toward a son who has become a man. And this irritation soon becomes, under the pen of the saint, a deliberate attack against those whom his father considers "real men", those "poor sons of the world" with whom he associates in his daily life and whose practices he imitates only too closely. And to be sure that his father understands his danger, the saint does not mince his words: "Will some of my friends and even my close relatives be among their number?" There can be no doubt, this time, that the blow was felt and that the irony of the moralist hit the very center of his target—the heart of his father.

In this same vein, we cannot pass over, in our attempts to understand the psychology of Charles Garnier, the fact that he was beardless. In Europe, this condition was considered a serious defect, but the Indians admired it as a most beautiful ornament. We have seen from the account of Jogues how greatly the savages detested those who were bald and those who were bearded—and how he suffered from both conditions. In this reversal of situations from one continent to another, Charles Garnier took a special delight in writing to his father: "I surely have one advantage in having left France, where you always twitted me because I had no beard. This is the big reason for my appeal to these savages" (*Rapport de l'archiviste*, p. 16). He certainly could not express himself more explicitly.

Thus, in regard to his relations with his father, Charles thinks that he has profited by separating himself from him in order to avoid a picayune, pricking attack—a useless and mortifying attack, capable of damaging very deeply the sensitive psyche of a child. But now the child is able to conquer his antagonist on his own plane and to ridicule his judgment. What is ugly on one side of the ocean became beauty on the other. What, then, is the value of the opinion of men, who contradict each other on points that seem to them to be fundamental and basic! I accept your challenge from here on, and it is I who will emerge as victor! Charles Garnier feels the need of writing to his father and insisting almost too much on his new advantage; we are almost tempted to say that he is seeking revenge.

There is no doubt that this child's psyche had been damaged, perhaps seriously, by this struggle in the bosom of his family. Under the guise of goodness, there was the iron hand—sometimes even without the proverbial velvet glove. We find the same unwarranted insistences on his new superiority in the letters to Charles' brothers. He was a man whose health had never been robust, frail even in his appearance, accused of not even being a man, and this by his own father—all of these psychological forces combined to make him desire to prove his virility. This was the same manliness that Brébeuf, who really and truly possessed it, could afford to hide. But these same psychological forces drove Garnier to show himself in his apostolate as a man who could face all sorts of difficulties. Father Ragueneau, that excellent connoisseur of souls, wrote of him:

> During the ravages of contagious diseases, which closed all the rest of us up tight in our cabins and as a result of which the savages spoke of nothing but putting us to death, he boldly went out among them if he thought there was a soul to be saved for Heaven. In his excess of zeal and his industry in works of charity, he found means of opening before himself all the roads that were ordinarily closed against him, to overcome all obstacles, sometimes *with violence* (MS de 1652, p. 259).

This is a very significant trait in the character of Charles Garnier. It was not the easy things that interested him, not the humble works and the hidden life, such as haunted Jean de Brébeuf; nor was it, like Jogues, the voices of his dear friends that call out to him and tempt him to forget the others. The whole temperament of Garnier, as a sort of compensation, seeks the showy, the heroic, and forces him to confront the impossible. This temptation to choose for himself the most agonizing of difficulties, simply because they are difficult, prevented him from seeking virtue for its own sake.

All this serves to explain, on the one hand, the fact that Garnier has always been considered a saint, that the heroism of the virtues he acquired through his courage is very evident; but on the other hand, his very sanctity seems dull when compared to that of his companions. He received, unquestionably, great favors from God; he was comforted, as his letters reveal, by those consolations that the Holy Spirit pours out on the souls of those who are suffering for the Kingdom; however, the characteristic contemplative aspect of the spiritual life—union with God consciously sought—is notably lacking in him. When we read the texts of his friend Pierre Chastelain, who also gives us very few direct confidences, we are, nevertheless, aware of a perpetual freshness, a spontaneity, an exhilaration in his love. On the contrary, the emotional nature of Charles Garnier always remains more or less inhibited, incapable of soaring aloft, even in his relationships with God.

Because on the human plane, facility was difficult for him, he transferred this same withdrawal to the divine life within him and remained more attentive to the conditions demanded for union with God rather than to that union itself. As a result of this, his actions frequently assume an aspect of willfulness, perhaps even a little strained, without his being able to reach that spiritual spontaneity so manifest in the others. "I must make a special effort to convince myself of the love of God," he wrote to his brother, "to tell you that God loves us and will continue to love us, regardless of the road by which he leads us" (*Rapport de l'archiviste*, p. 13). Jogues, for his part, found himself flooded with the love of God during the anguish of his captivity; it was never necessary for him to force himself to love.

Perhaps we may be accused of insisting too much on the aspects of the psychology of Garnier at the risk of tarnishing his portrait. But why should we avoid facing facts? Why should we be afraid to show that a warped personality is not a handicap to God's developing high sanctity in a man? The attraction that the saints have for us does not spring from their native endowments but from the triumph they achieve in Jesus Christ—or, rather, the success that Christ accomplishes in them. We are interested in the mysterious, supereminent manner by which the divine Teacher changes weakness to strength and transforms the wretchedness of humanity into glory. What the Holy Spirit silenced in Garnier was the infernal logic of his emotional constitution;

what it arrested in him was a destructive influence of familial mundane importance and thus gave him a new start. Even his vocation to the missions has its psychological roots in flight from his father. This does not mean, however, that he did not have a true missionary vocation from God. If he had not, he would not have been the happiest of men when he came to New France, nor would he have dedicated himself to his work with a zeal that became progressively more prudent and more fruitful. Likewise, if he had permitted his aggressiveness to take its course, he would have caused much suffering to his fellow religious and to the Indians in his charge. But all the evidence and testimonies concerning him agree in this: he never annoyed or offended anyone; his charity was always perfect and disinterested. Father Léonard Garreau commended this quality in him when he wrote:

> I often admired him for never making an unkind remark about any savage, no matter how impertinent he was. And when I—as I often did—mentioned some fault in the Indians that had annoyed me, he would either listen to me patiently and then make excuses for them or else he would say nothing at all. Not once, either in his words or in his actions, did I detect the least irritation or displeasure in reference to any savage (*MS de 1652*, p. 264).

Religious obedience could also have caused Garnier trouble, as it frequently does in consecrated souls of a less elevated sanctity. He could have manifested a poorly controlled desire for domination, a reaction to his struggles against his father. But the true situation is entirely contrary. On one occasion he wrote to his brother: "I would much prefer to perform a duty, even though it accomplished nothing, through obedience rather than to achieve great works through my own will" (*Rapport de l'archiviste*, p. 44). These are not idle words. Father Ragueneau tells us that all of Garnier's actions were in perfect harmony with that sentiment:

> He was frequently called from the mission work, in which he took such great pleasure, to plow a field, to work as a carriage driver, or even to drag the wagon over the snow, as a horse does the plow. Often, too, he was assigned to care for the sick, or to go out into the woods, looking high and low for wild grapes, sometimes walking for many leagues to accomplish this task and, after much labor, to bring back a quantity hardly sufficient to make enough wine for the Masses of the rest of the year. However, he never showed that it mattered to him what work he did, and to see him, one would think he had no inclination to do anything but the work he was actually engaged in and that this was the employment to which God had called him. (*MS de 1652*, pp. 261–62)

We could not wish for a truer or more perfect obedience.

Another sphere in which we perceive the triumph of grace in the soul of Charles Garnier is that of charity. He had suffered so much, in secret, from useless reproaches and from a lack of understanding of the depths of his soul, that he directed all his efforts to avoid similar pain to others. In one of his letters to his brother, he wrote:

> I do not think there is any affliction more difficult or more painful to bear than that of being an occasion of envy or irritation to others. There is no other suffering like it. And why should we be envious? God is our Master; he knows the pattern he has used for making each one of us. He knows also what place each of us can fill in his design, that he has made this type of person for this type of work and that type for another. It makes no difference whether or not we can see it.

This is surely wisdom that Garnier did not glean from books but from his own sad experience. He was wounded by the ignorance of others in his regard more than by anything else. He feared dealing the same blow to others. He realized that God had sent him this pain to free him from any desire he might have to dominate others or to overrule them by his aggressiveness. That is why his charity led him, as Ragueneau said, "to enter deeply into the hearts of others, not only to love them, as his father had also lavished affection on him, but rather to understand them".

How important he considered this understanding is revealed in a letter to his Father General in which the saint remarked of his superior, Father Jérôme Lalemant: "Our superior is a man of outstanding virtue, very prudent, and devoted to his men. There is only one quality that he lacks: he does not enter far enough into their hearts" (Thw. 25:82). Jérôme Lalemant, indeed, was attracted to heroic virtue and was inclined to demand it of his inferiors. He even went so far, when he was appointed superior of the Huron mission, as to reproach the Fathers working there for not having been martyred! We suspect that Garnier, in this veiled criticism of the man who had charge over him, perceived not only his own image but also the man he was determined not to become. His sanctity, a sanctity developed in God, grew from the knowledge that he must bring forth in himself the quality for whose absence he reproached Jérôme Lalemant.

When we read Garnier's correspondence very attentively, we discover more and more clearly how God took the initiative in him. When his brother entered the Carmelites in 1632, Charles wrote to him from the village of Eu, where Charles was teaching, insisting, certainly, that his brother give thanks to God for all his favors, but he also harangued at great length on the necessity for self-examination and the uprooting of his brother's faults. We see, though, as the years pass, that Charles Garnier becomes just as strongly insistent on the mistrust of oneself, and having absolute trust in God. One of his letters, quoted by Ragueneau, summarizes very succinctly Garnier's whole religious attitude:

> We can do absolutely nothing for the salvation of souls unless God is on our side. When we rely on him alone, through our obedience, he is obliged to help us. And with him, we accomplish all that he expects of us. On the other hand, when we ourselves choose our work, even though it be the holiest on earth, God has no obligation to give us aid. He leaves us to ourselves. And of ourselves, what can we do? Nothing at all, or—what is even worse—sin (*MS de 1652*, p. 262).

The spiritual doctrine that Garnier outlined to his brother is always very well balanced, very simple. He distinguished very clearly, this man who continually sought difficult things to do, between the crosses that he had taken on himself and those that God sent him. His humility was based precisely on the fact that he knew that he was unable to bear the least hardship without the help of God and that it is better to ask God to deliver us from all suffering rather than to seek it too boldly for ourselves. The very best course is to abandon ourselves to the all-wise Providence, who knows what we can bear.

However, the individuality of the spiritual notes left us by Garnier retain the marks of his psychological inhibitions that we suggested earlier. Unlike in Jogues' writings, it is rare that Garnier's own personal experience takes on such a particular identity that no one else could have said exactly the same thing. Very often, because his emotional powers were not fully delineated, he could not interpret his own life except in the form of general ideas; yet, when he was moved, his warmth was quickly transformed into eloquence.

Garnier did not know how to exult; it was not his nature to burst into a paean of praise. However, in the last few months of his life, as his martyrdom drew near, the accents of his voice changed and swelled into that magnificent avowal in which, three days before his death, he asserted his determination to unite himself to the love of Christ: "I shall never descend from the cross to which his goodness has fastened me" (Thw. 35:128).

LETTER TO HIS BROTHER

June 25, 1632

My dearest brother in Our Lord:

May the peace and love of Jesus be with you!

At last, at last you have gone out of Egypt, out of that Babylon, and have entered the promised land, Holy Jerusalem. At last, after having traveled throughout the world and reveled in the fruitless pursuits of the age, you have entered the house of rest and have said with assurance: "Here is my resting place forevermore; here will I dwell, for I have chosen it" (Ps 131 [132]:14). Congratulations, my dear brother! I embrace you affectionately in your new habit; in spirit I kiss the livery of Our Lord. I bless this day so full of happiness for you and thank the Most Holy Trinity for this moment marked by your first step into an earthly paradise. I thank our good Lord, who purchased this house and holy habit for you with his Precious Blood. And I ask all the angels of Heaven to sing thousands and thousands of hymns of praise to God and to his holy Mother, that guiding Star, who, I am firmly convinced, led you to your haven of happiness. I offer myself body and soul to Saint Joseph in gratitude for deigning to receive you among his servants and children; I also thank your guardian angel, who has with-

---

Rapport de l'archiviste, pp. 44–45. Garnier was at that time a teacher at the college at Eu, before taking up his theological studies in Paris.

drawn you from the occasions of losing your soul in the stormy tempests of the world. In short, I feel infinitely grateful to any and all who have contributed to the fulfillment of this holy plan. May Jesus live, may Jesus reign forever in our hearts and in that of our dear father, who did not resist the Holy Spirit!

But it is of no great worth to wish all these things with our lips if our hearts do not vehemently desire them and work at accomplishing them with all our strength. O my brother, I beg you—and myself also—let us hasten our steps, for we are always too late, toward loving so good a Master. You are blessed in being at the beginning of your new life, and I almost envy you because you have an opportunity of using so well the time that I have lost—that is, the period of the novitiate, and all the years since my entrance into religion. Indeed, I regret it bitterly, and that is why I wish with all my heart that you may be wiser than I—I am speaking quite frankly—and that you may spend your time as I would like to have spent mine. Would to God that in leaving the world I had strengthened my will, made it unshakable in its determination to serve God purely, perfectly, and solely, rooted it deeply in eternity by meditating on and pondering over the immeasurable obligations we owe to the Father of love. Would to God also that I had devoted myself seriously and entirely, throughout the time of my novitiate and all the time after that, to a full and clear knowledge and understanding of my passions and bad habits, all my imperfections. And in the third place, would to God that I had generously combated these vices one by one, granting myself no respite from the battle. I almost forgot one of my special wishes—that I had wept unceasingly over the sins that I committed while still in the world. That is a summary of what I would like to have done and what I beg you to do, insofar as your superiors find it good. It is especially important that you follow the will of your superior as a shadow follows a substance.

First of all, firmly and constantly resolve to serve God with all your heart and with sincere contrition for not having done so in the past.

Secondly, keep a faithful, careful watch over your heart, examining at every opportunity the movements of your soul, so as to achieve a complete knowledge of yourself. It is very useful to write down the results of these examens, particularly any inclinations toward sin that you may have.

Thirdly, include with these examinations of your soul a lively sorrow for those faults that you discover at that time and contrition for all your past sins.

Fourthly, root out these faults one by one, seeking help from your spiritual director and from books, but especially from prayer. On the other hand, be especially careful not to become scrupulous in these examinations. A good rule to follow is this: reveal candidly to your superiors what you are doing and how you are proceeding; then believe them as you do God himself.

Let us commend each other to God!

Your dear brother,

Charles Garnier

I forgot to include one thing that might cause you trouble unless you are careful; that is to drive from your heart every tendency toward haste, sadness, or anxiety. I think it is by these feelings that the devil harms us more than by any other means, and unless you are extremely watchful, you will fall into his snares. Let us serve Our Lord with filial love since he is such a good Father. I beg you not to forget me for a single day in your prayers and your Holy Communions on feast days, nor will I forget you, please God. If you see our father and brother, give them my fondest regards. I will write you again when I have an opportunity. Until then, I am, dear brother, etc.

Eu, June 25, 1632

LETTER TO HIS BROTHER

March 31, 1636

J.M.J.

My dearest brother:

May the peace and love of Our Lord be with you!

I thank you most affectionately for the two letters I have received from you since I left Paris. Monsieur Lucien brought me one a day or two before I left Amiens. The other I received the very day I arrived here at Dieppe, that is, Easter Monday. May God be blessed for all the news you gave me, and especially for letting me know that my father sends his blessing. I am asking for it again in a letter that I am addressing to you and that I beg you to give him when you think best. It is on this occasion, my dearest brother, that I must embrace you from the bottom of my heart, or to express it better, it is on this occasion that, renouncing this soiled heart, I embrace you in that of our good Master, where you have agreed to meet me. I embrace you there in order to unite myself to you there, rather than separate myself from you, for that is where I wish to live henceforth. I feel as though I am breathing a pestilential air when I leave it. But, alas, I need a very strong bond to keep me there. I hope that the Precious Blood, which I take daily, will bring me this blessing, my dearest brother. I am devoted to you, and if, therefore, it pleases Our Lord that this tree, hitherto

---

Rapport de l'archiviste, pp. 9–10.

unfruitful, should bring forth fruit, assure yourself that so far as lies in my power, this harvest shall be yours. I do not promise you any special prayers, because I feel that I do more by sacrificing myself entirely for you and making the resolution that I am preparing right now before Our Lord, his holy Mother, and her dear spouse, that as often as I can, I shall offer my Masses and other devotions notably and particularly to ask of God the petitions you have recommended to me. I also ask for nothing special from you. I do this with the simple assurance that you give yourself to me in our Lord, and thus we shall accomplish more for each other than if we limit our spiritual communication in any way. I am entirely at your disposal. God grant that I may be of some benefit to you, though I am worthless, good for nothing, and you are truly poor if you have nothing else. I hope that our good Master has not accepted me in so blessed and favorable a fashion unless he intends to change me. If he has not, there is very little likelihood that I shall acquire any virtue, for alas! Among several imperfections that make me incapable of this apostolic vocation, there are two that would make me lose courage a thousand times a day if I did not keep my eyes on him who leads me. One is a habitual state of distraction, the other a shameful cowardice in undertaking the desires of my Master. Do you have any desire to offer yourself as a victim for the savages? May the holy will of God be done and whatever is for his greater glory! It is a very noble, a most sublime calling to be a victim for sinners; it is the one Christ chose for himself.

I am in something of a hurry because the man who is going to take our letters to Paris is already here. I hope to have the joy of writing to you again soon. We expect to leave Wednesday or Thursday. Father Chastelain, one of our

Brothers, and I are to travel in the ship of Monsieur Duplessis Bochard, the leader of the fleet. The name of his vessel is the Saint Joseph. It was on Saint Joseph's Day that I left Amiens for Eu, when I made that long, difficult journey in a single day. However, it was so late in the evening when I arrived that the city gates were already closed. God in his goodness arranged that an influential person arrived at the same time, for whom, contrary to custom, the gates were opened. So I made myself small and slipped in behind him.

>Farewell, my dear brother!

Dieppe, March 31, 1636

LETTER TO HIS BROTHER

July 20, 1636

J. M. J.

My dearest brother:

May the grace and love of Our Lord Jesus Christ be with you!

Will you please help me bless and praise most fervently our great God, who looks down from Heaven's heights on even the lowest of creatures! It will take all eternity for us to realize the depths of the mercies of God in regard to him who is one with us in him. He has at long last led me to this delightful paradise, to which he called me, or, rather, he had me carried here in the arms of his most holy Mother and his own faithful guardian, Saint Joseph. He has given me so many proofs of his excessive love for me that I can do nothing but invite all creatures to join with me in saying, "Extol the Lord with me; in chorus let us glorify his name!" (Ps 33:4 [34:3]) and put you at the head of the choir. Let us truly magnify him, my dear brother, but more by the language of the heart—by love—than by mere words. Let us extol him, let us glorify him, not only for his sake, but for us and in ourselves, giving him a much larger place deep in our heart than he has ever had before. Let us enlarge those little cabins; let us increase them by our faithful love and by an unlimited confidence and courage. For if we are

---

Rapport de l'archiviste, pp. 10–11. This letter was written partly in Quebec and partly in Three Rivers.

indebted to him for the graces he has given me by bringing me here, what must I do to prepare myself to use the still greater grace he is making ready for me by sending me to the Hurons? For if to me Canada is a holy temple and a most sacred spot that God has built for me in this world, the Huron region is its holy of holies. This is the field from which our Fathers hope to reap the richest harvest of all the places where we are working, because it is a stabilized nation, not migratory like most of the others. It is a secret chamber in which one enjoys the chaste embraces of the holy Spouse, and where he is completely attached to the Cross, because Jesus and the Cross are inseparably united. Let us then leap for joy in this land of benediction!

But alas! What can a cowardly heart do in the midst of all these crosses? What can I, weak as I am, do in this holy of holies? I who, to tell the truth, have not yet learned to pray to God in thirteen years of conversation with him? That is why I am ashamed to go take the place of someone who would do the work of God so much better. So I beg you to obtain for me the gift of prayer and a mortified spirit. And do not say that you do not have enough credit in Heaven to obtain these favors for me. For even if that should be the case, which I do not believe, I shall use the power and influence that I have over your heart in virtue of our love, to command you to sanctify your heart so that it can steal these graces for me from the hands of our good Master. Command me, in turn, to contribute on my part all that I can to transform myself into him whose name is He Who Is and to consider myself as nothing until this is accomplished. Command me, my brother, to belong entirely to Jesus, but give me these orders chiefly when, as a sign of the power that God has given you, you hold in your hands him who, although he is almighty, is obliged to come down from Heaven into your hands whenever you wish him to do so. For it is especially at that time that I beg you to be mindful of me, to exorcise my heart and those of our savages, and to place me in the wounded side of him you are holding. And I, for my part, promise you that, with the help of my God, I shall always hold you pressed tightly to my heart in that cavern of our Spouse, and that daily I shall try to unite myself more perfectly to you in our Lord—or rather, to unite both of us to him, not separating my desires of giving myself completely to him from yours. May he hear from both of us the prayer that our Master himself made to his Father on the eve of his death: "All are to be one; just as you, Father, are in me and I am in you, so they, too, are to be one in us" (Jn 17:21). I am, then, one with you, in God the Father, the Son, and the Holy Spirit.[1]

---

[1] Then follows a postscript in which Garnier gives news of the mission.

LETTER TO
REVEREND FATHER LE JEUNE

August 8, 1636

May God be forever blessed! Since yesterday, we have been here among the Nipissings—so happy and in such good health that I am ashamed of it. For if I had had enough heart and courage, I do not doubt that our Lord would have given me one end of his Cross to bear, as he did to our Fathers who went before us. If he had done me this favor, I would be a little more cast down than I am. May he be blessed by all the angels! He has treated the child as a child: I did not paddle; I carried only my own baggage, except for three days during the portages, when I carried a little package that someone offered me because one of our savages fell ill. Is not that being treated like a child? The trouble is that he who complains of not suffering much receives with a great deal of cowardice the sufferings that Our Lord does send him; but what else can I do but cast my poor, weak, wretched heart into the arms of my good Master and beg you to bless the Lord with all your strength, because he "thrones on high and sees what is below" (Ps 112:6 [113:5–6]) and because he gives me hope that someday I shall be entirely his. We arrived at the island on the eve of the Feast of Saint Ignatius. We

---

Thw. 12:128–30. Garnier had just arrived in Canada. He was on his way to the Huron region and had made the regular stop at Lake Nipissing. Chastelain wrote to Father Le Jeune the same day.

bought some Indian corn because our peas gave out. This corn lasted us until we reached here. Our savages did not have any—at least, they found only one cache of it. Up to the present, we have found but few fish. We are expecting Father Davost here today. Farewell, Reverend Father; make me, through your Holy Masses, such as I ought to be in the place where you send me in the name of God.

LETTER TO HIS BROTHER

April 30, 1637

J. M. J.

My dearest brother:

May our Lord give you his holy love and peace!

Thanks be to God! Today I offered Holy Mass for you because I remembered that you have special devotion to the great Saint Catherine of Siena, whose feast we are celebrating today. You tell me, dear brother, that your infirmities are increasing daily. Blessed be God, if that be his holy will. Nevertheless, since we are not sure that this suffering is for his greater glory, we can pray that you may be relieved of your pains if they are not. But we must remember to pray with a perfect indifference and to realize that even when God afflicts us to the extreme, he will also give us the grace to bear up well in the end and show us how to derive profit from our pain. It would certainly be an unhappy thought to feel that we must inevitably succumb. I have reason to think that both of us commit the same fault when we do not trust that no matter what we ask from God, he will always surpass our hopes. Let us open our hearts to him as much as we can; let us raise our hopes and our desires as high as we can! This is the way to glorify God. This is the way that some theologians explain the words of

---

Rapport de l'archiviste, pp. 12–13. This letter was sent from the town of Immaculate Conception.

Our Lady: "My soul magnifies the Lord." And we make a serious mistake to fear that we shall succumb under the burden that the Lord puts on our shoulders. It is certainly to have a poor opinion of Our Lord to think that he would do what a man who was only moderately good would not do. It is on such occasions that we must be careful not to look with one eye at our own weakness and impotence and with the other at the omnipotence, the goodness, and the infinite wisdom of him who sees all and orders all. And it is a certain testimony that God loves us if he permits us to carry the Cross of his Son. How can we think that he would abandon us in our weakness and powerlessness? All of that, however, does not prevent us from begging God to deliver us, if that is for his greater glory. But let us remember the way we should make this prayer, following the example of our Lord in the Garden of Olives and trying to pray with the same interior dispositions that, if God does not wish to take this chalice from us, he will surely give us strength and will even send an angel from Heaven to support us if that be necessary; for that reason we must kiss the chalice, bearing in mind that it is, as we said in the beginning, a signal favor from God that we are permitted to share the sufferings of his Son.

It seems that there is no affliction that is more painful or more difficult to bear than to be a cause of envy or irritation to another. I know of nothing like it. And why? God is our Master; he knows from what stamp he has made each of us, and perhaps he would not have sent us to that sort of person who was unwilling to take the trouble to see what he has given to others. Courage, my brother! But what does that word mean? This is what I think it means: open your heart to receive the courage that God wishes to give you. Keep your eyes fastened on Jesus dying, and receive from him the sacred stigmata that he wishes to impress on your body, even though he does it in a way different from that in which he bestowed them on courageous Saint Catherine of Siena, that good and faithful friend of the cross. Read a little of the life of Saint Lydwina, if you will. It seems to me that it contains examples that fit you very well. Consider that God wants your body to bear the marks and effects of the corruption of your soul.

My dear brother, do not think that I am lacking compassion or tenderness of heart in speaking to you like this. It is not that at all. And I know very well that to talk is one thing and to do is an entirely different thing. Alas! My experiences every single day prove to me my own weakness, showing me how little able I am to bear any cross and convincing me that the true reason why God spares me is that he knows how I must force myself in telling you that God loves us and will continue to love us to the end, no matter by what road he leads us. Call to mind the desires that God gave you before, the will to be completely detached from all creatures. If you are prepared to accept all from the hand of God, only then can our divine Master ordain anything that pleases him.

As for the rest, I think you should overcome the diffidence you feel in accepting the help and service of others. They are necessary for you, and you must remember that your companions have virtue and that your only duty is to try to please God in the spirit of your Order and in preserving the regulations of the house, as long as the superiors do not command otherwise. And if God wishes to make use of you as an instrument in trying and strengthening the virtues of others, should you not also be content? And if you should find someone who is unusually mortified or who has a special attraction toward you, I think it would be a good thing to let him help and serve you, as long as the Rule and the superiors permit it. For without their permission, you may not flee your companions either, for that would be to tempt God. But, in a word, I would advise you to find a wise and virtuous person to take care of you. Perhaps Monsieur Chevalier would be able to do so; he might also be able to consult at the same time several others without your knowledge, should any difficulties arise. It is certainly necessary to have someone like that, and although in order to make a correct judgment in this matter it would be well to be on the scene, I think that you cannot solve anything at this point without the advice of someone else to whom you can explain at firsthand just what your sufferings are. That is the best advice I can give you, and it is very important, also. You will have no success if you do not follow it. One thing I surely think you should deliberate upon is the advisability of informing your immediate superior of the whole affair. I beg our Lord Jesus Christ to send you his Saint Joseph to advise you in all matters and to send you a faithful friend who knows how to interpret the movements of the Holy Spirit.

Farewell, my dearest brother. I beg you to write to me and tell me in what way our Lord inspires you to let me help you. Send me also the opinions of your Reverend superiors in regard to this matter and the means they think we should take concerning it, but let it be a matter between the two of us, for I think that is better. Pray for me, I beg you. I embrace you in spirit in the sacred side of Jesus Christ. I am entirely devoted to you in Our Lord Jesus Christ.

From the residence of l'Immaculée Conception de Notre-Dame, April 30, 1637

LETTER TO HIS FATHER

1638

J. M. J.

Dear Father:

May Our Lord give you his holy peace!

I learned from the letter you were so good to write to me that you are suffering a great deal from the infirmities of old age and that you are afflicted with still other pains. I beg the Holy Spirit to console and fortify you in these sufferings. It is he alone who can truly console our hearts. All that angels and men can say is incapable of bringing you a true and firm consolation unless the Holy Spirit puts his hand to it. And when it pleases him that men should hush and withdraw themselves so that he can speak and act all alone, oh, how much more we then gain than when men are involved in it! I have long been confirmed in my belief in this truth.

We had a very good proof of this after our arrival in this country, when it at once pleased the divine Goodness to send a contagious disease into our little cabin. I cannot tell you with what great joy the holy Consoler filled our hearts during this small affliction. He made us experience his consolations even more deeply in the persecutions heaped upon us during the past year. You should know, dear Father, that Our Lord gave us the honor of sharing his suffering. We

---

Rapport de l'archiviste, pp. 14–17.

were shouted at and maligned by the natives of this country as though we were the pestilence itself. Each one of us was looked upon as the cause of death to their tribe. Sometimes—almost always—they thought it was brought by holy pictures. Some said the pestilence was caused by the dead body of the little child we kept in our tabernacles. Almost all believed that we were the source of the contagion. They urged us to bring it out, whatever it was. I will let you judge whether or not the devil was acting in these calumnies. Isn't it true that a good Christian, but especially one who, by the grace of God, is bringing the Gospel to these far-off, barbarian countries, should feel his heart filled with joy when he sees that the devil is annoyed, and that a man in our profession is never completely satisfied until the devil begins to shout? If he feels this joy, it is through resignation to the will of God. Even when we feel that our work is fruitless, it is by these persecutions that we feel the strength and sweetness of the Consoler. You can understand this better by yourself than I can explain it to you.

Bless him, I beg you, and thank him because he has sheltered us under his wings during this time of danger. It would have been less easy for him to change the hearts of those who spoke of exterminating us than it was for him to fortify the hearts of his poor servants against the apprehensions that they felt in their hearts. May he be forever blessed and loved by all men!

My special request to you, dear Father, is that, if you truly love me, to banish from your heart all the worries and disquiet that your paternal affection causes you in my regard. Drive out these pricks of pain as soon as you notice them entering your heart, because you realize that I am in good hands. He to whom nothing is impossible takes a thousand times better care of me than you ever could; he has led me to a place over which he holds his hands outstretched day and night to protect us in a very special manner. In the second place, I beg you also to place yourself in the hands of this adorable Consoler in all your sufferings and afflictions. In brief, I beg you to devote all your attention and energy to removing these cares from your heart and replacing them with all that he loves, or, rather, to allowing him to fill it with whatever he wills. Oh, how happy you will be when he has filled it with himself, as he desires to do, since, with the exception of this divine Consoler, all that we can have in our hearts is nothing but filth, which must be purged from them as soon as possible, and before our death. And if we do not do it in this life, alas! That delay will cost us dearly in that burning furnace, the very thought of which gives me a new impetus to urge that you accept all these afflictions for the love of God. Each one of them has been moistened with the Blood of Jesus Christ and thus can noticeably shorten the time of our stay in Purgatory. And when we are no longer there, what honor, what a favor it is for us to be like to Jesus Christ. It is on this lovable image that we must keep our eyes fastened. In this vale of tears, let us ask God for each other; that he will grant us this grace; I beg you most humbly.

I have great need of this assistance from your prayers in a place where God gives me so many graces and so many satisfactions, and I do not think that men would be able to put me in a place where I would be anywhere nearly as happy and joyous as I am here. Perhaps I should say that I do not think anyone could put me in a place where I would not be unhappy because I was not here. Do not doubt at all that this feeling that I have in my heart comes from God. I am convinced of it, and as far as I can see, this conviction is confirmed by my confidence that God wants me here and nowhere else. That is why I feel so deeply indebted to his infinite goodness that I would like to consume myself completely in the flames of his love as a thank-offering for a favor that to me seems so generous that my heart is lost in the consideration of it. That is why also I am forced to break off this discourse, and also because I know that you are waiting for me to tell you about other things.

Since I last wrote you—a year ago, maybe a little longer—I have been in this village, which the French named La Rochelle. There are fifty cabins of Indians here who give us constant testimony of their affection for us. I am here with three of ours, namely, Father Brébeuf, our superior, Father Mercier, and Father Ragueneau. You remember the last named; it was he who visited you shortly before his departure from France and who brought me so much consolation with definite news of you. He asked me to remember him to you most humbly. If you would like to do something for him, thank God for having called him here and given him so much happiness, as well as Father Mercier and all of us who are here. My daily work is to visit the cabins of these savages in order to make the acquaintance of those who are ill, to instruct and baptize them when they are in danger of death. Most of the sick are close to death; many of the savages of our village have already died. You know what it costs me to do the work of a surgeon. That is one of my duties here: not just to bleed them, but to dress their suppurating wounds and their little bumps and burns. But, to come to the baptisms. In this single village, we have already baptized, thank God, a hundred souls. At the time of my writing this, of these hundred, forty-four died shortly afterward; that is, twenty-four adults and twenty infants who had not yet been weaned.

May God forgive me if I dare to say, wretched sinner that I am, that his goodness has seen fit to make use of me to baptize a goodly number of the above-mentioned. He knows my intention in speaking of it; it is for your consolation and to make you admit that God wants me here. It is also that you can help thank him for me for his infinite kindness and so that you can pray for me more fervently still to obtain from God the forgiveness of my sins, and grace to begin to be truly grateful for all the many favors he has bestowed upon me. Alas, my dear and honored father, as long as I serve God as poorly as I do and as long as I love him so little, I am an object of scorn to any who love him at all. May they have pity on me! I hope that the sovereign goodness of our Lord will someday take pity on me and grant me the grace to correspond more perfectly with his favors.

I almost forgot to tell you about the savage that we have in our village who has given us much consolation. We baptized him last year during an illness, and ever since then he has been a source of happiness to us. Even in France, one would be proud of him, he is so virtuous. And that is all the more reason why we hold him in such great esteem, namely, that he is a savage. It is God alone who can make such Christians! He has a nephew who imitates him very closely. His wife also gives us much joy. You will read more about them in the *Relation*. I hope that God will give us many more like them. Pray for them earnestly, I beg you.

But remember also that we live here in a fortress that has no equal in France. We are surrounded by a wall that is not much different from that of the Bastille. Yesterday we finished one of the towers. Your fear of the Spanish cannons is much stronger than our fears here. Some malicious person may tell you that it is because no cannon can approach closer than thirty leagues here, and that our rampart consists of a citadel of palings ten or twelve feet high and six inches wide, and that our tower is built of thirty posts planted in a corner of this citadel to defend two sides of it, and that they are going to build another to defend the other two sides. It is sufficient warning for you to know what great malice the spies are capable of, that our own Hurons think, while admiring our fortifications, that those in France must be quite like them. That shows how different their ideas and opinions are from yours.

You see how much I have gained in leaving France, where you were constantly making war against me for not having a beard, for that is the very reason why these savages think I am handsome. I see that you are afraid I am suffering much inconvenience and discomfort here. Let me assure you that I have never enjoyed such good health as I do here. When I was in France, there was hardly a year when I did not suffer from a cold, catarrh, or some such ailment; I assure you that, since I assured you of my good health in my last letter, I have not had any illness, neither a cold nor catarrh. So do you not think it foolish for those poor sons of this earth to treat their bodies so delicately and to go to so much trouble for their physical comfort? Alas! Would that they would realize how much they offend God by their disordered effeminacy—to the extent that the poor, who could live on their superfluities, die in poverty—and by putting on so much weight, which, instead of doing them good, sends them to bed with all sorts of pains and infirmities. And the sad part of it all is that they are just paving the way to Hell for themselves. Alas! Will there be any of my relatives or close friends in this number? God grant that there will not!

Another thing that bothers you is that I am progressing in my study of the language and that I can make myself understood. Yes, thank God, I can perform passably. I always keep a little notebook handy, in which I write any new words that I hear. But even though I have the book at hand, I am not always free to write. Sometimes people in France think that we have time and leisure to devote to our friends, but that is a mistake. I do not have even a good quarter-hour during the day in which to study, because of the frequent visits we must make and the multitude of savages that interrupt us in our cabin when we are at home. That is why I have to scratch out so much in this letter, a fault I beg you to excuse. At the moment, we are not in such great need to go to the cabins; the epidemic has abated since last March, and likewise, a great part of the irritation against us abated with it.[1]

---

[1] This is followed by a discussion of the events at the mission.

LETTER TO HIS BROTHER

June 23, 1641

J.M.J.

My dearest brother:

May Our Lord fill your heart with his holy love!

I am very happy not only to receive your letters but also to send you mine. I was therefore very sorry that you did not receive those that I wrote to you two years ago. I suppose they were lost. May God be blessed in all things! Without doubt, I would have more consolation in writing to you if I had made some notable progress that I could report to you—either in my individual perfection or in the conversion of the savages—as you think I have done. But patience! My real consolation is that I know that, whatever I tell you, you will find a way of praising, honoring, and loving God more because of it. I am engaged in a work that is wholly divine. Bless God for it forever! And bless him with all your heart! His infinite mercy grants me thousands upon thousands of graces to lead me to the perfection that this occupation requires. Let your heart break in the transports of love that you pour forth to his sovereign goodness. I am very faithless in responding to these innumerable favors; be angry at me! With David, admire the patience of God and console yourself that we have so good a Master to deal with

---

Rapport de l'archiviste, pp. 24–25. This letter was written at Sainte-Marie des Hurons.

us, one who wearies not in calling us to himself. He is not repelled by our stupidities, impertinences, and evil actions.

Courage, my dearest brother! If we have spent two years, even six, even thirty—in turning a deaf ear, let us hope that tomorrow we shall begin to open our ears to this voice, so gracious and so patient. And why, I beg you, should we not believe this, since we see and know that our patient Jesus still calls us? It is with a loving call, and one that will gain the day for us, only we know not when. Let us hope, at all events, that it will be as soon as possible. Oh, I do not believe that we can commit a greater fault in the service of God than to lose courage and to allow our hearts to be cast down by distrust and pusillanimity. All other sins are nothing in comparison with that one—at least, there is none that so much impedes our progress as this low estimate of the goodness of God toward us. Very often it is by that sin that the devil takes possession of our hearts, which he then lays open to all the others.

My dear brother, let us not be alarmed at not having advanced, or even for having receded; there is hardly any soul to which that does not sometimes happen. But let us consider the reasons God has for deriving his glory from these unfaithful actions. Your sufferings and inconveniences will purge your heart. Hope for this, therefore, although it may seem to you that you have borne them very ungracefully. I pray God that you may find peace of heart. I think you would find consolation in reading the other works of Monsieur de Sales. I do not know whether or not you have seen a certain little book entitled....[1] It is a little treasure of consolation. But the source of all sweetness and the whole

---

[1] There is a lacuna in the manuscript here.

support of our hearts is Jesus in the Blessed Sacrament. Do not say that you do not relish this Bread of Life; it is good to converse with God for some time after Holy Mass and to visit him in the Blessed Sacrament when your occupations permit you to do this. Let us adore and embrace him; let us protest to him that we are his in spite of ourselves, and let him do with us what he pleases.

Pardon me, my dear brother—consider that it is to myself alone that I speak in this letter and not to you; thus, you will know that I am a lunatic. It is true that I rave; but beg God to change me, and then, perhaps, I shall write you something good. Such as I am, I do not fail to entreat God for you and for our poor prodigal brother;[2] and I really pray for you often. Did you both receive my letters last year, in which I informed you that I was asking our Lord to accept my intention that a certain number of Masses I would say at the time of both of your deaths—should you depart before me—should be applied to you. Alas, will this poor prodigal come to his senses? Let us pray the Father and the Mother of mercies to have pity on him.[3]

---

[2] He is talking about his other brother, who later became a Capuchin.
[3] There follows a discussion of news of the mission.

LETTER TO HIS BROTHER

May 22, 1642

My dearest brother:

The peace of Our Lord Jesus Christ be with you!

It was a Heaven-sent affliction to me when I learned last September that the letter I had written to you during the summer had reached Quebec, with several others, after the departure of the vessels returning to France. The only thing that made it easy for me to resign myself to the will of God was that I was sure I could not have written my letter any sooner. I hope that our Lord will have abundantly compensated you for any consolation he might have given you through my letters, since you say that he has used them before to bring you some. I hope that this letter will join, at Quebec, the one I wrote you last year. First I will answer the one I received from you last summer, dated at Jalaix, March 4. Continue, I beg you, more and more to bless God for the favors that he has shown me and continues to show me from day to day. It is one of the principal proofs that you can give me of your love toward me; or, to speak more correctly, since there is nothing that can separate us two, and since we are but one heart, it is a very holy and profitable conversation for us to thank God continually for the favors he has bestowed on us, for I regard them as common to us both.

Rapport de l'archiviste, pp. 26–28. This letter was written at *Teanaostaiae*.

It is only my sins, my ingratitude, and my continued unfaithfulness that you do not share; however, I beg you with my whole heart to take some part in them out of charity, not that you will be burdened with them, but that you feel some obligation to try constantly to abolish them by your Holy Masses, prayers, and devotional exercises. I can assure you that if you do so, you are indeed promoting the glory of God among the Hurons. For God, in his goodness, has given me some advantages of grace and nature to serve him in this mission. I am sure that the abuse that I make of his graces and the negligence with which I serve him greatly hinder the profitable employment of the talents he has given me. Be that as it may, my dear brother, I beg you to treat your heart gently, never to humble it by the consideration of your imperfections without also raising it up by means of a filial confidence in our good Master. I surely hope to receive some letters from you this year in which you will tell me that our Lord has put some stability and firmness into your heart. I pray that he will do the same for me as soon as possible.

I have noticed, by the grace of God, that one of the things that hindered me from serving God was that I required too much of myself and that when I made my plans, I considered more what was desired of me than what I was able to do—that I didn't have sufficient perception of the state of perfection and virtue that I was in and of the measure of grace that God was giving me. There is no question that this is a very important consideration and that we should not try to be the sole guide of our hearts. If Our Lord would inspire me with some holy thought for your edification, I would gladly pass it on to you, because that is what you wish. This will come when God wishes it. But I still complain that you send me no word that can help me. Since you are not studying, you have more facility and fewer distractions for talking to God. God disposes everything for our good. I bless him for it with all my heart and beg him to lead you to whatever point of perfection he desires for you. I must confess that I have always found it difficult to understand how there could be persons in good religions[1] who could not discover the means to keep themselves busy during those periods when they were not engaged in some prescribed task. I do not know what such persons think of prayer or of reading the Bible, the works of the Fathers, and the lives of the saints. Sometimes they say that they have no love for study; surely they would never say they have no love for prayer. And even if they had an aversion for it, they ought to apply themselves to it, just a little—and after a little, then a little more. By so doing, I do not doubt that they would soon find pleasure in it. As for you, my dearest brother, I consider you most blessed if God has called you to this intimate communication with him. And if sometimes he casts you into a little doubt or perplexity, I beg you to take courage, for there is no duty in religion to which God calls us where we cannot and should not praise him. I hope that he will grant both of us the grace to do this and that he will place us where we ought to be. Let us not trouble ourselves about this, whether you are with Saint Peter or Saint John. What difference does it make? It is enough for us that he has placed us.

As to the request that the Holy Spirit made of you on the day of your profession, I thank his divine goodness that he confirms you in the hope of seeing it fulfilled some day. I pray with all my heart that he will fulfill it for his own

---

[1] He is referring to religious communities.

glory. Let us both go, my dear brother, to martyrdom: "Let us go along and die with him" (Jn 11:14). We must put our entire confidence in his goodness and mercy. And as for seeing you once more, that indeed would be a very special consolation for me; I beg God only that he direct this matter for his greater glory. Let us try, in all events, whenever we remember each other, to direct and fasten our gaze on Jesus Christ. In him we find all our consolation, strength, and virtue.

If I were concerned only for my own interest, I would desire that your Reverend Father provincial should send you as companion to your preachers, so that, not having a sacristan, you would give me a greater share in your Holy Masses. I thank you very much for those you have offered for me. As you request of me, let us continue to pray for our poor prodigal brother. Truly, he arouses great compassion in me. He sent me word that he has been much consoled by my letters and that he has read and reread them in order to prolong in his heart my good instruction and to open the door of his heart to God. He said that he felt that God was speaking to him with my lips. He also offered to send me whatever I would ask of him. "I am wholly yours," he said, "and whatever I possess is yours, too (even though I ought not possess it)." Let us pray ceaselessly, and have others pray also, to God for him. Try to arrange that some of your Fathers go to see him; I will try to do the same.

My cousin Bué, her son-in-law, and my cousin Chaufourneau have all written to me; I shall write to them also, God willing.[2]

---

[2] This is followed by news of the mission.

LETTER TO HIS BROTHER

May 14, 1646

J.M.J.

My dearest brother:

May Our Lord fill your heart with his holy love!

Our Lord saw fit to deprive me of the consolation of your letters last year. I do not know by what accident this was brought about, but I am sure that it was not at all your fault. I did not receive any from Aunt Chaufourneau or Cousin Bué, which makes me think that the whole packet was lost. I think, too, that the letters from our aunt, the nun, was with them; at least, I did not receive any from her either. We will have to send all these losses to eternity; there we will see all things in God, and the delay in reading those letters there will really not be long. This is the thought by which God frequently consoles me.

When, in the midst of some slight necessity here, I remember the delights of France, then I send these little hardships before me to eternity, which thought brings me great consolation and makes these privations the sweetest on earth. Oh, my dear brother, what happiness we will have when we can enjoy God! Then, by his grace, I firmly hope we will find all in him, and he will grant us every blessing and every pleasure. Courage, my dear brother! Let us bear in this hope all our troubles, and even our imperfections. Let

---

Rapport de l'archiviste, pp. 34–35. This letter was written from *Teanaostaiae*.

us bear them, if not joyfully, at least without anxiety, because not only can we reach God with them, but they even provide the means for us to approach closer to him. I mean by bearing with ourselves, in whatever state we may be, no matter how imperfect we are, provided that our poor little heart always retracts its evil and always renews its desire to do better. Excuse me for speaking to you thus, ignorant as I am of what state of grace God has raised you to since I last had news of you, but I speak as to myself; and if what I write here can be of use to you, I beg you to notice also that I am in a state low enough to have need of your prayers. For even while I write that I must always renew my good intentions, I find myself covered with shame and confusion in that I seem to feel a lack of this desire, pricking at me, to seek God always. I feel it, as I say, but not so much, it seems, as I formerly felt it. Nevertheless, I ardently desire thus to desire; I beg God to have mercy on me. Certainly, feeling my imperfections as I do, it seems to me that I would be very happy if God should call me to himself, where I would never again act through self-love but would love him alone, with never any backsliding. But—his holy will be done! He knows best what I need. But please make this request of him: that he grant me what he knows is best for me.

I suspect that you are condemning me a little for having so little zeal and so much cowardice in longing for Heaven so soon while there are still so many people in this land to be converted. But I confess, I do lack zeal for souls. Therefore, I beg you and your friends to obtain this grace for me from God. However, when my heart reproaches me for this fault, I answer that my imperfections prevent me in this life from gathering the fruits that God desires from me in regard to the salvation of my neighbor and that, in Heaven, the prayers that I could say for the savages would be much more useful to them than my presence. Thus it is that I confess that there is cowardice in my prayers—but that is the way they are.[1]

---

[1] This is followed by news of the mission.

LETTER TO HIS BROTHER

August 12, 1649

My dearest brother:

May Our Lord unite his heart to yours!

A month ago our good Master gave me the consolation of receiving the letters that I missed last year. Nevertheless, I did not receive the box of ...[1] the pictures and paintings that you sent the two preceding years. They are, however, still in the hands of Father Pierre Pijart in Three Rivers, but he says that he will send them on at the first opportunity. I thank you most sincerely for this kindness and for all the good things that you do for me. I beg our Lord to reward you for them in eternity. If you were moved by the sufferings of Father Isaac Jogues, you will be no less touched by those of Father Jean de Brébeuf and Father Gabriel Lalemant, about whom I wrote to you briefly last spring. The *Relation* will give you more details. Alas, my dear brother, if my conscience did not convince me and confound me because of my lack of fidelity in the service of our good Master, I would hope for some favor like the one he gave our blessed martyrs, with whom I had the blessing of conversing very often, in the same situations and the same dangers as they were. But justice makes me fear that I will

---

Rapport de l'archiviste, pp. 43–44.
[1] There is a lacuna in the manuscript.

always remain unworthy of such a crown. However, I hope that his goodness will give me the grace someday to love him with all my heart, and for me, that will be sufficient. That is what I beg you to ask him to send me. When he shall have granted me that, it will make no difference by what sort of death I leave this earth.

Courage, my dear brother! Let us aspire to this perfect love and this perfect resignation to all his holy desires, and you, in your sufferings, abandon yourself joyfully to the all-lovable Providence. Keep before your eyes his heart, which leads his paternal hand to chastise and afflict you during the short moment of your life only to crown you eternally with glory and a seat near him who has drunk long draughts from the chalice he is now presenting to you. Abandon yourself, my dear brother, to the hands of the Crucified and to the will of your superiors; be careful not to disobey in the least their directives to you, and if you propose to them something that seems necessary to you in your illness, do it without urgency, with great indifference. Take care that there be no self-love here, manifested by pressure. I would prefer to be in any duty whatever through obedience, even though I accomplish nothing in it, than to be employed in the greatest works through my own will, but I do not know where I....[2]

I beg God to give you two favors: first, a large heart with which to love Our Lord and to love him only; the second, a perfect abandonment to his hands and those of the superiors. I beg you to ask Our Lord for two favors for me: the first, that in all this disturbance, I may remain united to him; the second, that I place no obstacle to him in doing

---

[2] There is a lacuna in the manuscript.

whatever he wishes me to do for the salvation of these poor people. I must break off here, because the canoes are leaving. I am, dear brother, your. . . .

Fathers Chastelain, Poncet, and Menard recommend themselves to your Holy Masses and to your prayers; I, to those of your good Fathers and Brothers at Basses-Loges, if you are still there, or wherever you may be.

Please also take care of a letter I am enclosing for our brother the Capuchin, to see that he receives it.

Sainte-Marie, Ile de Saint-Joseph, August 12, 1649

FATHER FREMIN SAW FATHER GARNIER SAVED FROM A DRUNKEN INDIAN BY SQUAW. SEPTEMBER 1669

LETTER TO
REVEREND FATHER RAGUENEAU

December 4, 1649

It is true that I suffer something in regard to hunger, but it is not to death, and, thank God, my body and my spirit keep up all their vigor. I am not alarmed in that respect. What I fear more is leaving my flock in the time of their calamities and in the terrors of war—in a time when they need me more than ever. In such circumstances, I am afraid I would fail to see the opportunities God gives me of losing my life for him, and thus becoming unworthy of his favors. I am much too careful of myself; I would certainly come to you, Reverend Father, as you direct me to do, if I felt that my strength was failing me. I am always ready to leave everything, even to die, in the spirit of obedience, wherever God wills. Other than that, I will never come down from the cross on which his goodness has placed me.

Taken from the *Manuscrit de 1652*, p. 257. The following statement was written by Father Ragueneau, superior of the mission, as an introduction to this letter: "In the last letter he wrote me, three days before his death, in response to my questions concerning his health and whether or not he wished to leave his mission for a brief respite in order to return to us and to rest a little, he answered me at great length, advancing a long list of reasons that obliged him to remain at his mission, but reasons whose real force lay in the truly apostolic zeal and charity that filled him."

SAINT NOËL CHABANEL

INTRODUCTION

Father Noël Chabanel, born on February 2, 1613, in the diocese of Mende, entered the novitiate of the Society of Jesus at Toulouse, February 9, 1630. He completed his education in that city and later taught rhetoric there. He left for Canada in the spring of 1643 and arrived at Quebec on August 15 of the same year. He remained there for a year, then went to Sainte-Marie des Hurons.

The circumstances of Chabanel's death are rather obscure. He had been working with Father Charles Garnier, but in the beginning of the year 1649, he had received the order to go alone to the Petuns, because of the threatening Iroquois danger, to encourage the other missioners. It was during the course of this trip that he met his death. We do not know whether he was massacred by the Iroquois; it seems more probable that he was killed by a Huron apostate. The Jesuits preferred not to probe into this sad story. "If we had wished to pursue this affair," wrote Father Ragueneau, "I think we would have found convincing proof against his murderer. But, in the midst of the public miseries, we judged it more advisable to suppress whatever suspicions we had about it; we ourselves closed our eyes to what we were sure no one had seen. It is sufficient for us that God be served" (*MS de 1652*, pp. 174–75).

BRIEF SKETCH
OF THE LIFE OF
FATHER NOËL CHABANEL

Father Noël Chabanel came to us from the Province of Toulouse in 1643. He was received into our Society in 1630, when he was only seventeen years of age. God had given him a strong vocation to serve as a missioner in these countries; but in addition to the physical hardships of life among the savages, he found himself faced with another. Despite heroic efforts to learn the Indian language, he found his progress so slight after three, four, and even five years that he could hardly make himself understood in the most ordinary matters. This was no little mortification to a man who burned with a desire to bring the word of God to the savages and who was deficient neither in memory nor ability, as he had clearly demonstrated by his success in teaching rhetoric in France for some years.

This difficulty in understanding the language was accompanied—or perhaps caused—by a temperament so opposed to the customs and manners of the savages that he could find very little in common with them. Their very appearance and physical bearing irked him. He could not accustom himself to the food of the country; the daily life in the missions did such violence to his entire nature that he suffered extraordinary hardships without any consolation—at least any of those that we call sensible. Always to sleep on the bare ground, to live from morning to night in a little hell of smoke, to wake up in the morning covered with the

---

Title, *Abrégé de la vie du Père Noël Chabanel*, and text of Father Ragueneau, taken from the *Manuscrit de 1652*, pp. 277–84.

snow that drifted in on all sides of the cabins of the savages, to find yourself, despite all efforts to the contrary, providing hospitality to all types of vermin—this is only the beginning of the list. Each sense had its own special tortures: never anything but water to quench your thirst; the best food only a paste made with Indian cornmeal boiled in water; incessant work on an almost empty stomach; never one moment in the day to retire to a spot that is not public; no other room, no other apartment, not even a tiny hole in which to enjoy a little privacy, not even for study; no other light than that from a smoky fire—and that fire surrounded by ten or fifteen persons, including children of all ages, who scream, weep, and wrangle, persons who are busy about their cooking, their meals, their work, about everything, in a word, that is done in a house.

And besides all this, when God withdraws his sensible graces and hides himself from a person who longs only for him, when he leaves him a prey to sorrow, to disgusts, and repugnances of nature—these are trials that are not within the scope of ordinary virtue; the love of God must indeed be strong in a heart if it is not to be stifled by them. To make matters worse—if that were possible—there was the continual sight of dangers to which one was exposed at every moment: attack by a savage enemy who would subject you to the sufferings of a thousand deaths before death itself should come as a merciful release from fire, flames, and unheard of cruelties. Who can doubt that a heroic courage is needed, a courage worthy of the children of God, if one is not to lose heart in the midst of such abandonment?

This abandonment was the test by which God tried the fidelity of this good Father for five or six years. The devil never prevailed over him, although it was not for want of trying. Daily the wily Satan reminded the sufferer that by returning to France, he would find the peace, the repose, and the comfort that during all his past life he had enjoyed; that there would be no lack of employment better suited to his disposition, employment in which so many saintly souls nobly practiced the virtues of charity and zeal for souls and spent their lives for the salvation of their fellow men. Never, in spite of this, did our saint break away from the cross on which God had affixed him; never did he ask to be taken down from it. On the contrary, in order to bind himself more irrevocably, he obliged himself by vow to remain there until death, so that he might die upon the cross. These are the terms of his vow, as he himself wrote it:

> Jesus Christ, my Savior, who by a wonderful dispensation of your fatherly providence have willed that I, although completely unworthy, should be a helper of your holy apostles in this vineyard of the Hurons; impelled by the desire to fulfill the purposes of the Holy Spirit that I should help convert to the Faith the barbarians of the Huron country, I, Noël Chabanel, in the presence of the Most Holy Sacrament of your Body and your Precious Blood, the tabernacle of God among men, vow perpetual stability in this mission of the Hurons, provided this be in conformity with the will of the superiors of the Society in my regard. I implore you, therefore, O my Savior, to accept me as a perpetual servant of this mission and grant that I may be worthy of such sublime service. Amen.

He made this vow on the Feast of Corpus Christi 1647. This dedication in no way lessened the rebellions of his nature. His virtue continued to be taxed, yet grace always triumphed. God granted him the perseverance he so ardently desired.

The last time that he left us to go to the mission where he died, while he was embracing and saying good-bye to the Father who was his spiritual director,[1] he said to him: "My dear Father, may it be in earnest this time, that I give myself to God; and may I belong only to him." He uttered these words with so strong an emphasis and a countenance so bent upon true sanctity that the Father to whom he was speaking was deeply touched, and shortly after, when he met one of his friends, he could not refrain from saying to him: "Truly, I have just been deeply moved! Good Father Chabanel just now spoke to me with the look and tone of voice of a victim who immolates himself. I do not know what God wills for him, but I see that he is forming a great saint."

It was true. God was indeed preparing Chabanel for the final sacrifice and granting him some kind of premonition of it. He had remarked to one of his friends: "I do not know what is going on in my heart or what God wills to do with me; but in one respect I feel entirely changed. I am naturally very fearful, but now that I am going into the greatest danger and feel that death is not very far away, I no longer feel any fear. This frame of mind is certainly not from me."

When he set out from the mission of Saint Matthias, on the very day of his death, he said to the Father who was embracing him in farewell:[2] "I am going where obedience calls me; if I do not succeed here, I shall ask the superior to permit me to return to the mission to which I was first assigned. In any case, God must be served until death."

In the following letter, which he wrote to Father Pierre Chabanel, his brother, also a priest in our Society, we can perceive his great appreciation of suffering. He wrote:

---

[1] Written on the margin of the manuscript: "It was Father Chastelain."
[2] Written on the margin: "It was Father Léonard Garreau."

Judging from human appearances, you, Reverend Father, have been very near to possessing a brother martyr; but alas! In the mind of God, in order to merit the honor of martyrdom, a quality of virtue quite different from mine is needed. Reverend Father Gabriel Lalemant, one of the three whom the *Relation* mentions as having suffered for Jesus Christ, just a month before his death had taken my place in the village of Saint Louis. I, more robust of body, was sent on a more remote and laborious mission, one not so fruitful in palms and crowns. My cowardice has, in the sight of God, rendered me unworthy of these favors. My turn will come whenever divine Goodness pleases, provided that, in the meantime, I strive to make myself a pseudo-martyr, a martyr to my nature, a martyr without bloodshed. The ravages of the Iroquois throughout this country will, perhaps, someday bring me the red martyrdom, through the merits of all these saints with whom I now have the consolation of leading so peaceful an existence in the midst of such constant turmoil and danger. For news of other mission activities, the *Relation* will have to suffice for you. I have only enough paper and leisure to beg you, Reverend Father, and all our Fathers in the province, to remember me at the holy altar as a victim destined, perhaps, for the fires of the Iroquois. God grant that, with the help of his saints, I may emerge victorious from so fierce a struggle.

These are his words—words unquestionably worthy of a man who lived only for the moment of sacrifice.

PIERRE CHAUMONOT

INTRODUCTION

We still possess the picturesque autobiography[1] that Father Chaumonot wrote at the command of his superiors. He was born in 1611 and began his education at Châtillon-sur-Seine. Since he wished to continue his studies at Beaune, he pilfered a hundred sous from an uncle with whom he was living, and departed, accompanied by a lad of his own age. He soon found himself without resources but refused to return home at the risk of having fingers pointed at him as a petty thief. He then decided "to travel throughout the world like a vagabond" and set out for Rome as if on a pilgrimage. After a series of adventures that, according to his account, became progressively comical, he ended up at the college of Terni, where he finished his classical studies and became a teacher. In 1632 he entered the Society of Jesus in Rome. A few months later he was sent to Florence, where a new novitiate house was just being opened. This is how he himself relates his admission to first vows:

> Toward the end of my two-year period of noviceship, there was considerable doubt as to whether or not I would be permitted to take vows because of violent headaches, which had become chronic. My novice master told me that he feared I might be dismissed from the Society. My first impulse upon

---

[1] This *Autobiographie* was published with certain other documents that appeared for the first time in a collection made by Father Carayon (Poitiers, 1869), and was reissued by Father Félix Martin (Paris, 1885). We have given here the letter of Father Chaumonot to his confessor and the two letters to Saint John Eudes from the latter text.

being advised of my status was to implore the Father-Consultors, on whom, after God, my fate depended, to be favorable to me. But Our Lord inspired me with a more powerful alternative: to have recourse to Saint Joseph, virgin spouse of the Virgin Mother. No one could do more than he, the head of Christ's family, to secure my admission into the Society of Jesus. I was not mistaken in this attempt, because our Fathers, unable to decide whether they should receive me or send me away, sent for the community physician to obtain his opinion about my illness. The doctor immediately set himself up as a director of conscience, and in the presence of the assembled Father-Councilors, asked me: How did my meditations go? Could I apply myself to them when the headaches were severe? I answered him with all frankness, saying that, in truth, at the beginning of a period of prayer, I felt very bad; a while later, as soon as I entered deeply into my meditation, I no longer felt pain. The doctor had heard enough to pronounce this favorable decision: "My dear Fathers, he who contemplates well as a novice will teach well as a regent." Thereupon I was told to withdraw to my room, where I renewed my prayers to my powerful advocate, Saint Joseph. Soon my rector, visibly happy, brought me the good news of my reception; with many gestures of genuine friendship, he bade me prepare to make the first vows of the Society within a few days" (*Autobiographie*, pp. 31–32).

This same faith and almost naïve confidence characterized his approach to all the difficulties of his life.

Chaumonot was sent to Fermo, not far from Loretto, at the end of his novitiate. After two years of teaching, he was given a year to review his philosophy. He then begged to be sent to the Canadian mission. This time there was no difficulty about his acceptance; he was ordained priest without his knowing much theology, and he departed May 4, 1639. He arrived at Quebec on August 1 and left immediately for the Huron mission. He started out as companion to Father

Ragueneau, but when the latter was appointed superior, Chaumonot became the companion to Father Daniel, the future martyr, and then to Father Brébeuf, with whom he went to the Neutrals in 1640.[2] He quickly distinguished himself, not only by his simplicity of heart and by his charity, but also by his facility for learning languages. He tells us:

> When my superiors learned that I knew the Huron language well, they assigned me to the complete care of two different missions. At the same time, I applied myself to mastering the rules of this tongue, the most difficult of all the Indian languages of North America. God saw fit to bless my efforts, to the extent that there was no expression or subtlety that I did not know or understand. Perhaps this gift of tongues was Our Lord's way of rewarding me for the attraction to humility that I had experienced from the time of my noviceship. Perhaps Saint Jerome, to whom I had prayed for several months, also assisted me in these efforts. I was helped also by Father Charles Garnier, a Parisian, who was beaten to death with the butt of a rifle in 1649 while performing his work of good shepherd in the mission. He had been in Canada since 1636. I no sooner learned of his glorious death than I promised him all my good works for eight days on the condition that he would make me the heir of his perfect knowledge of the Huron language. In any case, this language is, so to speak, the mother tongue of several others, particularly of the five Iroquois languages (which I did not then know), and it took me only a month to learn them when I was sent among those Indians. I acknowledge that I have often noticed that, when their five nations were assembled in council, I understood them all by a special grace of God, although I had studied only the Onnontague (*Autobiographie*, pp. 80–82).

---

[2] Cf. the account that he gives of the accident of Jean de Brébeuf, pp. 125–26.

In 1649, after the destruction of the mission, Chaumonot accompanied the remainder of the Huron nation to Quebec and settled with them on the Ile d'Orléans in 1651. He was sent on a mission to the Iroquois from 1655 to 1658 and returned immediately afterward to his beloved Hurons. He died in Canada on February 21, 1693.

A simple and vigorous soul with a humility suited to any test, Chaumonot had a special devotion to the Blessed Virgin and to Saint Joseph. He had sought humiliation and suffering from the time of his novitiate days; he also received consolations that were never to leave him. He himself tells us:

> One of the first things that I requested of this ... master of novices was that, in punishment of my pride, he should publicly interrogate me concerning my parents' social status, my coming to Italy, and the activities in which I had been engaged. I hoped by this means to expiate to some extent my faults and particularly the inexactitudes I had fabricated to conceal the modesty of my extraction. He granted my request, and one day, while the entire novitiate was assembled, he questioned me on all these points. God gave me the grace to practice the humility he had inspired, and I publicly declared who I really was, how and why I had left France, and what my experiences in Italy had been. This holy man added to the acknowledgment I had proposed to make, another act of mortification that I was not expecting. He told me to sing one of the native songs of my village. I immediately started to obey, but the music did not last long. My memory could summon up only an old coach song, which I started to sing. The good Father stopped me at the end of the first couplet, crying out: "Enough of that ridiculous song! If you don't know any better than that, don't ever sing again!" Since this Father did not wish me to make a general confession to him—I had done so once, shortly after my entrance—I begged him to let me give him an account of my sins in writing, in

order that, by knowing my crimes, he would understand to which vices I was inclined and of which penances and mortifications I had greatest need; however, he did not wish to read my paper.

I do not know whether or not these small humiliations that God inspired in me caused him to begin to make me taste more than ever the sweetness of consolation, not only in prayer, but also everywhere else. I was consoled to such an extent that, even after going to bed, I often felt myself caressed by Our Lord, as is a child by his mother, who, to induce sleep more gently, has him savor the milk from her maternal breast.

From this time until 1688, when I am writing this, that is, during at least fifty-five years, I have never experienced either dryness or boredom or distaste in my prayers. Divine Goodness has always conducted herself with me as a pious and prudent lady, who shows more tenderness to the smaller and weaker of her children than to the older and stronger ones. It is not that she loves him more than them; it is simply that she knows that, without this help, which the others can well forego, he would only languish, if, indeed, he did not die (*Autobiographie*, pp. 27–29).

The priest's written communication to his director clearly shows that he drew divine consolations from the sacrifices of Christ. For him, to be the son of God, to pray, to live his Mass, to give thanks, to render glory to God—all of these were one and the same thing. Father Chaumonot, who had never made a detailed study of theology, had meditated sufficiently on the mysteries of the Faith and had lived them so adequately in the gift of himself that their unity seemed simple and rich to him in the unique sacrifice of Jesus Christ.

LETTER TO SAINT JOHN EUDES

October 14, 1660

Reverend and dear Father:

Pax Christi!

I was consoled to hear from Monsieur Forcapel of your holy ambition to surpass everyone in your love for Our Lady. May God grant that you can communicate this spirit to all on earth who desire it! May I dare to ask you, for the love of Mary, the Virgin Mother, whom you love so much, to obtain for me the favor of being admitted among the least of your associates in the service of this sovereign mistress, or, if you prefer, as the most insignificant of your brothers in adoption to this Mother of mercy? If you die before me, would you have the goodness of informing me, or of leaving me as your heir, so far as it is in your power, a part of the devotion which you have for her? In this way, it will continue on earth even after your death. Monsieur Forcapel will tell you in person how displeased I am that so many persons receive Our Lord in the Blessed Sacrament, with the immense gifts that he imparts, without giving any sign of gratitude to her who has given him to us. In order to remedy or to make up for this ingratitude in some small way, I would be extremely happy to learn that there was an association of chaplains of Our Lady. If only there were a good number of zealous priests who would make a promise of never saying Mass without

---

Text from the *Autobiographie*, Father Martin's edition, pp. 240–41.

having among other intentions that of honoring the Blessed Virgin and of offering God's adorable Son to him through her hands. In this way, Christ in the Host would ascend to his Father through the intermediary of the same person by whom he descended among us when he became man. I would not wish for the devotion to be limited to this one intention alone. I would further desire that, before and after Mass and Holy Communion, the greatest possible honor be paid to the Blessed Mother. For example, on the evening before Holy Communion, one could implore her to take possession of his heart in preparation for the reception of her Son. After Mass, one could thank her for having given us such a lovable Shepherd of Souls. I beg you, Reverend Father, to consult our good Mistress herself about these matters. If she makes it known that these practices would be agreeable to her, begin the work. Start this association, and kindly admit me to it. Since few souls are drawn to devotions unless they contain some attraction of spiritual interest, I leave it to your prudence, and to your fervent desire of increasing the cult of the Holy Virgin, to put in writing some means of attracting souls to this devotion. Send me a copy of your work. The love you have for Our Blessed Mother will serve as my excuse for having taken the liberty of writing to you so familiarly, for I am only a poor man and unknown to you.

I recommend myself to your prayers and Holy Masses, Reverend Father, and to those of your fervent associates.

Your humble servant in the Lord,

Joseph-Marie[1] Chaumonot

---

[1] Father Chaumonot took the names of Joseph and Mary because of his special devotion to them.

LETTER TO SAINT JOHN EUDES

September 27, 1661

Reverend and dear Father:

Pax Christi!

If the greatest of all monarchs should adopt me as his son with the intention of having me succeed him as the head of all his estates, I would not experience one thousandth of the joy that your promise, Reverend Father, gave me. To inform me of everything Our Lord has given you in the way of devotion, of veneration, and of zeal for the glory of his most amiable and admirable Mother! I, a poor, begging Lazarus, a peasant and a son of the soil—from where do I receive such gifts, if not from the immense goodness of this Mother of mercy, who takes pleasure in granting the greatest favors to the most unworthy? Oh, how I would like to see Christians of the future desire and contrive to obtain these benefices and these spiritual gifts from the servants of God instead of pursuing the goods of the world. May God grant me thoughts and words able and suited to discussing such a subject. May I incite everyone to cherish it!

It is to you, my dear Father, and to those like you, that our Master does this honor. He makes use of your pen and your writings to bathe the world with his love and with that of his holy Mother. Venerable Father, do not fail to

Autobiographie, pp. 242–43.

continue this holy practice. If the good God intended to give me fresh sentiments, sentiments suited to procuring an increase of honor for our good Queen and Mother, I beg him rather to bestow the gift upon you. You would make better use of it than I. What I desire to obtain from his infinite generosity, by means of your Holy Sacrifices, is that he provide me with a knowledge of the languages of the poor Hurons and of the Iroquois for the sake of their conversion. Also, may I persevere until death in the work to which God has called me, and in which I have now spent more than twenty-four years.

Please, Reverend Father, in your charity, recommend me to the prayers and the Holy Masses of all his holy missionaries, whom I embrace in the heart and countenance of Christ as my brothers and coassociates in the succession of honors that the Savior has communicated to you concerning his dear Mother.

LETTER OF FATHER CHAUMONOT TO HIS CONFESSOR

Since my spiritual Father has asked me to put in writing an account of the things that occupy my soul in prayer and those that raise it to God, I am going to try to obey him, reporting events as my memory serves me, with no concern for any other order.

More than thirty years ago, I was influenced by these words of the Savior: "I glorify my Father", and the rest of that account as it appears in Saint John. I resolved to fight against the enemies of the Son of God, as well as pagans, Jews, and heretics, and to honor Jesus Christ from the same motive that he always had—that of giving glory to the Father. This gave rise to an ardent desire sincerely to adore my Savior in the Blessed Sacrament, because it is there that he continues to give glory to his Father and mine in great humiliation. Prompted by my twofold desire of honoring him—that of showing him what great honor I think is due him in the Holy Sacrament, and in reparation for the irreverences I committed against Holy Church in my former years—I often licked the altar steps, making the Sign of the Cross with my tongue in the dust and other soiled spots there, saying mentally: "His enemies shall kiss the ground."

When I was before the altar, offering the Host with the words *Suscipe, Sancte Pater*, I would feel a tremendous joy at having in my Jesus, whom I was about to immolate, an immense treasure of satisfactions with which to expiate all

---

Autobiographie, pp. 246–66. This letter was written during the last years of Chaumonot's life.

my sins. By this sacrifice, I also returned to God a great deal more glory than I, the sinner, and all other sinners, were able to deprive him of. At the words *pro omnibus circumstantibus*, I rejoiced at being able to offer to my Creator the adoration and homage of his own Son to supply for those obligations of thanksgiving and worship that all of his creatures either cannot, will not, or do not know how to give him. At the words *ut mihi et illis proficiat ad salutem*, I would count myself blessed that, by offering the sacrifice of the Savior to the Eternal Father, I was giving him a new occasion to recognize the merits and works of his Son in the person of the latter's adopted brothers, whom Christ wishes to save. God gives them part of his glory and of his happiness out of love for his Son, the Son who so loved the Father. Christ did not immolate himself for the Father only once; he continues to do so every day, a million times, for his Father's glory.

When it is time to offer the Host that is on the paten, I shall remember that it is made of several grains of wheat, which, taken all together, constitute a single particle of bread. This represents the unity of the Church to me; all the faithful make up but one family or one body, whose parts are united by the same bonds of Faith and all the truths of Holy Church. When I have finished this reflection, I can then consider that the Host I am to offer to God takes the place of all who have ever been Christians, those who are now, and those who will be. It is with such intentions that I joyfully offer this great and illustrious gathering to the Lord. The assembly is led by Jesus Christ, the Leader of all men. They render him due homage. Oh, divine Savior! How worthy you are of love and praise, to sacrifice your Body thus! And not only your Body, but your Blood, and all your greatness in order to obtain salvation for so many members of the human race for your Father. You offer these sacrifices to him, immolating yourself on our altars, an infinite number of times each day. Zeal for God's glory is not satiated by offering these to him only in Heaven, on behalf of those who have shown themselves faithful vassals and true adorers of his perfections. Let me have in my power all the hearts on earth! I will oblige them to direct all the love and respect of which they are capable to congratulating you on the conquests you have made over the souls you have created, souls you have made subject to your Father to increase his Kingdom—glorify the Lord with me! These are the words you say to them at every moment. Oh, what joy they have in thus uniting themselves to you to pay their just debts!

When I pronounce the words of Consecration, in addition to the intention of changing the substance of bread and wine into the substance of the Body and Blood of Jesus Christ, I wish with all my heart to transform all the faithful and myself—all mystically represented by the Host—into Jesus and God himself. Would that our priests could accomplish as effectively in the mystical or spiritual body of Christ what they accomplish in the bread and wine. What joy would they have if, when offering the sacramental words, they could produce not only Jesus Christ on our altars but bring forth in the world once more an infinity of children for this God of love. How much greater a King would he be were these priests to give him so many more subjects—or, rather, more kings as subjects, and even more kings divinized by their participation in his God-Body and his God-Soul. Oh, how ravished with joy I would be to see this happy transformation, to be able to say to these elite souls: You are all gods, and children of the Most High!

I will admit here that on the fifth of June, 1687, I was extraordinarily enamored of God and was struck with an intense desire to love as perfectly as I could this Savior who furnished me in the Holy Sacrament the means of repairing all the honor I had failed to pay to my God. During the time of this holy movement in my soul, I could not repeat often enough: *Suscipe, Sancte Pater, hanc immaculatam hostiam!*—Accept, Holy Father, this immaculate Host! No matter how often I said these words, I could not satiate my joy with their repetition.

After a long time had passed, as I grew progressively inflamed with love because of this great favor, I experienced an incredible urge to see my Creator as soon as possible in order to thank him for his favors. Moved by these desires, I turned to Our Lady, and I do not know how many times I called upon her with the prayer of Holy Church: *Eia, ergo, advocata nostra*—Turn, then, most gracious advocate, thine eyes of mercy toward us, and after this our exile, show unto us the blessed fruit of thy womb, Jesus.

If I were the son of a great monarch who loved me more than a good father loves his children, and for whom, because of my disorderly conduct, I had been the cause of his losing all his wealth, with how much regret would I not be penetrated! If, later, all his treasures were restored to him by another king, how much love would I not pour out on this latter, and what rejoicing would we not make together! Indeed, the sorrow I should feel for having wronged my God should be much greater than what I felt for having ruined this earthly monarch. Likewise, my gratitude toward him who restored the wealth would be much less than that which is due to my Savior, who, every hour and every moment, in a million places, honors infinitely more his Father and mine than I and all sinners together could have dishonored him.

In that same month of June, in the same year, I received a light that revealed to me the infinite lovableness of my God and at the same time exposed my total inability to love him, to adore him, to bless him, to glorify him as much as I would have liked and as much as he deserved. In this intense desire that sought to glorify him, I wished that I could increase to infinity the number of angels and saints so that they could praise him with their lips and love him with their hearts. Oh, what pleas I could have poured out to the Holy Spirit in order to obtain my burning desire, begging him to sanctify an immense number of the faithful, to whom I could unite myself in order to love and honor my God! Then, realizing that I had already before me in the Blessed Sacrament more than I was asking for, since the Son of God was sacrificing himself in an infinity of churches, I was greatly consoled that, by uniting myself to Jesus, I had the means of giving to my God all the honor and all the love that he deserved. And not only I, but all creatures, have this same power through the same means. O Lord, how sweet is your Spirit, filling us with blessings, poor servants that we are! That is why you have distributed to us all that you have merited, you give us a share of all you have done for the glory of your Father, so that we may offer it to him as a fruit produced by ourselves. Ah, if what Saint Paul said is true—and it really is—that whoever unites himself to God becomes the same Spirit with him, let me keep myself united always, either in reality or in my thoughts and in my love, to the tabernacles, to the altars, to the Hosts, in which this perfect adorer of my God reposes, so that, with my spirit united to his, we may jointly and constantly praise our divine Father!

If there were ever a kingdom that was elective, and the electors were unable to agree on a choice for a king, and if, by some chance, they should give me the privilege of placing the crown on the head of him I thought most worthy of it, what joy would be mine to place this crown on the head of my own father, the one most deserving of it! How happy then, are priests, who, every single day, can place on the head of God himself the crowns of all the true kings of the world—his saints—and place them there while representing him at Mass, giving him all the homage that these kings receive on earth! Besides, I, if I had raised my own father to royalty, would see to it that his kingdom were increased, either by bringing in a much larger and flourishing court or by securing for him a greater number of subjects and provinces in his realm. That is what the priest does for his Creator, by offering him the Holy Sacrifice, at which all the angels and all the orders of saints are present as payers of tribute. Oh, what glory and what consolation for God to see all of them, as a result of the actions of his priest, prostrate before his throne, with his adorable Son, who immolates himself again, in their company, to the supreme majesty of his Father!

It gives much pleasure to the saints to see the priest represent what, according to the example of Jesus and as his followers, they themselves did on earth to give glory to the Father. On the other hand, if they were able to feel any regret, it would pain them if the priest did not mention them at Mass, since he would prevent them, by his silence, from being congratulated during this magnificent ceremony for having contributed something to the glory of our God.

The priest should pay special attention to this prayer in the Canon of the Mass, the part that begins with the words *Communicantes et memoriam venerantes in primis gloriosae Virginis*

Mariae, since he ought to rejoice in his heart in union with these saints that he mentions by name and all those others, because during their lifetime, they merited the honor of accompanying, after their death, their divine Master in this divine mystery. This is the most noble embassy there could possibly be!

Jesus is called the Crown of the Eternal Father, and this crown is, as it were, loaded and embellished by the glory of the saints, which we can regard as so many rubies, pearls, and diamonds! Oh, how great is the joy and honor for these just souls to see themselves united to Jesus, either in Heaven or on our altars, as are the precious stones in this rich diadem!

The Savior appeared to Saint Peter of Alexandria in a robe that was all torn. He told Peter that this garment represented his Church, which the heretic Arius had reduced to such a wretched state. The priest, equally as effective as the heretic but in a contrary direction, can remedy all this evil by offering the Sacred Host in expiation for all sins and for the conversion of all sinners. This is possible because, through the merits of Jesus Christ, all the greatest enemies of the Church can be united there, just as Saint Paul, who had been the greatest persecutor of the Church, became her greatest advocate. Could it be that the divine Mercy could not take pity on a few poor sinners or heretics at each Mass, in which he is offered all the merits of his Son, of his Mother, and even of all the saints! *Tantus labor non sit cassus!* Let not such great work be in vain! Oh, may these illustrious saints continue to feel an obligation to the priest, who makes their satisfactions of value with those of Jesus Christ for the deliverance of the souls in Purgatory! Would I not be guilty of an unworthy cowardice if I did not join some mortifications, some acts of charity, or some victory over my base nature to the good works of these holy ones?

In our letters from France, they tell us that our king has armies composed of three or four hundred thousand men. That is certainly glorious for him. But if he himself were able to be multiplied that many times by a miraculous reproduction, he would be able to have that large an army composed of himself alone, and he alone could go out and wage war against all his enemies. That is exactly what Jesus Christ does in the Holy Eucharist, where, multiplied an infinite number of times, he is, so to speak, a whole army of Jesus Christs, an army that disarms the justice of God, an army that puts the demons to flight, an army that even triumphs over hearts. And certainly, if we say that the Church is like an army in battle array, she holds this glorious advantage from the Savior, her spouse; then, since he gives it to her, he must have the power to do so and, therefore, must be greater than she. The Italians call by the name "glory" an apparatus that they construct for Forty Hours' Devotions in which they expose the Blessed Sacrament; and since this vessel is very beautiful, they say to each other, in the greatest admiration, "*O bella, bella gloria!*" Likewise, when the angels see a priest preparing to celebrate the Holy Mysteries, or a layman prepared to the best of his ability to receive his sweet Savior, they must surely cry out: "*O bella, bella gloria!* May the glory of this celebrant or this communicant give great glory to Jesus!"

A friend would owe us much gratitude if we were able to use some of his goods that he had entrusted to us as a means of procuring greater profit for him. Likewise, he would have reason to be angry if we had neglected to take advantage of a favorable opportunity for securing much profit or great glory for him.

The Holy Sacrifice, and even Holy Communion, put the treasures of Jesus Christ and of his saints at the disposition of the faithful. Oh, how much pleasure we would give to God by offering to him these immense riches for the redemption of souls—either those in Purgatory or those still on earth. The Gospel story describes for us how rigorously that servant was punished when he did not have his talent produce any profit. The priest will, then, be even more rigorously punished if, when he has so much wealth at his disposal, he does not use it to help his poor friends!

The priest should rejoice extremely when he says these words of the Canon: *Supra quae propitio ac sereno vultu respicere digneris* ... since at each Mass that he says he has the honor of presenting to God so large a number of his ancestors, his friends, his officers, who have spent their lives and given their blood even to the last drop, for his glory. Hence, it is quite just that the priest should intend not only to renew the pleasure that the Lord received from the sacrifices of Abel, Abraham, Melchizedek, and all the other saints of the Old Testament, but he should also offer him the divine Victim who was prefigured by all of these. How much love does not our Savior deserve, who, to fulfill more worthily his office of Mediator of all men, multiplies himself at every hour an infinite number of times in the hands of his priests. By this multiplication of his Body and Blood, he wishes to unite to his own merits all the actions and sufferings of his mystical members!

Indeed, when Jesus spoke about that mysterious fire that he had come to kindle in our hearts, he could have been speaking about the Holy Eucharist alone. May every priest who holds that divine fire between his hands and in his bosom be kindled with it, so that by its flame, he may consume all the sins of the world!

One day, during my morning prayers, I experienced a most extraordinary feeling of joy. It was caused by a very forceful thought that at every Mass that is said, the holy humanity of Jesus receives new glory from his Father in thanksgiving for the humility that he practices in the Blessed Sacrament. In addition, I was assured at the same time that, through the Savior's representation in this sacrifice of what the saints have contributed to the glory of God, they, in turn, receive an accidental glory, which comes to them from the heavenly Father's pleasure in what they have done and said in the fervor of their service.

When the priest repeats the same idea in several words that have almost the same meaning, such as *Haec dona, haec munera, haec sancta sacrificia; hostiam puram, hostiam sanctam, hostiam immaculatam*, he ought to do it with an excess of joy, as if declaring by this means that he cannot find enough terms to express his thought. It is just like the case of the lover who, in his attempts to show how deeply enamored of his beloved he is, does not stop at calling her "my love", but also adds, "my heart", "my life", "my delight"—and many more.

For my part, I never have enough words to express to my Creator my joy at his having found so beautiful a manner of being honored by his creatures. He so loved the world that he gave to it his only Son, and the world, in turn, loves him so much that it returns to him that same Son. I know of no greater honor for a creature than the ability to give his Creator all the homage, thanks, and satisfactions due to him. Nevertheless, that is what we do by offering God, on our altars, his dearly beloved Son. All creatures have some part in this offering, since, in addition to the holy humanity that is offered, the Blessed Virgin whose Son is sacrificed, the angels who join the priest in offering him to God, the consecrated ministers and the faithful people who belong to the royal priesthood of Christ—in addition to all of these, the bread and wine that are changed there to the Body and Blood of our Savior, the water that is mingled with the wine to signify the union of God with his people, the stone that is used for the altar, the white cloths that are symbolic of the purity with which we should communicate, as well as the candles, which by their light and their fire show us what should be the nature of our faith and our fervor, also have their share in it. Besides all these, there are the earth, the air, the sun, the stars, the farmers, the winemakers, the millers, the bakers, the workers of all sorts—all these, too, contribute to the glory of God and have their part in this offering. Never has there been an ambassador who bore to any monarch such great presents from so many nations as the priest offers every day to God in the mystery of our altars. If, for example, the ambassadors from Siam pleased our king Louis le Grand so delightfully that they received honors in so many cities of France as well as from the king himself, what honor and glory will not a good priest receive, he who has so often honorably fulfilled his embassy in the name of Jesus Christ! *Pro Christo ergo legatione fungimur.* Will there not be present a choir of angels, an order of saints, by whom he will be regaled, even as he is at the present time? Oh, how great is the dignity of a priest! How much gratitude I owe to God for having called me thus to serve him, for having withdrawn me from the slavery of Satan, to whom I had made myself subject by my sins! Every day I become increasingly convinced that Our Lord, at the Holy Sacrifice, not only offers to God the holocaust of himself, but joins all of us—all his members and all his creatures—with him, as if we were sanctified by him. *Quoniam omnia coaugmentata erant in eo*—because everything was increased in union with him, said one of the Fathers of the Church. Would it be possible for him who is the All in all to withhold from the sacrifice of himself anything that would contribute to God's glory, no matter how small? Would he, our Leader, wish to separate us from his person after he had so perfectly united us to himself?

If a generous man should find an immense treasure, he would be delighted to enrich all his relatives and friends with it. The priest, at every Mass he says, has an infinite treasure that can enrich millions of worlds. Would he not, then, be guilty of a great wrong if he did not share it with all creatures, if he did not invite them to express their gratitude for it to God? That is the feeling that animates me when, in leaving the altar, I recite the *Benedicite omnia opera Domini Domino* (Dan 3:57). What consolation it is to have an infinite number of associates to honor, to love, to serve my God! For that reason, I would wish to offer the Eucharistic Sacrifice at every moment! And since I am not able to do this so often myself, I shall do so *in voto*—by my desires—by uniting my intentions with all the priests who now or who ever will offer this holy sacrifice, even to the end of the world. A priest should never approach the altar for Mass unless he has first performed an act of mortification or an act of charity, in order by this to increase the sacrifice that he is preparing to offer—the sacrifice of all that his God has done and suffered for him.

When I consider the honor Jesus Christ gives to his Father by immolating himself for him so many times every day, I would like to be able to unite myself to him so as to be completely penetrated by him—body and soul, members and faculties. But because I realize how unworthy I am, I beg the Eternal Father to lodge me in his bosom, the only place perfectly worthy of him. Then, at the end of my thanksgiving, I am filled with joy by the thought that the divine Father and the divine Son, loving each other infinitely, cause each other an unspeakable happiness. One day, when I was rejoicing with these two adorable Persons, I heard within my heart: "Enter into the joy of your Lord" (Mt 25:23). Oh, what an immense blessing it was for me to enter!

When the centurion witnessed the death Jesus suffered in obedience to God the Father, he exclaimed: "Truly that man was the Son of God!" In the same way, the mystical death of the Savior, renewed so often on our altars through obedience to the priest, ought to transport us also to the extent that we cry out when he elevates the Host: *Vere Filius Dei erat iste!* It is thus that we realize that, of the two Persons, one is the Father and one is the Son when the latter offers to the former all sorts of deference and submission.

I do not believe that there is a better way of causing pleasure to a grateful and affectionate person than to furnish him the opportunity for just gratitude toward an unimportant person. It is that pleasure my dear Jesus gives to me every day by placing in my hands all possible treasures, even to the fullness of his satisfactions, his graces, and his spirit, so that by them I can gratify, so to speak, my God. When I arise in the morning, I would like my Savior to repeat to me in the depths of my heart: "Courage, my child! See, I am placing in your power all my worth and my whole Person for you to dispose of as you will." Oh, what joy would then be mine! What thanks I would pour out! "No, not to us, Lord, not to us: but to your name give glory" (Ps 113 [115]:1).

It is considered a high honor to be admitted to the table of important men to celebrate some unusual occasion, or to the council of the king to discuss some unusual affair. The priest should, then, consider his happiness at being present at the table of his God, there to discuss matters with him in the company of the very angels and the saints.

Oh! How they wish for prosperity for his Kingdom! How the souls in Purgatory long for their liberty! How burning is the zeal of the just on earth for the conversion of sinners!

The dignity of an ambassador is determined by the importance of the person who delegates him, by the power of the monarch to whom he is sent, by the gravity of the matter he is to discuss, and by the value of the presents he bears. But where can all these conditions be fulfilled more perfectly than in the Sacrifice of the Mass? "We are, therefore, Christ's ambassadors" (2 Cor 5:20), sent by God, his Father, with the most divine of all presents, to discuss the satisfaction owed to God by the sinner and to procure the salvation of mankind.

"LAST YEAR THEY BAPTIZED 350 'IROQUOIS" 1673

Bibliography
of Works Cited

Alegambe, Philippe. *Mortes illustres et gesta eorum de Societate Jesu qui in odium fidei . . . ab ethnicis, haereticis, vel aliis necati sunt.* Rome: ex typis Varesii, 1657.

Campeau, Lucien. *La mission des Jésuites chez les Hurons, 1634–1650.* Montreal: Éditions Bellarmin, 1987.

Carayon, Auguste. *Le P. Pierre Chaumonot de la Compagnie de Jésus, autobiographie et pièces inédites.* Poitiers: Éditions Chaumonot, 1869.

Catherine of Siena, *Livre de dialogues.* Translated from the original Italian, with an introduction to the study of mysticism, by Algar Thorold. London: Kegan, Trench, 1896.

Chastelain, Pierre. *Affectus amantis Christum Jesum, seu exercitium amoris erga Dominum Jesum pro tota hebdomada.* Paris: D. Bechet, 1648.

Gerson, Johannis. *De Imitatione Christi et de contemptu omnium vanitatum mundi.* Venice: P. Loesslein de Langencenn, 1483.

Jamet, Albert. *Écrits spirituels et historiques de Marie de l'Incarnation.* 4 vols. Paris: Desclée de Brouwer; Quebec: L'Action Sociale, 1929–39.

Larivière, Florian. *La vie ardente de saint Charles Garnier.* Montreal: Éditions Bellarmin, 1957.

Latourelle, René. *Brébeuf.* Coll. "Classiques Canadiens" Montreal and Paris: Éditions Fides, 1958.

———. *Étude sur les écrits de saint Jean de Brébeuf.* 2 vols. Montreal: Éditions de l'Immaculée-Conception, 1952.

Leclercq, Jacques. *Études sur saint Bernard et le texte de ses écrits.* Rome: Curia Generalis Sacri Ordinis Cistercienses, 1953.

Lettres du Bas-Canada (Montreal), periodical published annually.

Manuscrit de 1652: Mémoires touchant la mort et les vertus des Pères Isaac Jogues, Anne de Nouë, Antoine Daniel, Jean de Brébeuf, Gabriel Lallemant, Charles Garnier, Noël Chabanel, et un séculier, René Goupil. Montreal: Collège Sainte-Marie.

Martin, Félix. *Relation abrégée de quelques missions des Pères de la Compagnie de Jésus.* Montreal: John Lovell, 1852.

Migne, Jacques-Paul. *Patrologiae Latinae cursus completus.* Rotterdam: De Forel, 1952.

Pottier, Aloÿs. *Le Père Louis Lallemant et les grands spirituels de son temps.* Paris: Téqui, 1927–29.

Pouliot, Léon. *Étude sur les Relations des Jésuites de la Nouvelle-France, 1632–1672.* Paris: Desclée de Brouwer, 1940.

Rapport de l'archiviste: Collection de manuscrits contenant lettres, mémoires, archives et autres documents relatif à la Nouvelle-France, recueillis aux archives de la province de Québec, mis en ordre et édits sous les auspices de la Législature de Québec. A. Coté, 1883–85.

Rigault, Georges, et G. Guyau. *Martyrs de la Nouvelle-France.* Paris: Spes, 1925.

Rochemonteix, Camille de. *Les Jésuites de la Nouvelle-France au XVIIe siècle.* 3 vols. Paris: Letouzey et Ané, 1895–96.

Rouquette, Robert. *Textes des Martyrs de la Nouvelle-France.* Paris: Éditions du Seuil, 1947.

Schurhammer, Georg. *Franz Xaver.* Freiburg: Herder, 1955.

Sommervogel, Carlos. *Bibliothèque de la Compagnie de Jésus*. Brussels: Schepens; Paris: A. Picard, 1890–1932.

Thwaites, Reuben Gold. *The Jesuit Relations and Allied Documents*. Cleveland, 1896–1901.

Vaumas, Guillaume de. *L'Éveil missionnaire de la France au XVIIe siècle*. Paris: Bloud et Gay, 1959.

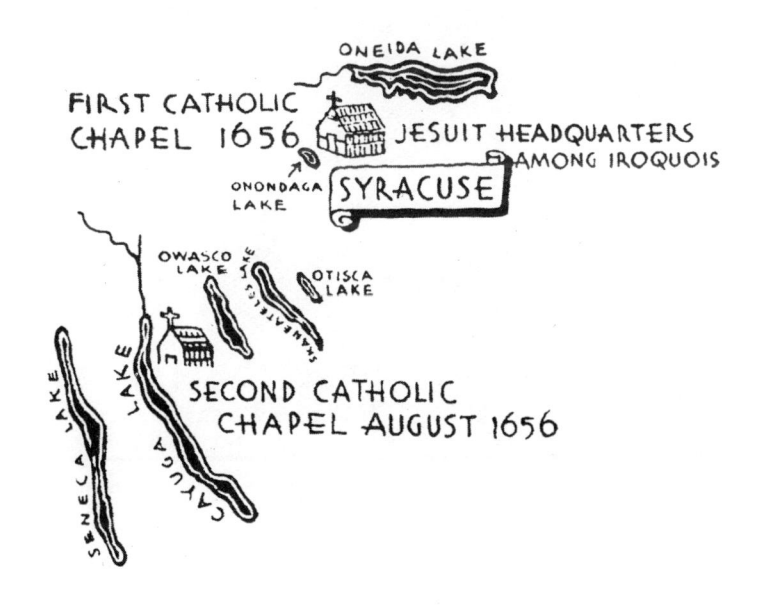

Index

Abenaquis, 30
Acadia colony, 21–24, 41, 111–13
Acarie, Madame, 46
Ahatsistari, Eustache, 250, 251, 266
Alacoque, Saint Margaret Mary, 10
Algonquins, 30, 62
Amyot, Jacques, 11
Anchieta, Joseph, 166
Andastes, 30
Aristotle, 12
Attikamegues, 30

Baltasar, Christopher, 115n2
Beaune, Jesuit college at, 395
Bernières, Jean de, 10
Bertrix, Jacques, 162, 240
Bérulle, Pierre de, 10, 46
Biard, Pierre
    letters of, 41
    and Massé, 21, 23, 111–12, 115n2
Binet, Étienne, 240
Blackfeet, 14
Bossuet, Jacques-Bénigne, 10
Boucher, Pierre, 169
Bourbon, Charles de, 24
Bourbon, Henri de, 24
Bourdalou, Louis, 10

Bourges, Jesuit college at, 59, 137–38
Brébeuf, Saint Jean de, 9, 121–84
    accident of, 125–26
    birth of, 123
    character and personality of, 123, 125, 126–31
    and Chaumonot, 169, 397
    in contrast to Jogues, 127, 129
    devotion to the Holy Eucharist, 49–50
    dreams of, 215
    early missionary activity of, 21–22, 24–25, 35–37, 38
    gentleness of, 123, 127, 128
    and Huron mission, 32–33, 124–25, 126, 139–52
    and Marie de l'Incarnation, 52
    and Indian mentality, 35–37, 62
    Jesuit studies and career in Europe, 123–24
    and Gabriel Lalemant, 137–38
    and Louis Lallemant, 45, 46
    language studies of, 25, 124, 126
    martyrdom of, 34, 126, 176–84, 206n2
    martyrdom preparations and vow, 124, 131, 133–34, 135, 137, 174–75

Brébeuf, Saint Jean de (*continued*)
  and the means of the cross, 131, 132
  and the Neutral nation, 125–26, 135–36
  persecution of, 135–36
  and Ragueneau, 46, 126–27, 159, 160–75
  return to France, 134–35
  spiritual development and mystical ascent of, 131–34, 137
  spiritual journal of, 127–28, 134n1, 136–36, 160–75
  temptations of, 129–31
  visions and mysticism of, 127–31, 132, 135, 160–75
  will of, 124–25
Brébeuf, Saint Jean de (writings)
  Important Advice for Those Whom It Shall Please God to Call to New France, Especially to the Country of the Hurons, 139–52
  Instructions for the Fathers of Our Society Who Will Be Sent to the Hurons, 153–56
  Letter to Reverend Father Le Jeune, 157–59
  Graces, Visions, Illustrations, and Comments Excerpted from the Writings of Father Jean de Brébeuf, 160–75
  The Holy Deaths of Father Jean de Brébeuf and Father Gabriel Lalemant, 176–84
Bremond, Henri, 46
Bressani, Father, 30, 32, 219, 221
Breve Relatione, 221

Bruno, Saint, 277
Burel, Gilbert, 24
Buteux, Father, 49

Caen, Jesuit college at, 59
Calvinists, 23–24, 26–27, 28
Campeau, Lucien, 111, 206, 219, 327
Capuchins, 28, 38
Carayon, Father, 395n1
Carmelites, 338, 345–46
Cartier, Jacques, 22
Castillon, Father, 327–29
Catherine of Siena, Saint, 147, 360, 362
Chabanel, Saint Noël, 385–92
  Jesuit studies of, 387
  language studies of, 388
  martyrdom of, 34, 206n2, 387
Chabanel, Saint Noël (writings)
  Brief Sketch of the Life of Father Noël Chabanel, 388–92
Chabanel, Pierre, 391
Champlain, Samuel, 22–28, 33
  on arrival of Jesuits, 25–26
  exploration by, 23–24
Chantal, Saint Jeanne de, 10
Charton, François, 24
Chastelain, Pierre, 185–202
  birth of, 187
  and Brébeuf, 135, 159
  devotion to the Eucharist, 50
  and Garnier, 187, 335, 336
  and Huron mission, 187–88
  and Marie de l'Incarnation, 188, 190
  Jesuit studies of, 187

and Jogues, 206, 231
and Louis Lallemant, 45–46
theological doctrine and spiritual formulae of, 49,
189–90
Chastelain, Pierre (writings),
188–92
Affectus amantis Christum Jesum,
188–89, 195
Letter to Reverend Father Le
Jeune (August 8, 1636),
190–91, 193–94
The Love of Christ, 195–202
Chaumonot, Pierre, 393–417
death of, 398
devotion to the Blessed Virgin,
398, 400–401, 402–3
devotion to the Eucharist, 50,
401, 404–17
dreams of, 215
and the French mystics, 47
Huron language studies of,
397–98
and Huron mission, 34,
396–98
and Iroquois mission, 398
Jesuit studies of, 395–96
and Neutral mission, 125–26,
136, 397
spiritual concerns of, 50,
398–99
Chaumonot, Pierre (writings),
50, 395n1
Autobiographie, 395
Letter of Father Chaumonot to
His Confessor, 404–17
Letter to Saint John Eudes
(October 14, 1660),
400–401

Letter to Saint John Eudes
(September 27, 1661), 402–3
Chiwatenwa, Joseph, 170n16, 171
Cicero, 12
Coadjutor Brothers, 22, 24, 129
Coeur d'Alènes, 14
Colbert, Jean-Baptiste, 27
Collège de Clermont, 59, 205,
336
Collège Sainte-Marie (Montreal),
220n9
Colombière, Saint Claude de la,
10
Company of One Hundred Associates (Company of New
France), 27
Condren, Charles de, 10, 46, 47
Congregation of Propaganda, 42
Constitutions of the Society, 41
Corneille, Pierre, 11
Coton, Pierre, 112, 173, 240
Couture, Guillaume, 251–52,
264, 267, 270, 280, 298

Daniel, Saint Antoine
and Chaumonot, 397
and Louis Lallemant, 45
martyrdom of, 9, 34, 206n2
De Nouë, Father, 25, 66, 68
De Smet, Peter, 14
Desjardins, Paul, 44n17
disease and the Huron mission,
33, 124, 171–72
donnés, 219n6, 271n12

École Sainte-Geneviève (Paris),
220n9
Écrits spirituels et historiques (Marie
de l'Incarnation), 50n21, 51

Eries, 30
Étude sur les écrits de saint Jean de Brébeuf (Latourelle), 123
Eu, Jesuit college at, 45, 124, 336
Eucharist
    Brébeuf and, 49–50
    Chastelain and, 50
    Chaumonot and, 50, 401, 404–17
Eudes, Saint John, 10, 46, 47
    Chaumonot's letters to, 400–401, 402–3

Favre, Saint Peter, 39–40
Flatheads, 14
Forest, Abbé J. B. Pierre, 219–20
Fort Richelieu, 295–96
François I, 22
fur trade, 22–24

Garnier, Saint Charles, 333–84
    beardlessness of, 339–40
    and Brébeuf, 159
    character and personality of, 337, 339–45
    charity of, 344–45
    and Chastelain, 187, 335, 336, 342
    early life of, 335, 337
    and Huron mission, 43n16, 336
    and Marie de l'Incarnation, 52, 335n2
    Jesuit studies of, 336–37
    and Jérôme Lalemant, 345
    and Louis Lallemant, 45–46
    martyrdom of, 9, 34, 206n2, 336
    and Petun mission, 336
    Ragueneau on, 335, 337, 341, 344, 345, 384
    relations with his father, 335, 336–40, 364–70
Garnier, Saint Charles (writings), 47, 336–47
    Letter to His Brother (June 25, 1632), 348–51
    Letter to His Brother (March 31, 1636), 352–54
    Letter to His Brother (July 20, 1636), 355–57
    Letter to Reverend Father Le Jeune (August 8, 1636), 358–59
    Letter His Brother (April 30, 1637), 360–63
    Letter to His Father (1638), 364–70
    Letter to His Brother (June 23, 1641), 371–73
    Letter to His Brother (May 22, 1642), 374–77
    Letter to His Brother (May 14, 1646), 378–80
    Letter to His Brother (August 12, 1649), 381–83
    Letter to Reverend Father Ragueneau (December 4, 1649), 384
Garnier, Jean, 336–39
Garreau, Léonard, 343
Gaufestre, Brother, 25
Godeau, Antoine, 277
Gonzaga University, 15
Goupil, Saint René
    captivity by the Iroquois, 212, 250–52, 258, 259, 260, 264, 268, 270, 271–72

martyrdom of, 9, 206n2, 207,
  271–72, 297–98, 310,
  311–20
 writing of, 12
Goyau, G., 42n14
Guercheville, Madame de, 23

Haye, Father de la, 50
Henri IV, 23, 112, 173n18
*Histoire littéraire du sentiment
  religieux en France* (Bremond),
  46
history of French Jesuit missionaries in New France, 21–55
 assessing successes and failures
   of, 34–38
 and the Calvinists, 23–24,
   26–27, 28
 and Champlain, 22–28, 33
 and colonization, 27
 and conditions of life, 31–32
 and cultivation of the land, 25,
   26, 28
 descriptions of Indian habits,
   customs, and beliefs, 37
 earliest Acadia missions, 22–24,
   111–13
 and England's war with New
   France, 27–28
 and French mysticism, 46–47,
   50–55
 and fur trade, 22–24
 and the Huron mission, 13,
   30–34, 43–47
 and Marie de l'Incarnation,
   50–55
 and Louis Lallemant, 44–46
 and the Recollets, 24–25, 28, 38
 and rules and practices of the
   Jesuit order, 38
 and study of the Indian languages, 25, 28
 and surrender of Quebec
   (1629), 27
 understanding of the Indian
   mentality, 35–37, 62
 See also missionary narratives
   and letters
Huby, Vincent, 46
humanism, 11
Huron mission, 13, 30–34,
  43–47
 Brébeuf and, 32–33, 124–25,
   126, 139–52
 Chastelain and, 187–88
 Chaumonot and, 34, 396–98
 disease and, 33, 124, 171–72
 Garnier and, 43n16, 336
 at Ile d'Orléans, 34, 398
 Iroquois control of, 13, 33–34
 Jogues and, 206
 Jérôme Lalemant and, 32
 Louis Lallemant and, 44–46
 Le Jeune and, 30–31
 meager success of, 32–33
 missionary narratives of, 43–44
 population size of, 30–31,
   32–33
Hurons
 and the Iroquois nation, 13,
   31, 33–34
 relations with neighboring
   tribes, 30

Ignatius, Saint, and Jesuit letter-writing tradition, 39–40

Ile d'Orléans, Huron mission at, 34, 398
Imitation of Christ (Thomas à Kempis), 173–74, 190, 279, 301n3
Incarnation, Marie de l', 10, 46, 50–55
  and Chastelain, 188, 190
  and French mysticism, 50–55
  and Garnier, 52, 335n2
  and Jérôme Lalemant, 53–54
  and Le Jeune, 61
  spiritual life for, 53–55
  writings of, 50n21, 51–55
Iroquois nation, 13–15
  and captivity of Goupil, 212, 250–52, 258, 259, 260, 264, 268, 270, 271–72
  and captivity of Jogues, 207, 208–10, 211, 214–17, 244–46, 250–93, 342
  and Chaumonot, 398
  and the Huron mission, 13, 31, 33–34
  Jogues and Iroquois language, 38, 207, 218, 283, 285
  Jogues's return to, 218, 308–10
  and martyrdom of Brébeuf, 126
  and martyrdom of Chabanel, 387
  and martyrdom of Garnier, 336

Jamet, Dom, 51
The Jesuit Relations and Allied Documents (Thwaites, ed.), 17, 37, 39–42
  Chastelain and, 187

Jogues and, 212, 221, 244
Le Jeune and, 41–42, 60
Jogues, Saint Isaac, 9, 203–331
  birth of, 205
  and Brébeuf, 127, 129, 159
  captivity by the Iroquois, 207, 208–10, 211, 214–17, 244–46, 250–93, 342
  character and personality of, 127, 206–7, 210–12
  dreams of, 207–8, 213, 215–16, 231–33, 234–39
  escape from captivity, 217, 294–304
  and Garnier, 224n3, 336
  and Huron mission, 206
  illness of, 229n7
  and Iroquois language, 38, 207, 218, 283, 285
  Jesuit studies of, 205
  journey to New France, 224–25, 227–28
  and joy in suffering, 213, 214–15
  and Louis Lallemant, 45
  martyrdom of, 206, 219
  and martyrdom of René Goupil, 206n2, 207, 271–72, 297–98, 310, 311–20
  post-captivity, return to France, 217–18, 305–7
  return to New France and the Iroquois mission, 218, 308–10
  writing style/qualities, 208–9
Jogues, Saint Isaac (writings)
  copies and textual concerns, 219–21

Letters to His Mother (1636–1637), 205–6, 210–11, 217, 219–20, 222–30
In the Land of the Hurons: A Dream (1638), 207–8, 231–33
Prisoner of the Iroquois: A Dream, (1642), 234–39
Prisoner of the Iroquois: Several Visions (1642–1643), 240–43
Prisoner of the Iroquois: Letter to the Governor of New France (June 30, 1643), 244–46
Prisoner of the Iroquois: Letter to His Provincial in France (August 5, 1643), 247–93
Account of His Escape: Letter to Father Jérôme Lalemant (August 30, 1643), 294–304
After His Return to France: Letter to a Priest (January 5, 1644), 305–6
After His Return to France: Letter to Father Charles Lalemant (January 6, 1644), 307
Mission to the Iroquois: Letter to Father Jérôme Lalemant (May 2, 1646), 308–10
Martyrdom of René Goupil by the Iroquois, 311–20
New Holland, 321–26
Final Departure: Letter to Father Castillon (September 12, 1646), 327–29

Final Departure: Letter to a Fellow Jesuit (September 1646), 330–31
Juby, Vincent, 226

Kertk, Admiral, 27

La Flèche, Jesuit college at, 59, 112, 137
La Rochelle, siege of (1628), 27
La Lande, Saint Jean de, 9, 206n2, 219
Lalemant, Charles
and cultivation of the land, 25, 26
early letters to his brother Jérôme, 41–42
early missionary activity of, 21–22, 24–25
Jogues' letter to, 307
and Le Jeune, 66
and Massé, 112
Lalemant, Saint Gabriel, 51, 137–38
and Brébeuf, 137–38, 176–84
martyrdom of, 34, 138, 176–84, 206n2
Lalemant, Jérôme, 32
and Brébeuf, 125
early letters of Charles Lalemant to, 41–42
and Garnier, 345
and Huron mission, 125
and Marie de l'Incarnation, 53–54
Jogues' letters to, 294–304, 308–10

Lallemant, Louis, 10, 12, 213n5
    and Huron mission, 44–46
    and Le Jeune, 59
Larivière, Florian, 188, 335n2, 336n3
Latourelle, Father, 123, 131, 165nn10–11
Le Brun, Charles, 11
Le Gaudier, Antoine, 46
Le Jeune, Paul, 57–108
    birth of, 59
    Brébeuf's letter to, 157–59
    Chastelain's letter to, 190–91, 193–94
    conversion of, 59
    death of, 65
    and difficult winter of 1633, 64, 71–84
    dreams of, 37n10, 215
    and earliest *Relations*, 41–42, 60
    early missionary activity of, 28–31
    and Garnier, 335n2
    and Marie de l'Incarnation, 61
    and Indian cultural differences, 61–62
    Jesuit career in Europe, 59
    and Louis Lallemant, 44–45, 59
    language studies of, 62
    and Massé, 112
    missionary projects of, 28–30, 59–61
    and Silléry compound, 28–30
    writing style/qualities, 47, 48, 62–65
Le Jeune, Paul (writings)
    A Brief Account of the Voyage to New France, 66–70
    Hardships We Must Be Ready to Endure When Wintering with the Savages, 71–84
    Diary of the Trip, 85–96
    Various Thoughts and Feelings of the Fathers in New France, 97–108
Lettres annuelles (Saint Francis Xavier), 41
Lettres édifiantes et curieuses (Saint Francis Xavier), 41
Louis XIII, 27–28
Louis XIV, 42
Lyons, 111

Manoir, Julien, 10
Manuscrit de 1652, 44n17, 221, 308–10, 384
Maquas, 248
Marco Polo, 41
Marillac, Saint Louise de, 10
Martin, Dom Claude, 51
Martin, Félix
    and writings of Chastelain, 188
    and writings of Chaumonot, 395n1
    and writings of Jogues, 219, 220
martyrs, Jesuit, 9, 206
Martyrs de la Nouvelle-France (Rigault and Goyau), 42n14
Massé, Enemond, 109–20
    and Biard, 21, 23, 111–12, 115n2
    death of, 112
    early missionary activity of, 21–22, 23, 111–13
    Jesuit studies and career in Europe, 111, 112

Le Jeune on, 112
return to France, 112
writing style/qualities, 111
Massé, Enemond (writings)
   Letter to Reverend Father General (December 8, 1608), 114–16
   Letter to Reverend Father General (June 10, 1611), 117–18
   Spiritual Notes, 119–20
Maunoir, Julien, 46, 336
Mazarin, Jules, 33
Médicis, Marie de, 23
Megapolensis, John, 302n4
Melançon, Arthur, 44n17
Mercier, François Joseph le, 140, 159
Mercure de France, 41
missionary narratives and letters, 39–44, 47–50
   audience for, 40–41
   and devotion to the Holy Eucharist, 49–50
   earliest *Relations*, 41–42
   and Huron mission, 43–44
   and Jesuit tradition of letter writing, 39–41
   literary quality and stylistic aspects, 47–50
   spiritual characteristics of, 43–44, 48–50
   See also *The Jesuit Relations and Allied Documents* (Thwaites, ed.)
Missions Étrangères seminary (Paris), 13
Moliére, 11
Montagnais, 124

Montaigne, Michel de, 11
Montfort, Saint Louis Grignion de, 10
Montmagny, Monsieur le Chevalier de, 296
Montmorency, Duke de, 24, 27
Moulins, 137–38
Municipal Library at Orléans, 220
mysticism, French, 46–47, 50–55

Neutrals, 30
   Brébeuf and, 125–26, 135–36
   Chaumonot and, 125–26, 136, 397
Nevers, Jesuit college at, 59
New Holland, 321–26
Newfoundland. *See* Acadia colony
Nipissings, 30, 358
Nobili, Robert de, 34–35
Nouë, Anne de, 112
Noyrot, Father, 25–27

Olier, Jean-Jacques, 10
Ondihoahorea, 169
Ononhoraton, Paul, 267
Oregon Territory, 14
Ottawas, 30

Parkman, Francis, 208
Paul, Saint Vincent de, 10, 47
Peltrie, Madame de la, 47
Petuns, 30, 336, 387
Pijart, Pierre, 140, 159, 206, 232, 381
Pius XI, Pope, 206n2

Point, Nicolas, 14–15
Pontoise, 112, 123
Port Royal, 111

Quebec, surrender of (1629), 27

Racine, Jean, 11
Ragueneau, Paul, 43–44, 45n19
  and Brébeuf, 46, 126–27, 159, 160–75
  on Chabanel, 387, 388–92
  and Chaumonot, 396–97
  and Garnier, 335, 337, 341, 344, 345, 367, 384
  and Louis Lallemant, 45
  on martyrdom of Gabriel Lalemant, 138
  and Massé, 112
Recollets, 24–25, 28, 38
Regis, Francis, 10
Relations. See *The Jesuit Relations and Allied Documents* (Thwaites, ed.)
Rennes, Jesuit college at, 13, 59
Ricci, Matteo, 34–35
Richelieu, Armand Jean du Plessis de, 26, 27, 28, 33
Rigault, G., 42n14
Rigoleuc, Father, 45
Rochemonteix, Father de, 37n10
Rocky Mountain Mission, 14–15
Rouen, Jesuit college at
  Brébeuf and, 123–24
  Jogues and, 205
  Louis Lallemant and, 45
  Le Jeune and, 59
  Massé and, 112
Rouquette, Father, 42n14

Ruellan, Louis, 15
Ruggieri, Michele, 34–35

Sagard, Father, 37
Saint-Augustin, Catherine de, 188
Saint-German-en-Laye, peace of (1632), 28
Saint-Jean-de-Terre-Neuve, 22
Saint-Jure, Jean-Baptiste, 46
Saint-Pierre-et-Miquelon, 22
Sales, Saint Francis de, 10
Sévigné, Madame de, 11
Silléry, mission compound at, 28–30
Sire de Monts, 23
Sodalities of Our Lady in France, 187
Sokokiois, 299
Spiritual Exercises, 134n1
Sulpicians, 38

Teanaostaiae, 168n13, 170
Tekakwitha, Kateri, 14
Teresa of Avila, Saint, 52n23, 151
Terni, Jesuit college at, 395
Textes des martyrs de la Nouvelle-France (Rouquette), 42n14
Three Rivers compound
  Algonquin families at, 30
  Jogues at, 218–19, 249, 312, 327–29
Tournon, Jesuit college at, 111

University of Paris, 42
Ursulines, 31, 66
  See also Incarnation, Marie de l'

Valignano, Alessandro, 34–35
Verrazano, Giovanni da, 22
Ventadour, Duke de, 24, 26, 27
Vie de R. P. Isaac Jogues d'Orléans (Forest), 220
Vimont, Barthélemy, 112, 311

Xavier, Saint Francis
    Brébeuf on, 148–49, 150, 152
    Le Jeune on, 106
    letters of, 40–41

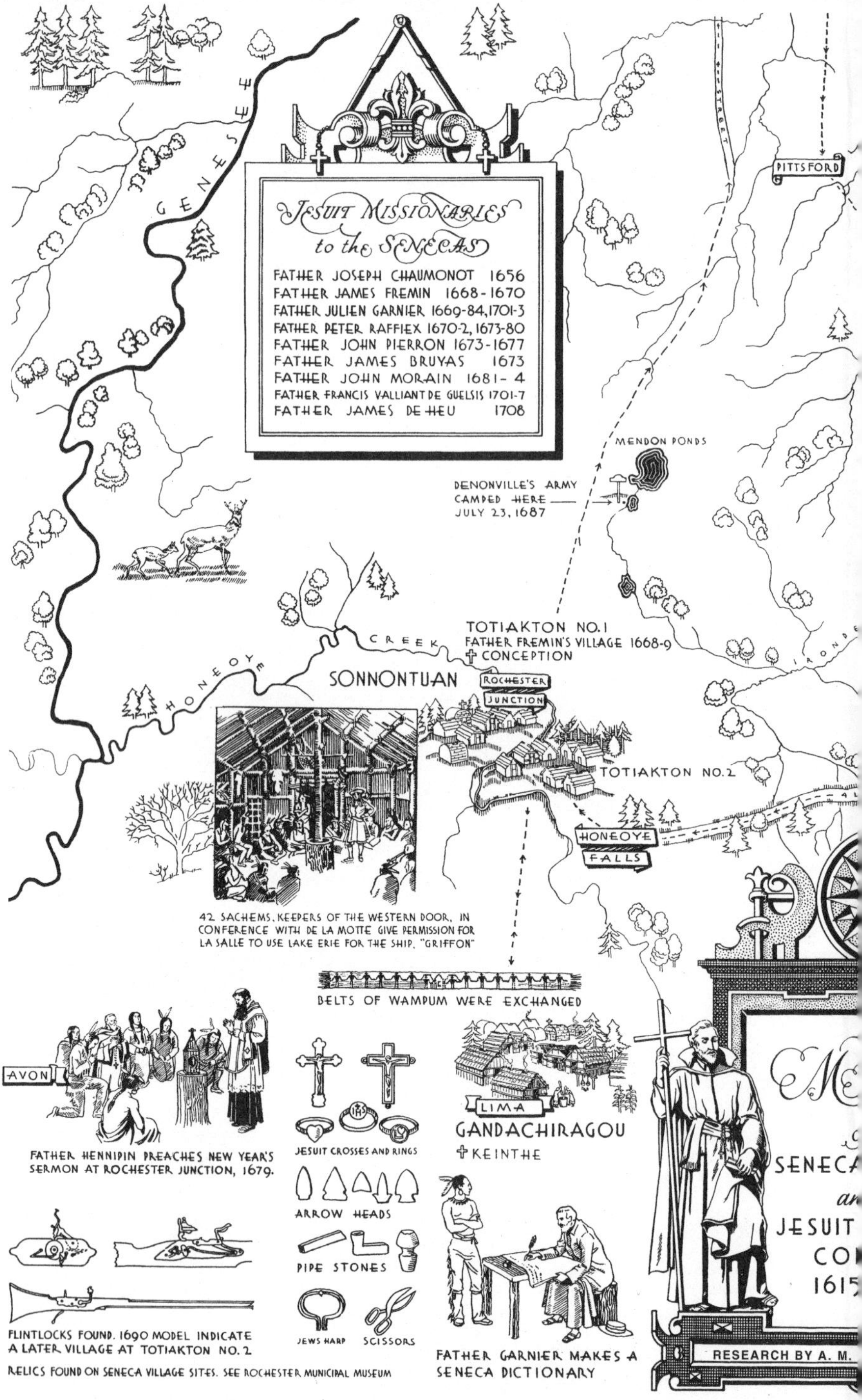
JESUIT MISSIONARIES to the SENECAS
FATHER JOSEPH CHAUMONOT 1656
FATHER JAMES FREMIN 1668-1670
FATHER JULIEN GARNIER 1669-84, 1701-3
FATHER PETER RAFFIEX 1670-2, 1673-80
FATHER JOHN PIERRON 1673-1677
FATHER JAMES BRUYAS 1673
FATHER JOHN MORAIN 1681-4
FATHER FRANCIS VALLIANT DE GUELSIS 1701-7
FATHER JAMES DE HEU 1708
GENESEE
STREET
PITTSFORD
MENDON PONDS
DENONVILLE'S ARMY CAMPED HERE JULY 23, 1687
TOTIAKTON NO. 1
FATHER FREMIN'S VILLAGE 1668-9
CONCEPTION
HONEOYE
CREEK
SONNONTUAN
ROCHESTER JUNCTION
TOTIAKTON NO. 2
HONEOYE FALLS
42 SACHEMS, KEEPERS OF THE WESTERN DOOR, IN CONFERENCE WITH DE LA MOTTE GIVE PERMISSION FOR LA SALLE TO USE LAKE ERIE FOR THE SHIP, "GRIFFON"
BELTS OF WAMPUM WERE EXCHANGED
AVON
FATHER HENNIPIN PREACHES NEW YEAR'S SERMON AT ROCHESTER JUNCTION, 1679.
JESUIT CROSSES AND RINGS
LIMA
GANDACHIRAGOU
KEINTHE
ARROW HEADS
PIPE STONES
JEWS HARP
SCISSORS
FLINTLOCKS FOUND. 1690 MODEL INDICATE A LATER VILLAGE AT TOTIAKTON NO. 2
RELICS FOUND ON SENECA VILLAGE SITES. SEE ROCHESTER MUNICIPAL MUSEUM
FATHER GARNIER MAKES A SENECA DICTIONARY
SENECA
JESUIT
CO
1615
RESEARCH BY A. M.

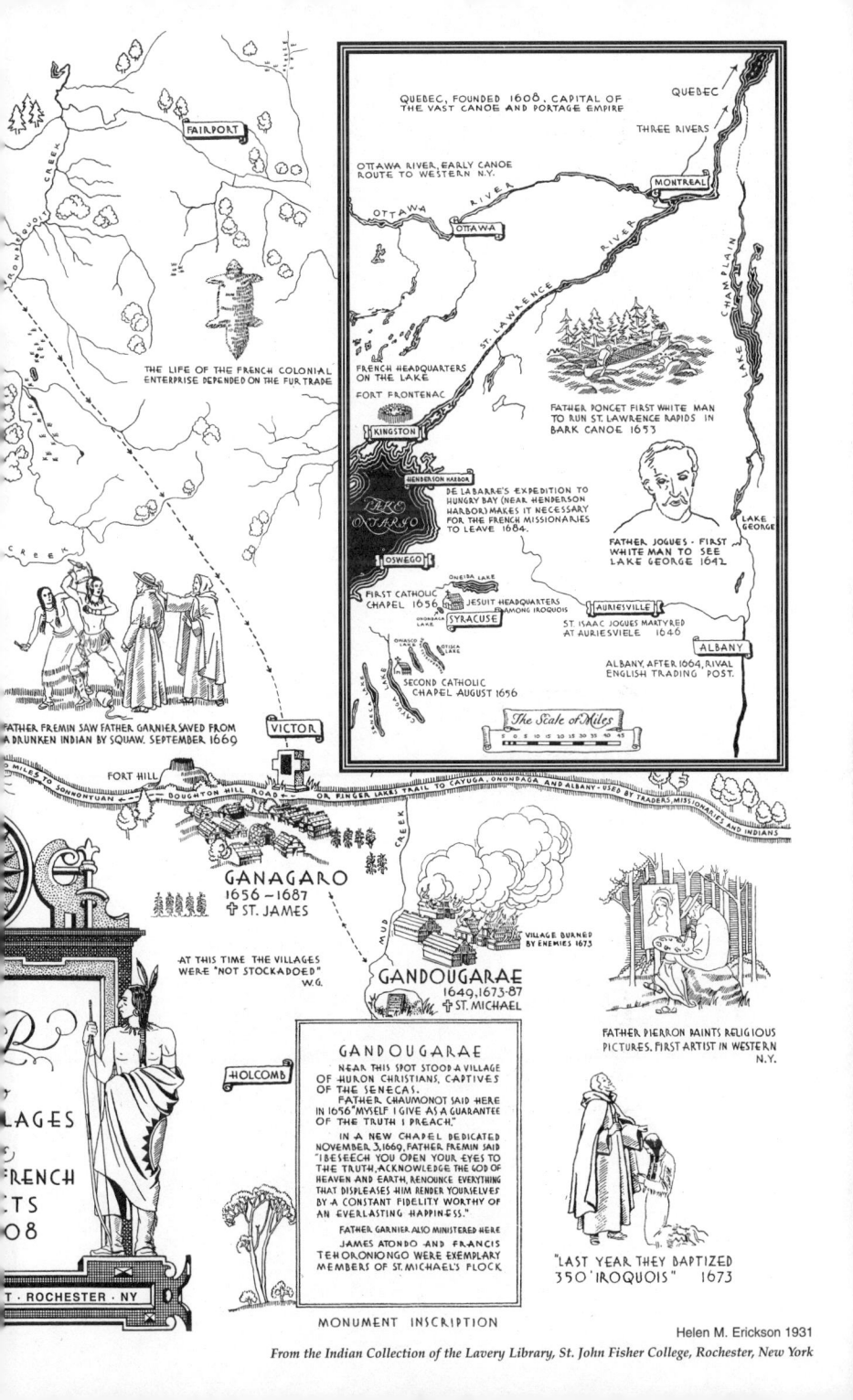

QUEBEC, FOUNDED 1608, CAPITAL OF THE VAST CANOE AND PORTAGE EMPIRE

QUEBEC
THREE RIVERS
MONTREAL

OTTAWA RIVER, EARLY CANOE ROUTE TO WESTERN N.Y.

FAIRPORT

THE LIFE OF THE FRENCH COLONIAL ENTERPRISE DEPENDED ON THE FUR TRADE

FRENCH HEADQUARTERS ON THE LAKE
FORT FRONTENAC
KINGSTON

FATHER PONCET FIRST WHITE MAN TO RUN ST. LAWRENCE RAPIDS IN BARK CANOE 1653

LAKE ONTARIO
HENDERSON HARBOR

DE LABARRE'S EXPEDITION TO HUNGRY BAY (NEAR HENDERSON HARBOR) MAKES IT NECESSARY FOR THE FRENCH MISSIONARIES TO LEAVE 1684.

OSWEGO

FATHER JOGUES – FIRST WHITE MAN TO SEE LAKE GEORGE 1642

LAKE GEORGE

ONEIDA LAKE
FIRST CATHOLIC CHAPEL 1656
JESUIT HEADQUARTERS AMONG IROQUOIS
SYRACUSE
ONONDAGA LAKE

AURIESVILLE
ST. ISAAC JOGUES MARTYRED AT AURIESVIELE 1646

ALBANY
ALBANY, AFTER 1664, RIVAL ENGLISH TRADING POST.

OWASCO LAKE
OTISCO LAKE
SKANEATELES LAKE
CAYUGA LAKE
SECOND CATHOLIC CHAPEL AUGUST 1656

The Scale of Miles

FATHER FREMIN SAW FATHER GARNIER SAVED FROM A DRUNKEN INDIAN BY SQUAW. SEPTEMBER 1669

VICTOR
FORT HILL
BOUGHTON HILL ROAD OR FINGER LAKE TRAIL TO CAYUGA, ONONDAGA AND ALBANY – USED BY TRADERS, MISSIONARIES AND INDIANS

GANAGARO
1656–1687
✠ ST. JAMES

AT THIS TIME THE VILLAGES WERE "NOT STOCKADOED"
W.G.

MUD CREEK

VILLAGE BURNED BY ENEMIES 1673

GANDOUGARAE
1649, 1673-87
✠ ST. MICHAEL

HOLCOMB

FATHER PIERRON PAINTS RELIGIOUS PICTURES. FIRST ARTIST IN WESTERN N.Y.

GANDOUGARAE

NEAR THIS SPOT STOOD A VILLAGE OF HURON CHRISTIANS, CAPTIVES OF THE SENECAS.

FATHER CHAUMONOT SAID HERE IN 1656 "MYSELF I GIVE AS A GUARANTEE OF THE TRUTH I PREACH."

IN A NEW CHAPEL DEDICATED NOVEMBER 3, 1669, FATHER FREMIN SAID "I BESEECH YOU OPEN YOUR EYES TO THE TRUTH, ACKNOWLEDGE THE GOD OF HEAVEN AND EARTH, RENOUNCE EVERYTHING THAT DISPLEASES HIM, RENDER YOURSELVES BY A CONSTANT FIDELITY WORTHY OF AN EVERLASTING HAPPINESS."

FATHER GARNIER ALSO MINISTERED HERE

JAMES ATONDO AND FRANCIS TEHORONIONGO WERE EXEMPLARY MEMBERS OF ST. MICHAEL'S FLOCK

"LAST YEAR THEY BAPTIZED 350 IROQUOIS" 1673

MONUMENT INSCRIPTION

Helen M. Erickson 1931

From the Indian Collection of the Lavery Library, St. John Fisher College, Rochester, New York